专业硕士研究生英语

自学手册

English For Professional Master's Degree Candidates

A Reference Book

主编　王爱华　李淑静

编著者　程英　高虹　李淑静
　　　　陆蓉蕾　王爱华

英文审校　Sheryl Small

北京大学出版社

PEKING UNIVERSITY PRESS

图书在版编目(CIP)数据

专业硕士研究生英语自学手册 / 王爱华,李淑静主编. —北京：北京大学出版社，2008.1

（研究生英语系列）

ISBN 978-7-301-12278-5

Ⅰ.专… Ⅱ.①王…②李… Ⅲ.英语–研究生–自学参考资料 Ⅳ.H31

中国版本图书馆 CIP 数据核字(2007)第 080639 号

书　　　　名：专业硕士研究生英语自学手册
著作责任者：王爱华　李淑静　主编
责 任 编 辑：徐万丽
标 准 书 号：ISBN 978-7-301-12278-5/H·1782
出 版 发 行：北京大学出版社
地　　　　址：北京市海淀区成府路 205 号　100871
网　　　　址：http://www.pup.cn
电　　　　话：邮购部 62752015　发行部 62750672　编辑部 62765014　出版部 62754962
电 子 邮 箱：xuwanli50@yahoo.com.cn
印　　刷　者：河北滦县鑫华书刊印刷厂
经　　销　者：新华书店

　　　　　　　730毫米×980毫米　16开本　18印张　362千字
　　　　　　　2008年1月第1版　2019年8月第7次印刷

定　　　　价：36.00元

未经许可，不得以任何方式复制或抄袭本书之部分或全部内容。
版权所有,侵权必究　　举报电话：010-62752024
　　　　　　　　　　　电子邮箱：fd@pup.pku.edu.cn

前 言

本书是与《专业硕士研究生英语》配套使用的教学辅助材料,主要是对《专业硕士研究生英语》主课文中出现的重要词汇、表达方法及重点语法现象做出注解,并提供所有练习的参考答案。同时,本书设计了巩固重要词汇及提高测试技能的自测练习,另外还增加了实用口语表达的内容,以加强听说能力的训练。

与《专业硕士研究生英语》相呼应,本书共包括十二个单元,每个单元又分为四个部分。具体编排模式如下:

第一部分 Language Points:对主课文中的重要词汇及词组进行中、英文注释,并给出相关例句。同时对课文中的重点语法现象进行说明。编者们在查阅多本辞典,比较多种释义,并结合课文内容的基础上,尽量使注解达到准确翔实。

第二部分 Key to Exercises:提供了课文练习及课后讨论题的参考答案。

第三部分 Self-check:设计了一些针对重点词汇、词组而又不同于教材中已有形式的练习,以便学习者检查自己对这些常用表达法的掌握情况。同时增加了完型填空及阅读理解两种练习形式。其中的素材是从包括互联网等多种渠道收集的,编写者们从中尽量挑选那些能提供主课文背景知识的短文,或提供一些与主课文题材或体裁相近的文章,一方面有益于学习者对主课文进行多方位、多角度的深入理解,同时又能有针对性地对这两种常用测试技能进行训练。

第四部分 Oral Expression:每单元围绕一个日常话题,如问候、自我介绍、饭店用餐、商场购物、银行取款、行车问路、体育娱乐、网上漫游等,为学习者介绍如何征求他人意见、如何表达自己看法、如何讨论不同意见、如何赞美他人以及如何向他人致谢等多种实际语言交际功能。目的是使学习者熟悉生活中常见情景中的常用语言,帮助学习者掌握基本的口语交际技能,提高学习者实际运用语言进行口头交流的能力。

本书的编写意图首先在于辅助学习者学好《专业硕士研究生英语》,同时又能提供更多实用的语言知识,从而促进学习者今后的英语学习。我们希望学习者通过此书的学习,能熟悉一些常见的测试形式,如完型填空和阅读理解,从而提高自己的测试成绩。我们对重点词组和词汇做了详细注解,期望学习者反复操练,进而促进英语词汇的学习。本书为课后讨论题以及关于课文内容的问答题提供的参考答案是编者们经过反复阅读课文,对文章全面准确地理解、把握之后写出的,有助于学习者更深刻地理解主课文。总之,这是一本既针对而又不局限于《专业硕士研究生英语》内容的辅助教材,对教师的教学具有参考价值,对学习者的自学具有指导意义。

本书由北京大学长期从事非英语专业研究生英语教学的骨干教师负责编写,由北京大学博士生英语教学负责人、美籍专家 Sheryl Smalligan 担任审校。

本书的编写和出版得到了北京大学 2006 年度教材建设立项的资助以及责任编辑徐万丽老师的宝贵意见,在此谨表示衷心感谢。由于编写仓促,缺点在所难免,我们诚挚地希望使用本教材的师生和读者提出批评和建议,以便在今后修订时改进和完善。

编 者
2007 年 11 月于北京

Contents

Unit One 1
  Text A   Colin Powell: Straight to the Top 1
    Part One: Language Points 1
    Part Two: Key to Exercises 8
    Part Three: Self-check 12
    Part Four: Oral Expression: Greetings and Introductions 18

Unit Two 24
    Text A   That Lean and Hungry Look 24
    Part One: Language Points 24
    Part Two: Key to Exercises 32
    Part Three: Self-check 36
    Part Four: Oral Expression: Entertaining 43

Unit Three 50
    Text A   Selling Our Innocence Abroad 50
    Part One: Language Points 50
    Part Two: Key to Exercises 58
    Part Three: Self-check 61
    Part Four: Oral Expression: Going Shopping 68

Unit Four 73
    Text A   The Right to Fail 73
    Part One: Language Points 73
    Part Two: Key to Exercises 80
    Part Three: Self-check 83
    Part Four: Oral Expression: At the Bank 90

Unit Five 94
    Text A   A Granddaughter's Fear 94
    Part One: Language Points 94
    Part Two: Key to Exercises 103
    Part Three: Self-check 106
    Part Four: Oral Expression: Transportation 113

Unit Six 117
    Text A   The Generation Lap 117
    Part One: Language Points 117
    Part Two: Key to Exercises 125
    Part Three: Self-check 128
    Part Four: Oral Expression: Getting Directions 135

Unit Seven 139
    Text A   Propaganda Techniques in Advertising 139
    Part One: Language Points 139
    Part Two: Key to Exercises 147
    Part Three: Self-check 151
    Part Four: Oral Expression: Asking for and Expressing Opinions 158

Unit Eight 162
    Text A   Nora Quealey 162
    Part One: Language Points 162
    Part Two: Key to Exercises 171
    Part Three: Self-check 174
    Part Four: Oral Expression: Going to the Movies 181

Unit Nine 185
    Text A   How to Deal with a Difficult Boss 185
    Part One: Language Points 185
    Part Two: Key to Exercises 195
    Part Three: Self-check 198
    Part Four: Oral Expression: Internet 205

Contents

Unit Ten 209
    Text A   Was America a Mistake? 209
    Part One: Language Points 209
    Part Two: Key to Exercises 218
    Part Three: Self-check 221
    Part Four: Oral Expression: Talking About Sports 228

Unit Eleven 233
    Text A   Any More Like You at Home? 233
    Part One: Language Points 233
    Part Two: Key to Exercises 243
    Part Three: Self-check 245
    Part Four: Oral Expression: Compliments/Thanks and Responses 253

Unit Twelve 256
    Text A   The Real Generation Gap 256
    Part One: Language Points 256
    Part Two: Key to Exercises 264
    Part Three: Self-check 267
    Part Four: Oral Expression: Discussing Different Points of View 274

Unit One

Text A

Colin Powell: Straight to the Top

Part One: Language Points

I. Vocabulary

1. There was no magic <u>shortcut</u>. (Para. 1)

   译文：没什么神奇的捷径。

   shortcut: *n.* a way of getting somewhere, doing something, etc. (thought to be) quicker than the usual or ordinary way （至某地，做某事的）近路，捷径

   e.g. *I think we should take a shortcut across the fields instead of going by the road.*
   我觉得我们不用走大路，我们可以从田里抄近路过去。

2. There is no <u>substitute</u> for hard work and study. (Para. 1)

   译文：什么也代替不了努力学习，认真工作。

   substitute: *n.* person or thing taking the place of, acting for or serving for another 代替者，代用品

   e.g. *Substitute for rubber can be made from petroleum.*
   石油中可制出橡胶的代用品。

3. Many blacks and other <u>minorities</u> live in Harlem. (Para. 2)

   译文：有很多黑人和一些其他少数民族住在哈莱姆区。

   minority: *n.* small racial, religious, etc. group in a community, nation, etc. （在一社会、国家等中之）少数民族，少数宗教等。

  e.g. *Gaelic is still spoken in Ireland by a tiny <u>minority</u>.*
     在爱尔兰仍有极少数人使用盖尔语。

4. But tears can still <u>cloud</u> his eyes when he speaks of his mother and father. (Para. 4)
  译文：当他提起他的父母时，眼泪仍会涌上他的双眼。
  cloud: *v.* to become, make, indistinct as through cloud （使）变模糊
  e.g. *Her eyes <u>were clouded</u> with tears.* 她泪眼婆娑。

5. "As I grow older," he has said, "I have greater and greater <u>affection</u> for my parents." (Para. 4)
  译文：他说："我年龄越大，对我父母的感情就越深。"
  affection: *n.* kindly feeling, love 亲爱，爱
  e.g. *Every mother has great <u>affection</u> for her children.*
     每位母亲都很爱自己的孩子。

6. Maud and Luther Powell were <u>serious</u> people with a dream. (Para. 5)
  译文：莫德和卢瑟·鲍威尔是有着自己梦想的认真严肃的人。
  serious: *adj.* solemn; thoughtful; not given to pleasure-seeking 严肃的，庄重的
  e.g. *You look very <u>serious</u>; is there anything the matter?*
     你看起来很严肃，怎么了？

7. If Maud Powell got <u>annoyed</u> at her husband, she would <u>remind</u> him just who had the high school diploma. (Para. 5)
  译文：如果莫德·鲍威尔和她丈夫生气，她就会提醒他记住是谁获得了高中文凭。
  annoy: *v.* to cause slight irritation to (another) by troublesome, often repeated acts 使生气，使烦恼；用烦人的、通常是重复性的行为使（别人）生气
  e.g. *She was <u>annoyed</u> with her husband because he didn't do the dishes.*
     她很生她丈夫的气，因为他没有刷碗。
  remind: *v.* to cause (sb.) to remember (to do sth., etc.); to cause (sb.) to think (of sth.) 提醒（某人）（做某事等）；使（某人）想起（某事物或某人）
  e.g. *Please <u>remind</u> him to turn off the lights before he leaves.*
     请提醒他走时别忘关灯。

8. Children watch their parents *live* values. (Para. 7)
  译文：孩子们观察父母言行中体现出的价值观。
  live: *v.* to practice in one's life 实行
  e.g. *He spent all his life to <u>live</u> his beliefs.*
     他毕其一生来实行他的信仰。

Unit One

9. She <u>recalls</u> that he was "really a pretty <u>average</u> boy"... (Para. 8)

   译文：她回忆到那时他其实是个很平常的孩子……

   recall: *v.* to bring back to the mind; to recollect　记起；忆起

   e.g.　*She didn't seem to <u>recall</u> where they met.*　她记不起他们在哪儿见过面了。

   average: *adj.* of the ordinary or usual standard　普通的，平常的

   e.g.　*There was nothing special about the movie, it was only <u>average</u>.*
   这部影片没什么特别之处——不过是一般的片子。

10. Actually, the military always <u>impressed</u> him. (Para. 12)

    译文：事实上，军队生活对他一直有很大的影响。

    impress: *v.* to have a strong influence on; to fix deeply (on the mind, memory)　给予强烈影响；使留深刻印象

    e.g.　*His book did not <u>impress</u> me at all, I did not think it good, useful, etc.*
    我对他的书没有很深的印象，我没觉得那本书很好或很有用等等。

11. They felt that, like most young men at the time, he would have been <u>drafted</u> into the military anyway. (Para. 16)

    译文：他们觉得，不管怎样，像当时大多数年轻人一样，他都可能被应征入伍。

    draft (into) AmE = **conscript:** *v.* to make someone serve in one of the armed forces by law　征(某人)入伍

    e.g.　*In that story, the old lady's three sons have all been <u>drafted</u> into military service.*
    在故事里，老太太的三个儿子都被应征入伍了。

12. Although I had to compete in my military schooling with West Pointers... My CCNY foundation was so <u>solid</u>, I never regretted going anywhere but to City. (Para. 18)

    译文：虽然在军事训练上我不得不跟西点军校毕业生比拼，但我在纽约市立大学打下的基础非常扎实，我从来都不后悔我上了纽约市立大学而不是其他任何学校。

    solid: *a.* firm and well made　坚固的；实在的

    e.g.　*There are <u>solid</u> reasons for believing that this is possible.*
    (我们)有坚实的理由相信这是可能的。

13. Don't let your blackness, your minority status, be a problem to you. Let it be a problem to somebody else... <u>Beat</u> them at it. Prove they're wrong. (Para. 20)

    译文：不要让你的黑皮肤，你的少数民族角色成为你的问题。让它们成为别人的问题……试图战胜他们。证明他们错了。

    beat: *v.* to defeat; to do better than　打败，超越

e.g. *She beat the other finalist and got the gold medal.*
决赛中她战胜对手，获得金牌。

II. Expressions

1. He grew up in a four-bedroom apartment on Kelly Street. (Para. 2)
   译文：他在凯利街上一个有四个卧室的公寓里长大。
   grow up: (of a person) to develop from childhood to adulthood; (of people of any age) to develop beyond childish thoughts and ways 长大，成年，成熟
   a) *Mary is growing up so fast, I think she's going to be a tall woman.*
   玛丽长得这么快，我看她一定能长得很高。
   b) *Stop acting like a child with your bad temper! Do grow up.*
   你该长大了。别再像个孩子似地发脾气。

2. But tears can still cloud his eyes when he speaks of his mother and father. (Para. 4)
   译文：当他提起他的父母时，眼泪仍会涌上他的双眼。
   speak of: to mention, talk about; to suggest the idea of 提起；谈到
   a) *She spoke of the government's plans for the unemployed.*
   她谈到政府关于安置失业人员的计划。
   b) *Everything at the party spoke of careful planning.*
   晚会上的一切都透露着精心设计的痕迹。

3. For the Powells, education was the key to a better life. (Para. 5)
   译文：对鲍威尔一家来说，要过上好日子，就要受教育。
   the key to: something that affords a means of access （喻）（问题或神秘事物之）解答；关键
   a) *The weather holds the key to our success or failure.*
   我们成功或失败的关键取决于天气。
   b) *The discovery of the murder weapon provided the key to the mystery.*
   谋杀凶器的发现为揭开这件案子之谜提供了重要线索。

4. Kids don't pick up training because parents sit around and talk to them about values. (Para. 7)
   译文：孩子们并不会因为父母坐着给他们讲讲价值观就受到教育了。
   pick up: to learn, often informally or by chance 自然学得
   a) *He has picked up some knowledge of physics.*
   他学到了一些物理知识。
   b) *I don't know where my children have picked up those rude words.*
   我不知道我孩子们从哪儿学到的那些粗话。

Unit One

sit around/about: to sit doing nothing, especially while waiting or while others are active 闲坐着,无所事事

a) *Some lucky people can sit around with nothing to do, while I do all the work.*
有些命好的人成天坐着什么也不干,而我要干所有的活。

b) *I got tired of sitting about waiting, so I went home.*
我坐在那里等烦了,就回家了。

5. He admits that at school he sometimes "horsed around." (Para. 10)
译文:他承认有时候他在学校里胡闹。

horse around: (informal) to play roughly and rather carelessly so that someone could be hurt or something damaged (俚)哄闹,胡闹,捣蛋

a) *You boys have been horsing around again, getting yourselves dirty.*
你们这些男孩子又在胡闹了,把自己弄得那么脏。

b) *He was horsing around in the kitchen and broke my favorite bowl.*
他在厨房里淘气,把我最喜欢的碗打碎了。

6. According to an old saying, some people "find a home in the army." (Para. 13)
译文:根据一句老话,有些人"在部队里找到了家。"

according to: as stated or shown by; in a way that agrees with 根据……所说(所示)

a) *According to David, she is really a good teacher.*
大卫觉得她真是一个好老师。

b) *We will be paid according to the amount of work we do.*
根据我们所做的工作的多少,我们会得到相应的报酬。

7. Colin Powell did not go to West Point. Yet he did make it to the top in the army. (Para. 18)
译文:鲍威尔没上过西点军校,但他仍然成功地获得了军队里的最高职位。

make it: to be successful at something, for example, in a job; to succeed in getting somewhere on time when getting there is difficult; to successfully deal with a difficult experience (非正式)取得成功

a) *So far, relatively few women have made it to the top in the business world.*
到目前为止,在商界里很少有女人取得成功。

b) *She couldn't have made it through those times without the support of her family.*
没有她家人的帮助,她不可能度过那段时光。

8. "Although I had to compete in my military schooling with West Pointers ... my CCNY foundation was so solid, I never regretted going anywhere but to City." (Para. 18)

译文:"虽然在军事训练上我不得不跟西点军校毕业生比拼,但我在纽约市立大学打下的基础非常扎实,我从来都不后悔我上了纽约市立大学而不是其他任何学校。"

compete with / against / for: to try to win something in competition with someone else 竞争,争夺

a) *Women can compete with men on an intellectual plane.*
女人和男人在智力上是可以比一比的。

b) *We try to make the trains run on time, but we can't compete against the weather.*
我们尽量想让火车正点运行,但我们也拿气候变化没办法。

c) *The two girls competed with each other for the highest mark.*
这两个女孩子争着拿第一。

9. It also helped, he added, that he "came along at a time of change, a time of growth in civil rights." (Para. 19)

译文:"当然,"他补充到,他"正处于变革中,正处于民权运动发展时期"。这一切对他都是有利的。

come along: to appear or arrive 偶然出现,产生

a) *I waited a long time until a script came along that I thought was genuinely funny.*
我等了很长一段时间,直到我等到了一个我觉得很有趣的剧本。

b) *Trouble comes along when you least expect it.*
麻烦总是在你最想不到的时候出现。

10. "In the army," he said, "I never felt I was looked down on by my white colleagues. I've been give the opportunity to compete fair and square with them." (Para. 19)

译文:"在军队里,我从来没有觉得我的白人同事轻视过我,同时,他们也给我机会和他们公平竞争。"

look down on: to have or show a low opinion of, especially of someone one considers socially inferior or unimportant; to despise 轻视,看不起

a) *She wouldn't let her daughter marry a boy from a poor family, as she looked down on him and thought he was not worthy of her daughter.*
她不让她女儿嫁给一个穷人的孩子,因为她很看不起他,认为他配不上她女儿。

b) *Women have gotten tired of being looked down on by employers.*
妇女们对雇主的歧视再也受不了了。

fair and square: winning a competition honestly and without cheating; conducting oneself with integrity 光明正大地;遵照规则地

a) *There are no excuses. We were beaten fair and square.*
没什么借口可找。我们实实在在地输了。

b) *He was admired for being fair and square in all his dealings.*
他因做什么都光明磊落而受到尊重。

11. If you work hard, do the best you can, take advantage of every opportunity that's put in front of you, success will come your way. (Para. 20)

    译文：如果你努力工作，竭尽你的全力，把握住每个机会，你一定会取得成功的。

    take advantage of: to make use of, profit from; to make unfair use of, to exploit
    利用

    a) *You'll want to take full advantage of this opportunity.*
    你应该充分利用这次机会。

    b) *She took advantage of his good nature.* 她利用了他的善良。

    c) *Many small investors are taking advantage of these attractive share offers to make a quick profit.*
    许多小投资者在利用这诱人的股价来快速赚一笔钱。

III. Grammar

1. People keep asking the secret of my success. (Para. 1)

    译文：人们不断问我成功的秘诀。

    keep (on) doing sth.: to continue doing sth.; to do sth. frequently or repeatedly
    继续做某事；不断或反复做某事

    e.g. *Don't keep giggling. You should go to sleep.*

    My shoe lace keeps (on) coming undone.

2. Nothing comes easy. (Para. 1)

    译文：(在这个世界上)没有什么唾手可得的东西。
    某些不及物动词后面可以直接跟形容词，用以说明状态。

    e.g. *He stood motionless.*

    He scares easy.

3. "As I grow older," he has said, "I have greater and greater affection for my parents." (Para. 4)

    译文：他说，我年龄越大，对我父母的感情就越深。

    As 意思是"at the same time"，比 when, while 更强调时间的同时性，用于两件事同时进行的场合。When 表示"做……的时候(瞬间)"这种一时的动作和状态，while 表示"做……的期间"这一期间。

4. ...there were few children his age in the neighborhood. (Para. 8)

   译文：周围和他一样大的孩子很少。

   his age: a children (of) his age 中 age 省略 of 的用法是形容宾格。起纯形容词作用的"of＋名词"中的 of 省略了，因此剩下的名词是宾格。从前用 of，现代英语通常省略，特别是在口语中。

5. If you work hard, do the best you can, take advantage of every opportunity that's put in front of you, success will come your way. (Para. 20)

   译文：如果你努力工作，竭尽所能，把握住每个机会，你一定会取得成功的。

   比较 "do/try one's best" 和 "as best one can"：

   do/try one's best: to make one's best effort or be in one's best state　尽最大的努力；处于最佳的状态；处于颠峰

   e.g.　I'll do my best.

   as best one can: as well as one can　尽最大努力，竭力

   e.g.　Do it as best you can.

   "do the best you can" 在文中意思为 to make your best efforts or to do as well as you can。

6. They felt that, like most young men at the time, he would have been drafted into the military anyway.

   译文：他们觉得，不管怎样，像当时大多数年轻人一样，他都可能被应征入伍。虚拟语气是一种特殊的动词形式，用来表示说话人所说的话不是一个事实，而只是一种愿望、假设、怀疑、建议、猜测、可能或纯粹的空想等。在此处表示鲍威尔父母的一种猜测。而且此处为省略了条件从句的虚拟语气结构。

Part Two: Key to Exercises

I. Suggested Answers to *Topics for Discussion*

1. **What specific qualities made Colin Powell successful?**

   First, Colin Powell was able to find the right career for himself, and, second, he worked hard at what he chose to do, doing the best he could. Backed with a solid education and possessing a strong mind and a strong sense of identity, this born leader made it to the top.

Unit One

2. What were the barriers on Powell's way to success?

   Powell (a) came from a poor black immigrant family; (b) when he was a student, he got only a grade average of "C"; and (c) in the army he had to compete with the West Point graduates who always held top positions in the army. All these factors worked against him. Yet he overcame all these obstacles and rose to the top.

3. From his advice to young black Americans and his description of the secret of his success, what can we learn about Colin Powell?

   In Paragraph 1, Powell says, "People keep asking the secret of my success. There isn't any secret. I work hard and spend long hours. It's as simple as that." He also says, "There is no substitute for hard work and study. Nothing comes easy." These quotations show that Powell is industrious and persistent. We can also see that he has a clear sense of reality. He does not believe in magic. He does not believe in shortcuts. He believes only in hard work. He knows that nothing can be obtained easily.

   In Paragraph 20, Powell advises young black Americans: "Don't let your blackness, your minority status, be a problem to you. Let it be a problem to somebody else.... Beat them at it. Prove they're wrong. If you work hard, do the best you can, take advantage of every opportunity that's put in front of you, success will come your way." Here he tries to say: Don't be too concerned about your differences. Don't be too sensitive. Assert yourself. Take a positive and active stance toward life. If you do your work and do it well, you will make it to the top.

4. In what way does Colin Powell embody the American Dream?

   The American Dream refers to traditional U.S. social ideals—that everyone in the United States has the chance to achieve success and prosperity. This ideal is expressed through self-betterment, wealth, and success through hard work and perseverance. Everyone can earn his or her version of the American Dream. We can say that in some ways Colin Powell embodies the American Dream, because he came up the hard way and he rose to the top purely through his hard work and perseverance. His achievements inspire young Americans to work hard to get to the top.

II. Key to Exercises
Text A
A.
1. See suggested answers to "Topics for Discussion."
2. The army offered the right profession for Colin Powell. He found a home there. There he discovered his life goals and began to show his talent.
3. In Paragraph 15, one of Powell's ROTC classmates at CCNY, Mitchell Strear, recalls, "Even back then Colin drew attention when he entered a room. At the age of eighteen, his bearing, manner, and presence were special. You just knew he would become a leader. The infantry has a motto: 'Follow me.' Colin's manner of acceptance of responsibility and leadership all said 'Follow me.'" According to Strear, Colin Powell was special even when he was very young. He drew attention to himself. He seemed to be a born leader. Others would follow him because he was ready to accept responsibility.
4. He is giving his perception of racial relationships and opportunities. We can see that he looks at the bright side, that he has an optimistic and positive attitude. We can say that he is sensible, that he does not want to bother himself with trifles.
5. (1) F (2) F (3) F (4) T (5) F (6) T (7) T (8) F

B.
1. not easy 2. a poor black immigrant family 3. seamstress 4. a shipping clerk
5. serious 6. was a key to a better life 7. really a pretty average boy
8. bloom 9. straight A's 10. at the top of 11. certain 12. made it

C.
1. C 2. B 3. C 4. D 5. D

D.
1. shortcut 2. substitute 3. were clouded 4. affection 5. was annoyed 6. recall
7. impressed 8. drafted 9. solid 10. beat

E.
1. has... grown up 2. speaks of 3. have picked up 4. sit around 5. According to
6. compete for 7. horsing around 8. make it 9. take advantage of
10. look down on

F.
1. comes my way 2. set a goal 3. have done your job well 4. get to the top
5. gives hopes to 6. just right for 7. draw... attention 8. comes with, comes with

9. a late bloomer   10. have found a home

G.

1. C   2. B   3. D   4. A   5. C   6. D   7. D   8. B   9. A   10. D

H.

1. Isn't she rather young to be a mother? She's hardly had time to grow up herself.

2. For some girls, marrying a rich man is the key to happiness.

3. Where did you pick up such ideas?

4. According to our records, the books you have borrowed should now be returned to the library.

5. Several advertising agencies are competing to get the contract.

6. As a child, she recalled, her parents had seemed very happy together.

7. Stop horsing around and get to work.

8. He was a late bloomer. He had made some academic achievements when he was in his forties.

9. What impressed the judges most was the originality in the dancer's performance.

10. I remember thinking then that nobody's ever going to see me cry again. I did not always make it.

11. The first two years at college provide a solid foundation for my English study.

12. They won the game fair and square.

13. His father told him to take every chance that comes along.

14. You should take advantage of the fine weather to paint the fence.

I.

1. 鲍威尔出生于一个贫穷的黑人移民家庭,他是如何成功地成为这个国家军队里的最高领导人的?并没有什么神奇的捷径。鲍威尔有一次说:"人们不断地问我成功的秘诀。并没有什么秘诀。我只是长时间地努力工作。就是这么简单。"他向年轻人提出忠告:"没有什么能替代努力工作和认真学习。(在这个世界上)没有什么是唾手可得的。"

2. 根据一句老话,有一些人"在军队里找到了家"。换句话说,有一些人生来就是到部队里当兵的。鲍威尔和军队似乎彼此青睐。

3. 不要让你的黑皮肤和你的少数民族角色成为你的问题。让它成为别人的问题。试图战胜他们。证明他们错了。如果你努力工作,竭尽所能,把握住每一个机会,你一定会取得成功的。

Text B
1. D 2. C 3. D 4. D 5. D

Part Three: Self-check

I. Choose the word that is closest in meaning to the underlined word in each sentence.

1. How did he rise to become the country's top military man? There was no magic <u>shortcut</u>.
   A. better method   B. secret   C. quicker way   D. detour
2. There is no <u>substitute</u> for hard work and study. Nothing comes easy.
   A. substance   B. institute   C. excuse   D. alternative
3. Many blacks and other <u>minorities</u> live in Harlem.
   A. small ethnic groups   B. groups   C. minors   D. majorities
4. But tears can still <u>cloud</u> his eyes when he speaks of his mother and father.
   A. cover   B. blind   C. fill   D. veil
5. "As I grow older," he has said, "I have greater and greater <u>affection</u> for my parents."
   A. feeling   B. love   C. care   D. effect
6. If Maud Powell got <u>annoyed</u> at her husband, she would remind him just *who* had the high school diploma.
   A. satisfied   B. anxious   C. worried   D. irritated
7. If Maud Powell got annoyed at her husband, she would <u>remind</u> him just *who* had the high school diploma.
   A. mind   B. recall   C. tell   D. make ... remember
8. Maud and Luther Powell were <u>serious</u> people with a dream.
   A. severe   B. earnest   C. kind   D. mysterious
9. Children watch their parents *live* values.
   A. practice   B. teach   C. fulfill   D. give
10. She <u>recalls</u> that he was "really a pretty average boy," but he always "had a sense of direction."
    A. remembers   B. calls   C. reminds   D. comments

Unit One

11. She recalls that he was "really a pretty average boy...."
    A. excellent   B. handsome   C. ordinary   D. standard
12. Actually, the military had always impressed him.
    A. depressed   B. imprinted
    C. pressed   D. influenced ... favorably
13. They felt that, like most young men at the time, he would have been drafted into the military anyway.
    A. drew   B. recruited   C. accepted   D. admitted
14. ... my CCNY foundation was so solid, I never regretted going anywhere but to City.
    A. deep   B. hard   C. strong   D. stupid
15. Let it be a problem to somebody else .... Beat them at it.
    A. Hit   B. Defeat   C. Strike   D. Bat

II. Choose the expression that best completes each sentence.

1. He _____ in a four-bedroom apartment on Kelly Street.
   A. stayed up   B. lived on   C. grew up   D. brought up
2. But tears can still cloud his eyes when he _____ his mother and father.
   A. speaks of   B. speaks up   C. speaks for   D. speaks out
3. For the Powells, education was _____ a better life.
   A. the way out   B. the key to   C. the solution to   D. the chance to
4. Kids don't _____ training because parents sit around and talk to them about values.
   A. put up   B. pick up   C. come by   D. get up
5. Some lucky people can _____ with nothing to do, while I do all the work.
   A. sit up   B. sit around   C. sit down   D. sit out
6. Colin was not an honor student. He admits that at school he sometimes "_____."
   A. hung up   B. passed off   C. horsed around   D. went off
7. _____ an old saying, some people "find a home in the army."
   A. Owing to   B. Because of   C. As for   D. According to
8. General Colin Powell did not go to West Point. Yet he did _____ to the top in the army.
   A. do it   B. make it   C. get it   D. go it

9. Although I had to _____ in my military schooling _____ West Pointers,... my CCNY foundation was so solid, I never regretted going anywhere but to City.
   A. deal...with   B. compete...with   C. argue...with   D. compare...with
10. It also helped, he added, that he "_____ at a time of change, a time of growth in civil rights."
    A. came along   B. came about   C. came in   D. came on
11. I never felt I was _____ by my white colleagues.
    A. looked up on   B. looked forward to
    C. looked back on   D. looked down on
12. I never felt I was looked down on by my white colleagues. I've been given the opportunity to compete _____ with them.
    A. by and large   B. far and wide   C. fair and square   D. pro and con
13. If you work hard, do the best you can, _____ every opportunity that's put in front of you, success will come your way.
    A. get rid of   B. pay attention to
    C. take advantage of   D. get away with
14. Luck had _____ at the very last moment.
    A. come his way   B. made her way
    C. gone her way   D. got her way
15. Colin Powell did not go to West Point. Yet he did make it _____ in the army.
    A. in the end   B. at the end   C. to the top   D. at their best

III. Read the following passage and fill in each blank with the most suitable word or expression.

My father adored my sister, Marilyn. Thanks to his job in the garment district, she was always well ___1___, and she led a sheltered life by Kelly Street ___2___. She ran with the good girls. The Teitelbaum sisters, ___3___ father owned the pharmacy on the corner, were Marilyn's closest friends. I played the role of pesky little brother. Marilyn's first ___4___ boyfriend was John Stevens, whose family was ___5___ active in St. Margaret's Church. John was ___6___ only child and was being groomed to become a doctor (he made it). He and Marilyn ___7___ by their parents. My idea of fun was to sneak up on them in amorous embrace and make a nuisance ___8___ myself. John would buy me off with a quarter. Marilyn would rage at her little brat brother. I thought of her in those days as a fink ___9___ turned me in for playing hooky, and I'm sure she found me a pain in the neck. __10__ the whole it was a normal sibling relationship.

1. A. worn   B. dressed   C. adorned   D. decorated
2. A. standards   B. rules   C. principles   D. custom
3. A. their   B. that   C. which   D. whose
4. A. serious   B. good   C. close   D. sincere
5. A. too   B. also   C. either   D. so
6. A. an   B. the   C. a   D. some
7. A. was matched up   B. were matched up
   C. matched up   D. have been matched up
8. A. about   B. at   C. of   D. on
9. A. and   B. she   C. who   D. he
10. A. As   B. On   C. Above   D. In

IV. Read the following passage and choose the best answer for each question.

I believe in America and I believe in our people.

Later this month, I will be participating in a ceremony at Ellis Island, where I will receive copies of the ship manifest and the immigration documents that record the arrival in America of my mother, Maud Ariel McKoy, from Jamaica aboard the motor ship Turialba in 1923. My father, Luther Powell, had arrived three years earlier at the Port of Philadelphia.

They met in New York City, married, became Americans, and raised a family. By their hard work and their love for this country, they enriched this nation and helped it grow and thrive. They instilled in their children and grandchildren that same love of country and a spirit of optimism.

My family's story is a common one that has been told by millions of Americans. We are a land of immigrants—a nation that has been touched by every nation—and we, in turn, touch every nation. And we are touched not just by immigrants but by the visitors who come to America and return home to tell of their experiences.

I believe that our greatest strength in dealing with the world is the openness of our society and the welcoming nature of our people. A good stay in our country is the best public diplomacy tool we have.

After 9/11 we realized that our country's openness was also its vulnerability. We needed to protect ourselves by knowing who was coming into the country, for what purpose, and when they left. This was entirely appropriate and reasonable. Unfortunately, to many foreigners we gave the impression that we were no longer a welcoming nation. They started to go to schools and hospitals in other countries, and, frankly, they started to take their business elsewhere. We can't allow that to happen. Our attitude has to be, we are glad you are here. We must be careful, but we must not be afraid.

As I traveled the world as Secretary of State, I encountered anti-American sentiment. But I also encountered an underlying respect and affection for America. People still want to come here. Refugees who have no home at all know that America is their land of dreams. Even with added scrutiny, people line up at our embassies to apply to come here.

You see, I believe that the America of 2005 is the same America that brought Maud Ariel McKoy and Luther Powell to these shores and so many millions of others. An America that each day gives new immigrants the same gift that my parents received. An America that lives by a Constitution that inspires freedom and democracy around the world. An America with a big, open, charitable heart that reaches out to people in need around the world. An America that sometimes seems confused and is always noisy. That noise has a name—it's called democracy and we use it to work through our confusion.

An America that is still the beacon of light to the darkest corner of the world.

1. What can we say about Colin Powell's father and mother?
   A. They were unusual immigrants from Jamaica.
   B. They became wealthy in America.
   C. They were pessimistic about the prospect of America.
   D. They were just common people in America.
2. What does Powell probably mean with the following statement: "We are a land of immigrants"?
   A. American society is dominated by immigrants.
   B. American society is mainly made up of immigrants.
   C. America and other nations are closely interrelated.
   D. All Americans are immigrants from other different nations.

Unit One

3. What does Colin Powell say about America's public policy?

   A. America has the best public policy in the world.

   B. America is still a welcoming nation.

   C. America is vulnerable because it is open to the whole world.

   D. Despite the need for security, visitors to the U.S. should not be tracked.

4. According to Powell, what is the world's general attitude toward America?

   A. Foreigners think it is dangerous to stay in America.

   B. Foreigners think they can no longer profit from doing business in America.

   C. Many foreigners still respect and like America.

   D. Foreigners no longer like to go to America.

5. Colin Powell believes that _____.

   A. America will give gifts to every immigrant every day

   B. America is a country in confusion

   C. America is a nation of freedom and democracy

   D. America can literally shed light in every corner of the world

V. Read the following passage and decide whether each statement is TRUE or FALSE.

Despite obstacles, African-Americans made political gains. By organizing at the state and local levels, African-Americans were able to increase black political representation. By 1968 nine African-Americans, including the first black woman, Shirley Chisholm, had been elected to Congress, the largest number since 1875. Twelve were elected in 1970, and the following year they formed the Congressional Black Caucus (核心小组会议) for a stronger voice in federal affairs.

Coalitions (联合) of blacks, Hispanics, and whites in the Democratic Party brought an impressive number of African-Americans to office in many major cities. In 1970 Kenneth Gibson was elected mayor of Newark; in 1973 Thomas Bradley was elected in Los Angeles, Maynard Jackson was elected in Atlanta, and Coleman Young was elected in Detroit. In 1983 Harold Washington was sworn in as the first black mayor of Chicago, and black victories continued in major and minor cities in the 1980s and 1990s.

Meanwhile, the number of blacks in Congress also grew. By 1994 the membership of the Congressional Black Caucus stood at forty, including Carol Moseley-Braun of Illinois, the first black woman to be elected to the U.S. Senate. In

1989 General Colin Powell became the first African-American Chairman of the Joint Chiefs of Staff, and L. Douglas Wilder was elected Governor of Virginia, the first elected black governor in American history.

One of the most hopeful signs of racial progress during the decade was civil rights leader Jesse Jackson's run for the Democratic presidential nomination in 1988. Jackson was the first black man to mount a serious campaign for a major party's presidential nomination. He won Virginia's Democratic primary and 6.6 million primary votes nationally. Jackson did not win the nomination, but he amassed (积聚) 1200 delegates (代表) at the Democratic convention and was recognized as a major power in the party.

In 1983 Vanessa Williams became the first African-American to win the Miss America Contest, and *The Color Purple* (1982) by black author Alice Walker won the Pulitzer Prize for literature. In 1988 Toni Morrison, another African-American writer, received the Pulitzer Prize for her novel *Beloved* (1987). Such black performers and sports stars as Michael Jackson, Michael Jordan, and Bill Cosby became national icons (偶像).

1. In spite of enormous barriers, African-Americans managed to increase black representation in the American government.
2. In 1968, Shirley Chisholm became the first black woman elected to the Senate.
3. Due to the great efforts of African-Americans, in the 1980s and 1990s many black people became mayors of major American cities.
4. Jesse Jackson's campaign for the Democratic presidential nomination raised the hopes of millions of black people.
5. So far, African-Americans have shown excellence only in art and sports.

Part Four: Oral Expression: Greetings and Introductions

I. Dialogues

Dialogue 1

Receptionist: Hello, Ms Anopow. How are you?

Anopow: Not too bad, thanks. And you?
Receptionist: Oh fine. How are things in Moscow?
Anopow: Oh, busy at the moment. In fact, we're about to open a new branch in St. Petersburg.

Dialogue 2

A: Interesting meeting, isn't it?
B: Yes, very. I thought the last speaker was especially good.
A: Let me introduce myself, by the way. My name's Thomas Bradley.
B: How do you do? I'm Ted Nugent.
A: Sorry, what was your last name again?
B: It's Nugent, N-U-G-E-N-T, but just call me Ted.
A: OK, I'm Tom.
B: Glad to meet you.
A: And what do you do, Ted?
B: Me? I'm in the car business.
A: Salesman?
B: Yes, that's right. And how about you?
A: I work for American Airlines.
B: Oh, really? What do you do there exactly?
A: I'm in the Personnel Department.

Dialogue 3

Woman: Hello, Giovanni. Good to see you again. How are things?
Giovanni: Just fine. And you?
Woman: Oh, not too bad. Giovanni, do you know Bryan Turner, our new personnel manager? Bryan, this is Giovanni Toncini. He's from Italy. He works in Milan.
Bryan: Pleased to meet you, Mr. Toncini.
Giovanni: Please, call me Giovanni.
Bryan: And I'm Bryan.
Woman: Have a seat, Giovanni.
Giovanni: Thank you.
Woman: How about some coffee, Giovanni?

Giovanni: Yes, please. Cream and sugar, please.

II. Useful Expressions

1. Greeting a Friend and Responding

Greeting a Friend	Responding
• Hello, Ms. Anopow. How are you?	• Not too bad, thanks. And you?
• Hello, Peter. How're you doing?	• Fine, just fine. And you?
• Hi, Jim. Nice to meet you here. How are you getting on with your new work?	
• Hello, Robert. I haven't seen you for a long time. What have you been doing since I saw you last?	
• Diana! Haven't seen you for ages. How have you been?	
• Hello, Joan. How is everything going?	
• Hi, Ken. What's up?	

2. Approaching a Stranger and Responding

Approaching a Stranger	Responding
• Interesting meeting, isn't it?	• Yes, very. I thought the last speaker was especially good.
• Great party, isn't it?	• Yeah, really.
• Hot in here, isn't it?	• Yeah, really.
• Hello.	• Hello.

3. Introducing Oneself and Responding

Introducing Oneself	Responding
• Let me introduce myself, by the way. My name's Thomas Bradley.	• How do you do? I'm Nick Nugent.
	• Nice to meet you. I'm Bev Marshall.
• May I introduce myself? My name is Thomas Bradley.	• Hi, I'm Susan Jackson.
• My name is Bill Peters, by the way.	

Unit One

4. Introducing Other People and Responding

Introducing Other People	Responding
• Giovanni, do you know Bryan Turner, our new personnel manager? Bryan, this is Giovanni Toncini. He's from Italy. He works in Milan.	• Pleased (nice, glad) to meet you, Mr. Toncini.
• Mr. Smith, allow me to introduce my good friend, David. David, John Smith.	• How do you do, Mr. Smith?
• Dr. Johnson, I'd like you to meet my friend and colleague, David. This is my advisor, Dr. Gerald Johnson.	• How do you do?

5. Taking Leave and Responding

Taking Leave	Responding
• It was nice meeting you.	• Nice meeting you too.
• I'm glad to have met you.	• I am also glad to have met you.
• I hope we'll meet again sometime.	• I hope very soon.
• I hope we can see each other again some time.	
• See you later.	• See you later.

III. Exercises

1. **Dialogue Completion**

   (1) Woman: Hello, Davis. How are you?
   Man: _____
   A. How are you?
   B. How do you do?
   C. Fine, thank you. And you?
   D. Nice to meet you.

   (2) Man: Great party, isn't it?
   Woman: _____
   A. Hello.
   B. Yeah, really.

C. Have we met before?

  D. It's hot in here.

(3) Man: Let me introduce myself, by the way. My name is Thomas Burgson.

  Woman: _____

  A. How do you do? I'm Tina Cook.

  B. Thank you. My name is Tina Cook.

  C. Sorry. I don't know you.

  D. Oh, really. I haven't seen you for ages.

2. **Dialogue Comprehension**

  (1) Woman: Great party, isn't it?

  Man: Sure is. Jane and Ted always have great parties.

  Woman: This is my first. I met Jane only last week. She and I teach at the same school.

  Question: Where did the conversation probably take place?

  A. At a meeting.

  B. At a hotel.

  C. In a theatre.

  D. At their friends' home.

  (2) Man: Hello, Ms. Girardin. It's nice to see you again.

  Woman: Nice to see you, too.

  Man: Is Mr. LeGrand with you as well?

  Woman: Er... no. He's still in London.

  Question: What can we say about the two speakers?

  A. They are meeting each other for the first time.

  B. They have met each other only once before.

  C. They haven't seen each other for some time.

  D. They don't know each other.

Key to Part Three and Part Four

Part Three:

I. Vocabulary: 1. C   2. D   3. A   4. D   5. B

                    6. D   7. D   8. B   9. A   10. A

                    11. C   12. D   13. B   14. C   15. B

Unit One

II. Expression: 1. C   2. A   3. B   4. B   5. B
                 6. C   7. D   8. B   9. B   10. A
                 11. D   12. C   13. C   14. A   15. C
III. Cloze: 1. B   2. A   3. D   4. A   5. B
                 6. A   7. B   8. C   9. C   10. B
IV. Reading: 1. D   2. C   3. B   4. C   5. C
V. Reading: 1. T   2. F   3. F   4. T   5. F

Part Four:
1. Dialogue Completion: (1) C   (2) B   (3) A
2. Dialogue Comprehension: (1) D   (2) C

Unit Two

Text A

That Lean and Hungry Look

Part One: Language Points

I. Vocabulary

1. When these narrow fellows <u>spring</u> at me, I <u>quiver</u> to my toes. (Para. 1)

   译文: 我突然碰到这些瘦家伙们时,我从头到脚都会发抖。

   spring: *v.* to jump suddenly from the ground; to move suddenly from rest, concealment, etc. 跳;跳出;突然活动

   e.g. He <u>sprang</u> to his feet. 他跳了起来。

   quiver: *v.* to shake with a slight, rapid, tremulous movement 颤动(以一种轻微快速颤抖的运动摆动)

   e.g. The little girl <u>quivered</u> with fear at the sound.
   那个小女孩听到这声音害怕得有点发抖。

2. Thin people <u>come</u> in all personalities, most of them menacing. (Para. 1)

   译文: 有各种各样的瘦子,但大多数瘦子让人望而生畏。

   come: *v.* (+*adv./prep.;+adj.*) to be offered, produced, sold, etc. 被供应(生产,出售等),此处为幽默用法

   e.g. Shoes <u>come</u> in many shapes and sizes.
   所供应的鞋子有许多的款式和不同的尺码。

3. They've got speedy little metabolisms that cause them to <u>bustle</u> briskly. (Para. 3)

   译文: 他们新陈代谢很快,整日轻快地忙碌着。

bustle: *v.* to be busily active, often with much noise   忙忙碌碌;熙熙攘攘

e.g. *Everyone was bustling in and out.* 人人都在匆匆忙忙地进进出出。

4. They're forever rubbing their bony hands together and <u>eying</u> new problems to "tackle." (Para. 3)

   译文:他们瘦骨嶙峋,却总在摩拳擦掌,寻找有待解决的问题。

   eye: *v.* to watch closely   注视;密切地观察

   e.g. *The boys stood on the corner eyeing the local girls.*
   男孩子们站在角落里,注视着那些本地女孩。

   tackle: *v.* to take on and wrestle with (an opponent or a problem, for example)
   着手处理;接受(比如一名对手或一个问题)的挑战并与之拼搏

   e.g. *What is the best way to tackle this problem?*
   什么是解决这个问题的最好方法?

5. I like to surround myself with <u>sluggish</u>, <u>inert</u>, easygoing fat people, the kind who believe that if you clean it up today, it'll just get dirty again tomorrow. (Para. 3)

   译文:我喜欢和那些懒洋洋、不爱动的、悠闲自在的胖子在一起。他们往往都认为即使你今天把屋子打扫干净了,明天还会脏的。

   sluggish: *adj.* displaying little movement or activity; slow; inactive   缓慢的,迟缓的;表现出很少的活动或活力的;慢的;不活跃的

   e.g. *This humid heat makes you feel rather sluggish.*
   这种湿热天气让人懒洋洋的。

   inert: *adj.* sluggish in action or motion; inactive   迟缓的;行动或运动时呆滞的;无生气的

   e.g. *He lay completely inert on the floor and we feared he was dead.*
   他一动不动地躺在地板上,我们怕他已经死了。

6. Thin people turn surly, mean, and hard at a young age because they never learn the value of a hot-fudge sundae for <u>easing</u> tension. (Para. 4)

   译文:瘦子年轻轻的就变得又吝啬又乖戾,心肠还很硬。他们从来就不知道用热乎乎的奶糖冰激凌来放松自己。

   ease: *v.* to give relief to (the body or mind) from pain, discomfort, anxiety   减轻(身心之痛苦,不安,忧虑)

   e.g. *Can I ease you of your burden?* 我能减轻你的负担吗?

7. They go straight to the heart of the matter while fat people let things stay all blurry and hazy and <u>vague</u>, the way things actually are. (Para. 4)

   译文:瘦子喜欢直入主题,而胖子却让什么都模糊不清(事情本来就应该是这

样)。

vague: *adj.* not clear or distinct　不清楚的;模糊的

e.g. *I haven't the vaguest idea what they want.*
我一点都不知道他们需要什么。

8. Fat people know happiness is elusive at best and even if they could get the kind thin people talk about, they wouldn't want it. (Para. 8)

译文:胖子觉得无论如何幸福都是不可把握的,即使他们可以得到瘦子所说的幸福,他们也不要。

elusive: *adj.* tending to elude capture, perception, comprehension, or memory　逃避的;不易被抓获、觉察、理解或记忆的

e.g. *Despite all their efforts, success remained elusive.*
尽管他们作了种种努力,成功的把握还是不大。

9. They are the ones acquainted with the night, with luck, with fate, with playing it by ear. (Para. 9)

译文:他们熟谙事物的混沌状态,能够随机应变。他们知道一切都是命运安排,一切都靠运气。

acquainted: *adj.* known by or familiar with another　了解的,熟悉的;为他人所了解的或熟悉他人的

e.g. *He was acquainted with his new duties.*　他非常清楚他的新的职责。

10. One thin person I know once suggested that we arrange all the parts of a jigsaw puzzle into groups according to size, shape, and color. (Para. 9)

译文:一次我认识的一个瘦子建议我们把所有拼图玩具块按大小、形状和颜色分类。

arrange: *v.* to put into a specific order or relation; to dispose　安排;放成有序或相关的(排列);整理

e.g. *In a dictionary the words are arranged in alphabetical order.*
词典里的词是按字母顺序编排的。

11. The main problem with thin people is they oppress. (Para. 10)

译文:瘦子的主要问题是他们让人感到压抑。

oppress: *v.* to make someone feel unhappy, worried, or uncomfortable　(通常用作及物动词)压迫,压抑

e.g. *The loneliness of her little apartment oppressed her.*
她的小房子让她感到又孤独又压抑。

12. Their good intentions, bony torsos, tight ships, neat corners, cerebral machinations and pat solutions loom like dark clouds over the loose,　comfortable,

Unit Two

spread-out, soft world of the fat. (Para. 10)

译文: 他们的良苦用心、瘦削身材、严格管理、干净整洁、机智狡猾、灵活应变和高效率像乌云一样笼罩在胖人闲散、舒适、柔软、开阔的世界的上空。

loom: *v.* to appear to the mind in a magnified and threatening form 赫然耸现：以放大的和有威胁性的形象出现在意识中

e.g. Fear of failure <u>loomed</u> large in his mind.

(喻) 害怕失败的情绪沉重地压在他的心头。

II. Expressions

1. They don't know how to <u>goof off</u>, at least in the best, fat sense of the word. (Para. 2)

   译文: 他们根本不知道如何消磨时间，至少从"消磨时间"这个词的最丰富的意义上来看是这样的。

   goof off: to waste time or avoid doing any work 消磨时间；浪费时间

   a) *My work duty is this afternoon, so I'm gonna <u>goof off</u> for a while.*
   我下午才当班，所以我还可以闲逛会儿。

   b) *They <u>goofed off</u> too much, and now they're not ready for the exam.*
   他们玩得太多了，所以他们现在没准备好考试。

2. I like to surround myself with sluggish, inert, easygoing fat people, the kind who believe that if you <u>clean it up</u> today, it'll just get dirty again tomorrow. (Para. 3)

   译文: 我喜欢和那些懒洋洋、不爱动、悠闲自在的胖子在一起。他们往往都认为即使你今天把屋子打扫干净了，明天还会脏的。

   clean up: to make a place completely clean and tidy 清理；使清洁或有秩序

   a) *We spent all Sunday morning <u>cleaning up</u> the mess from Saturday night.*
   星期天一上午我们都在清理星期六晚上造成的脏乱。

   b) *There was mud all over the carpet, and it took me a long time to <u>clean it up</u>.*
   地毯上到处都是泥，我用了很长时间才把它清理干净。

3. Thin people have a long list of logical things they are always <u>spouting off</u> to me. (Para. 7)

   译文: 瘦人有一长串"我们应该如何做"的单子，而且他们总在滔滔不绝地对我说这些事情。

   spout off: to talk a lot about something in a boring and annoying way 滔滔不绝地讲

   a) *I really don't want to listen to Peter <u>spouting off</u> all afternoon.*
   我真不想整个下午都听彼得在那儿滔滔不绝地闲聊。

b) *All too often the old lady is spouting off about matters which should not concern her.*
那个老太太突然滔滔不绝地说起了一些和她毫无关系的事。

4. They <u>hold up</u> one finger at a time as they <u>reel off</u> these things, so I won't lose track. (Para. 7)

译文：他们掰着手指一件一件地罗列这些事情，好让我能跟上他们的思路。

hold up: to raise; to keep raised 举起；抬起

a) *My husband has lost so much weight that he has to wear a belt to hold his trousers up.*
我丈夫瘦了很多，他现在得扎个皮带才能把裤子提上。

b) *You have held up your hand for some minutes. What do you want?*
你已经把手举了一会儿了，你想要干什么？

reel off: to recite a lot of information quickly and easily 熟练地、一口气地背出

a) *Mary reeled off the titles of a dozen or so novels.*
玛丽能熟练地说出一系列小说的名称。

b) *What is the point of teaching children to reel off the names of ancient kings if they know nothing of history?*
如果孩子不知道什么历史，让他们记住一系列古代国王的名字有什么用？

5. It contains tidbits like "get a grip on yourself," "cigarettes kill," "cholesterol clogs," "fit as a fiddle," "ducks in a row," "organize" and "sound fiscal management." (Para. 7)

译文：尽是些诸如"管住自己"、"吸烟有害健康"、"胆固醇堵塞血管"、"神采奕奕"、"井井有条"、"组织好一切"和"高效理财"之类的无稽之谈。

get a grip on oneself: to act in a more sensible, calm, and controlled manner 管住自己；理智、清醒地处理（事情）

a) *Pull yourself together, my boy! You must get a firmer grip on yourself.*
镇静些，我的孩子！你必须控制住自己。

b) *He has a good grip on himself and never gives way to anger.*
他总能很好地控制自己，而不让自己生气。

to be fit as a fiddle: to be perfectly healthy 神采奕奕；身体健壮

a) *The man was almost ninety years old but fit as a fiddle.*
那个老人已快九十了，但仍然精神矍铄。

b) *Today she's as fit as a fiddle—thanks to research funded by efforts such as Beefy's.*
今天她神采奕奕,主要归功于比菲等出资赞助所作的研究。

6. They think these 2,000-point plans lead to happiness. (Para. 8)
   译文:他们认为这两千条计划能给我们带来幸福。

   lead to: to open the way for something to happen   导致

   a) *A degree in English could lead to a career in journalism.*
   获得一个英语学位后可以在新闻界找个工作。

   b) *Disobeying the law could lead to trouble.*   不遵守法律就会有麻烦。

7. Wisely, fat people see that such programs are too dull, too hard, too off the mark. (Para. 8)
   译文:胖子非常明智地认为这样做太难,太沉闷了,也难以实现。

   off the mark / wide of the mark: not correct, inaccurate   不准确;不正确;相差甚远

   a) *John didn't think the story was so far off the mark.*
   约翰不认为那个说法有那么大的出入。

   b) *If that was meant to be an apology, your words were way off the mark.*
   如果那算是道歉的话,你的话也太不着边际了。

8. They are the ones acquainted with the night, with luck, with fate, with playing it by ear. (Para. 9)
   译文:他们熟谙事物的混沌状态,能够随机应变。他们知道一切都是命运安排,一切都靠运气。

   play it by ear: to decide what to say or do in a situation on the spot rather than by following a plan   见机行事;随机应变

   a) *We'll see what the weather is like and play it by ear.*
   我们看看天气情况再说吧。

   b) *Devil Rays officials head to the winter meetings in Dallas this morning not sure exactly what they're looking for—they plan to play it by ear there.*
   "魔鬼之光"队的官员们今天上午赶往达拉斯参加会议,他们也不清楚他们要什么——他们打算到那儿再见机行事。

9. One, I like to muddle through. (Para. 9)
   译文:首先,我就喜欢随意地玩。

   muddle through: to reach an end point in an indirect and disorganized fashion   胡乱应付过去

a) *There were some difficulties, but I managed to muddle through.*
有很多困难,但我们总算混过来了。

b) *I'm afraid I can't help you—you'll just have to muddle through on your own.*
恐怕我不能帮你,你只能自己想办法对付了。

10. My thin friend had no use for my list. (Para. 9)

    译文:我的瘦朋友对我列举的几条不以为然。

    have no use for: to have no liking or respect for 不需要;不喜欢;厌恶

    a) *I've no use for such old-fashioned methods. We must modernize at once.*
    我无法容忍这种老方法。咱们得使用现代方法。

    b) *The earnest young man had no use for jokes.*
    这个一本正经的年轻人不能容忍别人开玩笑。

11. Fat people are heavily into fits of laughter, slapping their thighs, and whooping it up, while thin people are still politely waiting for the punch line. (Para. 10)

    译文:瘦子还在等点题的妙语时,胖子已经拍着大腿前仰后合地开怀大笑。

    whoop it up / whoop things up: to enjoy oneself in a noisy and excited way
    (俚)欢闹;狂欢

    a) *They whooped it up after winning the game.*
    他们赢得了比赛后一起欢庆。

    b) *Let's go to the party and whoop it up together!*
    我们去参加晚会热闹热闹吧。

12. They will come up with a good reason why you never wrote the great American novel. (Para. 12)

    译文:他们能替你找出没能写出伟大的美国小说的理由。

    come up with: to think of an idea or solution 产生;发现(解决问题的办法、答案)

    a) *Is that the best excuse you can come up with?*
    这就是你能找出的最好借口吗?

    b) *Thirty years ago, scientists came up with the theory that protons and neutrons are composed of three smaller particles.*
    三十年前科学家们提出了质子和中子是由三个小粒子组成的理论。

13. They will let you off the hook. (Para. 12)

    译文:他们会帮你摆脱困境。

    let somebody off the hook: to allow or help somebody get out of a difficult situation (非正式)摆脱困境

a) *Robert has agreed to go to the party in my place so as to let me off the hook.*
罗伯特同意到我的住处参加晚会,帮我摆脱困境。

b) *His opponents have no intention of letting him off the hook until he agrees to leave office immediately.*
他如果不答应立即辞职,他的对手不会让他摆脱困境。

III. Grammar

1. I like to surround myself with sluggish, inert, easygoing fat people, the kind who believe that if you clean it up today, it'll just get dirty again tomorrow. (Para. 3)

   译文:我喜欢和那些懒洋洋、不爱动的、悠闲自在的胖子在一起。他们往往都认为即使你今天把屋子打扫干净了,明天还会脏的。

   划线部分为 fat people 的同位语,其中包含由 who 引导的定语从句修饰 the kind。

2. They go straight to the heart of the matter while fat people let things stay all blurry and hazy and vague, the way things actually are. (Para. 4)

   译文:瘦子喜欢直入主题,而胖子却让什么都模糊不清(事情本来就应该是这样)。

   the way=as, 常引导定语从句,起连接词的作用。在美国口语中,表示"as"意义的 the way 的用法可以认为是紧接在从句之前的 in the way 脱落了 in 而来的。比较:the moment=as soon as

   e.g. *I fixed things the way he wanted.*

3. The sides fat people see are rounded blobs, usually gray, always nebulous and truly not worth worrying about. (Para. 5)

   译文:胖子所看到的各个方面是圆圆的一团,通常是灰蒙蒙,模糊不清的而且也没什么值得操心的。

   worth+doing 在英语中为较特殊的结构。此处 worth 为形容词,doing 在意义上相当于 worth 的宾语。worth 后不能接不定式。除 worth 外,像动词和介词一样接宾语的有 opposite, near, like 等形容词。

   e.g. *Come and sit near me.*

4. If God were up there, fat people could have two doughnuts and a big orange drink anytime they wanted it. (Para. 6)

   译文:如果有上帝的话,胖子们就应该能什么时候想要甜圈饼就有甜圈饼,想要橘子汁就有橘子汁。

anytime 此处作为连词,相当于 when;比较: every time(每当)。

e.g. *Every time we had difficulties, he will come to help.*

Part Two: Key to Exercises

I. Suggested Answers to *Topics for Discussion*

1. What does the title suggest about the thesis of the essay?

   It is part of a comment Caesar made about one of the men conspiring against him in *Julius Caesar*, a play written by William Shakespeare. From the title we can see that the author holds a negative attitude towards thin people. She is making fun of thin people.

2. What bothers the author most about thin people?

   What bothers the author most is that thin people are always busy with something and that they just seem much more clever than fat people. Thin people exert pressure on other people.

3. Sum up the personalities typical of thin people and of fat people, according to the essay. What are the major differences between them?

   Thin people are always busy with something and always finding new problems to solve. They make other people feel tired and inadequate. They work very hard, trying to ascertain the absolute truth and putting everything into logical order. They see the world in black and white.

   Fat people, instead, believe that there is no absolute truth in this world. They think that life is illogical and unfair and that happiness is elusive. They know the mystery of life. And they know how to relax and enjoy themselves and have a good time.

4. Is the author serious in speaking against thin people? What is her underlying purpose in writing this essay?

   No. The author is criticizing thin people while showing her approval of fat people.

   In American culture, which is a "diet-crazy" culture, to be thin is to be perfect and much admired, to be in control. Fat people are judged as lacking self-discipline and being out of control. Britt, according to this piece, is a fat person who is fed up with the adulation of the thin. Her essay is "tongue in cheek," though, not to be taken seriously. If she is serious about anything, it is about the American tendency to admire the thin over the fat.

II. Key to Exercises
Text A
A.
1. The author suggests that thin people make others feel uncomfortable by their very presence. They are too superior, too much in control of any situation. They make others feel under great pressure by their constant bustle and hustle.
2. The "together" thin person is very confident, organized, and knows what he or she wants.
    The "tsk-tsk" thin person always shows disapproval of something and is too critical of others.
3. To "goof off" is perhaps to fully enjoy oneself, relax, and have a good time. According to Britt, a fat person is less controlling, less anxious, more able to relax, more able to let a good time "just happen" than is a thin person.
4. According to this essay, "things" are actually always blurry and vague, nebulous and complex. For fat people there is no need to get a clear image of things because "truth" is not a sharp, clear reality to be faced directly. Fat people do not "tackle" problems.
    Thin people see "things" differently. They think much more linearly in terms of problems and solutions, of black and white, of seeking a definitive "truth." Thin people "tackle" problems because they want to be in control, to overcome problems.
5. The mystery or meaning of life is elusive, as is acknowledged by the fat person, but not by the thin.
    At night everything is dark and indistinct, illogical and impossible to understand. Fat people are "acquainted with the night" because they see truth as elusive and life as illogical and incomprehensible.
6. The author spouts off a logical list, which is usually what thin people like to do.
7. "The main problem with thin people is they oppress." They consider themselves superior to fat people and try to impress them with their organized, logical, in-control lives.
8. The letter "p" is explosive and suggests action. The letter "g" is more guttural, sug-

gesting depth (from deep in the throat and stomach) and perhaps slowness and sluggishness rather than sharp action.
9. Fat people give space both to themselves and to others. They tolerate others' failures and provide emotional support for others.
10.

Adjectives Describing Thin People			Adjectives Describing Fat People		
menacing	dangerous	mechanical	sluggish	inert	easygoing
condescending	"together"	"tsk-tsk"	loose	comfortable	spread-out
efficiency-expert	speedy	wizened	soft	convivial	
shriveled	surly	mean			
hard	crunchy	dull			
bony	tight	neat			
cerebral	pat	skinny			

Verbs Related to Thin People	Verbs Related to Fat People
1. make one feel tired	1. believe that if you clean it up today, it'll just get dirty again tomorrow
2. bustle briskly	2. know there is no truth
3. believe in logic	3. see gray, nebulous, rounded blobs which are not worth worrying about
4. see all sides	4. realize that life is illogical and unfair
5. want to face the truth	5. know happiness is elusive
6. always staring at complex, unsolvable problems	6. know all about the mystery of life
7. always spout off a long list of logical things to othersit	7. be acquainted with luck, fate, and playing by ear
8. oppress	8. let things stay all blurry and hazy and vague
9. like math and morality and reasoned evaluation of the limitation of human beings	

11. (1) F (2) T (3) T (4) F (5) F (6) T (7) F (8) T

B.

1. goof off ... make her tired
2. the logical things in life ... rounded blobs, usually gray, always nebulous and truly

Unit Two

not worth worrying about ... illogical and unfair ... elusive at best ... luck ... fate ... playing it by ear

C.
1. D 2. B 3. C 4. D 5. D 6. C

D.
1. ease 2. loomed 3. sprang 4. bustled 5. tackle 6. arranging 7. sluggish
8. elusive 9. acquainted 10. vague 11. oppress 12. eying 13. quivered
14. inert 15. comes

E.
1. goofing off 2. clean up 3. stare at 4. spouting off 5. Hold up 6. lead to
7. muddle through 8. came up with 9. at best 10. has no use for
11. take ... in 12. reeled off 13. play it by ear

F.
1. the things that
2. the way she wants them
3. as if for
4. isn't the important thing. The important thing is
5. The fact is (that)
6. Long after ... were still

G.
1. D 2. C 3. B 4. A 5. C 6. D 7. A 8. B 9. C 10. D

H.
1. Tian'anmen square is a favorite place for people to whoop it up on National Day.
2. He got fired because he kept goofing off on his job.
3. I always have the image of my mother bustling in and out.
4. The government set up a task force to tackle the rising crime rate in this city.
5. He often spouts off about the funny things that happened when he was in the army.
6. This five-year-old boy can reel off the names of more than a hundred countries.
7. The problem is that we are short of funds. What you said is off the mark.
8. We could not do it according to plan. We have to play it by ear.
9. I myself don't know how I muddled through the four years at college.
10. She said she has no use for those who idle around all days.
11. He can always come up with excuses for being late.
12. I owed him a lot for letting me off the hook.

I.
1. 有各种各样的瘦子,但大多数瘦子让人望而生畏。有镇定自若的瘦子,有呆板机械的瘦子,有屈尊俯就的瘦子,有不停指责别人的瘦子,还有是效率专家的瘦子。
2. 瘦子喜欢直入主题,而胖子却让什么都模糊不清(事情本来就应该是这样)。
3. 瘦子相信逻辑。胖子看到的是事物的各个侧面。胖子所看到的各个侧面是圆圆的一团,通常是灰蒙蒙、模糊不清的而也没什么值得操心的。
4. 胖子非常了解生活的秘密。他们熟谙事物的混沌状态,能够随机应变。他们知道一切都是命运安排,一切都靠运气。
5. 瘦子的主要问题是他们让人感到压抑。他们有良好的意图,瘦削的身材。(他们对事情)有严格的管理,到处都收拾得很干净。做事情足智多谋,雷厉风行。这一切都像乌云一样笼罩在胖子柔软舒适、悠闲而又开阔的世界的上空。

Text B
1. B   2. D   3. B   4. D   5. A

Part Three: Self-check

I. Choose the word that is closest in meaning to the underlined word in each sentence.

1. When these narrow fellows spring at me, I quiver to my toes.
   A. come   B. speak   C. jump   D. scream
2. The little girl quivered with fear at the sound.
   A. trembled   B. quaked   C. cried   D. listened
3. Thin people come in all personalities, most of them menacing.
   A. move   B. arrive   C. reach   D. exist
4. They've got speedy little metabolisms that cause them to bustle briskly.
   A. hustle   B. walk   C. work   D. proceed
5. They're forever rubbing their bony hands together and eyeing new problems to "tackle."
   A. looking for   B. studying   C. seeing   D. glimpsing
6. What is the best way to tackle this problem?
   A. create   B. present   C. approach   D. cause

Unit Two

7. I like to surround myself with sluggish, inert, easygoing fat people, the kind who believe that if you clean it up today, it'll just get dirty again tomorrow.
   A. slow-moving   B. lazy   C. stupid   D. snobbish

8. He lay completely inert on the floor, and we feared he was dead.
   A. inactive   B. dumb   C. quiet   D. sad

9. Thin people turn surly, mean, and hard at a young age because they never learn the value of a hot-fudge sundae for easing tension.
   A. adding   B. building   C. feeling   D. relieving

10. They go straight to the heart of the matter while fat people let things stay all blurry and hazy and vague, the way things actually are.
    A. weak   B. vain   C. indistinct   D. vacant

11. Fat people know happiness is elusive at best and even if they could get the kind thin people talk about, they wouldn't want it.
    A. illusive   B. illogical   C. intriguing   D. evasive

12. They are the ones acquainted with the night, with luck, with fate, with playing it by ear.
    A. annoyed   B. familiar   C. impatient   D. upset

13. One thin person I know once suggested that we arrange all the parts of a jigsaw puzzle into groups according to size, shape, and color.
    A. organize   B. mix   C. break   D. array

14. The main problem with thin people is they oppress.
    A. press   B. oppose   C. depress   D. dismiss

15. Their good intentions, bony torsos, tight ships, neat corners, cerebral machinations and pat solutions loom like dark clouds over the loose, comfortable, spread-out, soft world of the fat.
    A. appear   B. weave   C. threaten   D. grow

II. Choose the expression that best completes each sentence.

1. They don't know how to _____ at least in the best, fat sense of the word. They've always got to be adoing.
   A. spout off   B. reel off   C. goof off   D. take off

2. I like to surround myself with sluggish, inert, easygoing fat people, the kind who believe that if you _____ today, it'll just get dirty again tomorrow.
   A. clean it down   B. clean it out   C. clean it up   D. clean if away

3. Thin people have a long list of logical things they are always _____ to me.
   A. bugging out   B. spouting off   C. making up   D. taking up
4. They _____ one finger at a time as they reel off these things, so I won't lose track.
   A. hold up   B. hold out   C. hold onto   D. hold forth
5. What is the point of teaching children to _____ the names of ancient kings if they know nothing of history?
   A. reel off   B. write off   C. speak out   D. speak up
6. He _____ himself and never gives way to anger.
   A. lets it be   B. keeps a grip on   C. holds onto   D. picks up
7. The man was almost ninety years old but _____.
   A. fit as a fiddle   B. neat as a pin   C. smart as a whip   D. deaf as a post
8. A degree in English could _____ a career in journalism.
   A. stem from   B. rest on   C. lead to   D. add to
9. If that was meant to be an apology, your words were way _____.
   A. off the mark   B. out of control   C. to the point   D. out of mind
10. Devil Rays officials head to the winter meetings in Dallas this morning, not sure exactly what they're looking for—they plan to _____ there.
    A. play the fool   B. play it by ear   C. play the game   D. play it cool
11. One thin person I know once suggested that we arrange all parts of a jigsaw puzzle into groups according to size, shape, and color. I said I wouldn't do it. One, I like to _____.
    A. muddle up   B. muddle along   C. muddle on   D. muddle through
12. The earnest young man _____ jokes.
    A. made use of   B. had no use for
    C. took advantage of   D. make nonsense of
13. Fat people are heavily into fits of laughter, slapping their thighs, and _____ while thin people are still politely waiting for the punch line.
    A. whooping it up   B. going it alone
    C. making it to the top   D. playing it by ear
14. They will _____ a good reason why you never wrote the great American novel.
    A. come up with   B. put up with
    C. keep up with   D. catch up with

15. His opponents have no intention of letting him _____ until he agrees to leave office immediately.

   A. off the mark   B. off the hook   C. off the point   D. out of the way

III. Read the following passage and fill in each blank with the best choice from the words or expressions given.

I want a wife who will take care of my physical needs. I want a wife who will __1__ my house clean. A wife who will pick up after my children, a wife who will pick up after me. I want a wife who will keep my clothes clean, ironed, mended, replaced when need be, and who will __2__ it that my personal things are kept in their proper place __3__ I can find what I need the minute I need it. I want a wife who cooks the meals, a wife who is a good cook. I want a wife who will plan the menus, __4__ the necessary grocery shopping, prepare the meals, serve them pleasantly, and then do the cleaning up __5__ I do the studying. I want a wife who will care for me when I am sick and sympathize with my pain and loss of time from school.

I want a wife who will take care of the details of my social life. When my wife and I are __6__ out by my friends, I want a wife who will take care of the babysitting arrangements. When I meet people at school that I like and want to __7__, I want a wife who will have the house clean, prepare a meal, serve it to me and my friends, and not __8__ when I talk about things that interest me and my friends. I want a wife who will have arranged that the children are fed and ready for bed before my guests arrive so that the children do not bother us. I want a wife who will take care of the __9__ of my guests so that they feel comfortable, who makes sure that they have an ashtray, that they are offered a second helping of the food, that their wine glasses are replenished (再装满) when __10__, that their coffee is served to them as they like it.

1. A. make	B. get	C. keep	D. render
2. A. see to	B. see over	C. see round	D. see through
3. A. in order to	B. so that	C. so long as	D. in so far as
4. A. go	B. do	C. make	D. take
5. A. since	B. as	C. while	D. until
6. A. wanted	B. invited	C. pleaded	D. inquired
7. A. entertain	B. meet	C. inform	D. chat

8. A. cut   B. interrupt   C. break   D. interfere
9. A. requirements B. demands   C. requests   D. needs
10. A. useful   B. necessary   C. proper   D. good

IV. Read the following passage and choose the best answer for each question.

Despite this shift, mothers are by and large still shown as the primary caregivers and, more important, as the primary nurturers of their children. Men in the books—if they're shown at all—still come home late after work and participate in the child rearing by bouncing baby around for five minutes before putting the child to bed.

I recently spent an entire day on the children's floor of the local library trying to find out whether these same negative stereotypes (典型, 形象) are found in the more recent classics-to-be. The librarian gave me a list of the twenty most popular contemporary picture books, and I read every one of them. Of the twenty, seven don't mention a parent at all. Of the remaining thirteen, four portray fathers as much less loving and caring than mothers. In Little Gorilla, we are told that the little gorilla's "mother loves him" and we see Mama Gorilla giving her little one a warm hug. On the next page we're also told that his "father loves him," but in the illustration, father and son aren't even touching. Six of the remaining nine books mention or portray mothers as the only parent, and only three of the twenty have what could be considered "equal" treatment of mothers and fathers.

The same negative stereotypes also show up in literature aimed at the parents of small children. In *What to Expect the First Year*, the authors answer almost every question the parents of a newborn or toddler could have in the first year of their child's life. They are meticulous (小心翼翼的) in alternating (轮流) between references to boys and girls. At the same time, they refer almost exclusively to "mother" or "mommy." Men, and their feelings about parenting, are relegated (归入) to a nine-page chapter just before the recipe (食谱) section.

Unfortunately, it's still true that, in our society, women do the bulk of childcare and that, thanks to men abandoning their families, there are too many single mothers out there. Nevertheless, to say that portraying fathers as un-nurturing or completely absent is simply "a reflection of reality" is unacceptable. If children's literature only reflected reality, it would be like prime-time TV and we'd have books filled with child abusers, wife beaters, and criminals.

    Young children believe what they hear—especially from a parent figure. And since, for the first few years of a child's life, adults select the reading material, children's literature should be held to a high standard. Ignoring men who share equally in raising their children and continuing to show nothing but part-time or no-time fathers is only going to create yet another generation of men who have been told—since boyhood—that mothers are the truer parents and that fathers play, at best, a secondary role in the home. We've taken major steps to root out discrimination in what our children read. Let's finish the job.

1. How are mothers usually portrayed in children's literature?
   A. They are shown as the weak personalities in the family.
   B. They can tolerate all the wrongdoings of their children.
   C. They work hard to give their children a better life.
   D. They are the main caregivers.
2. What is the usual image of fathers in children's literature?
   A. They are not loving and caring to their children.
   B. They are only bread-winners.
   C. They are not as involved in child raising.
   D. They are bad-tempered.
3. How are fathers represented in children's literature?
   A. They are under-represented in children's literature.
   B. About half the books talk mainly about fathers.
   C. Most books treat both mothers and fathers equally.
   D. None of the children's books mention fathers.
4. What is the author's point about children's literature?
   A. Children's literature should reflect reality.
   B. Children's literature should not reflect reality.
   C. Children's literature must reflect reality.
   D. We should apply a high standard to children's literature.
5. What does the author think about men's role in childraising?
   A. Men are part-time or no-time fathers.
   B. Fathers should share equally in raising their children.
   C. Fathers do the bulk of childcare.
   D. Fathers shrink from giving care to their children.

V. Read the following passage and decide whether each statement is TRUE or FALSE.

And that, perhaps, is where the contrast between Grant and Lee becomes most striking. The Virginia aristocrat, inevitably, saw himself in relation to his own region. He lived in a static society which could endure almost anything except change. Instinctively, his first loyalty would go to the locality in which that society existed. He would fight to the limit of endurance to defend it, because in defending it he was defending everything that gave his own life its deepest meaning.

The Westerner, on the other hand, would fight with an equal tenacity for the broader concept of society. He fought so because everything he lived by was tied to growth, expansion, and a constantly widening horizon. What he lived by would survive or fall with the nation itself. He could not possibly stand by unmoved in the face of an attempt to destroy the Union. He would combat it with everything he had, because he could only see it as an effort to cut the ground out from under his feet.

So Grant and Lee were in complete contrast, representing two diametrically opposed elements in American life. Grant was the modern man emerging; beyond him, ready to come on the stage, was the great age of steel and machinery, of crowded cities and a restless burgeoning vitality. Lee might have ridden down from the old age of chivalry, lance in hand, silken banner fluttering over his head. Each man was the perfect champion of his cause, drawing both his strengths and his weaknesses from the people he led.

Yet it was not all contrast, after all. Different as they were—in background, in personality, in underlying aspiration—these two great soldiers had much in common. Under everything else, they were marvelous fighters. Furthermore, their fighting qualities were really very much alike.

1. Grant and Lee had little in common. They stood in complete contrast.
2. Grant and Lee represented two conflicting currents in American life. Lee stood for the great age of steel and machinery.
3. Lee, the Virginia aristocrat would defend his own nation to the limit of his endurance.
4. Grant had an acute stake in the continued growth and development of his country.
5. Both Grant and Lee were great fighters, possessing great fighting qualities.

Unit Two

Part Four: Oral Expression: Entertaining

I. Dialogues

Dialogue 1

Ruffer: Good morning.

Harris: Hello. This is Alicia Harris. I'd like to speak to Mr. Ruffer.

Ruffer: Speaking. How are you, Mrs. Harris?

Harris: Fine, fine. I'd like to discuss our new product with you. Would you like to have lunch at the Atlas some time next week?

Ruffer: That sounds nice. When exactly?

Harris: Well, how about Tuesday?

Ruffer: That's very kind of you, but I'm afraid I can't make Tuesday. I've got to go to the head office.

Harris: That's a pity. Does Thursday suit you?

Ruffer: Yes, that would be fine. What time?

Harris: Shall we say 12:30?

Ruffer: Yes, that's fine. Next Thursday at 12:30 at the Atlas. I'll look forward to it.

Dialogue 2

Carter: Everything looks good. What are you going to have, Jackie?

Jackie: I think I'll have the spaghetti and a salad. How about you? What are you having?

Carter: Spaghetti sounds good, but I feel like a steak. I guess we're ready to order.

Excuse me!

Waitress: Good evening. Have you decided yet?

Jackie: Yes. I'll have the spaghetti and a salad.

Waitress: And what kind of dressing would you like on your salad?

Jackie: I'd like oil and vinegar.

Waitress: OK. And what would you like, sir?

Carter: I'd like a steak, medium-rare, please.

Waitress:	Would you like soup or salad with that?
Carter:	What kind of soup do you have tonight?
Waitress:	Cream of mushroom and clam chowder.
Carter:	Clam chowder, please. And I'll have a baked potato and carrots.
Waitress:	I'll be right back with your soup and salad.
Jackie:	Thank you.

Dialogue 3

Waiter:	Shall I bring you some more coffee?
Woman:	Please. I'd love some.
Waiter:	Here you are, ma'am.
Woman:	And could I get a little more cream, please?
Waiter:	Of course. Anything else?
Woman:	I think ... just the check, thanks.
Waiter:	Right away.

II. Useful Expressions

1. **Extending an Invitation**

Inviting	Responding
• Would you like to go to lunch Saturday? (informal)	• Oh, that's a great idea.
• Do you want to have lunch together tomorrow? (informal)	• That sounds nice.
• Would you like to have lunch at the Atlas some time next week? (more formal)	• Oh, yes. I'd love to.
• I was wondering if you'd like to go to lunch tomorrow? (more formal)	• Oh, I'd love to, but I don't think I can.

2. **Suggesting Another Time**

Suggesting Another Time	Responding
• That's very kind of you, but I'm afraid I can't make Tuesday.	• That's too bad. Does Thursday suit you?
• I'm really sorry. I can't make it.	• OK. Maybe we can do it some other time then.

Unit Two

3. **Setting the Time and Place**

Setting the Time and Place	Responding
• What time should we meet? • What time should be good for you? • Would 12:30 be all right?	• Is 7:00 OK? • Shall we say 12:30? • Yes, that's fine. Next Thursday at 12:30 at the Atlas. I'll look forward to it.

4. **Ordering in a Restaurant**

Ordering for Others	Ordering for Oneself
• Everything looks good. What are you going to have, Jackie? • How about you? What are you having?	• I think I'll have the spaghetti and a salad. • Spaghetti sounds good, but I feel like a steak.

5. **Speaking to a Waiter/Waitress**

Waiter/Waitress	Customer
• What would you like, Sir? • What will you have, Ma'am? • Are you ready to order, Miss?	• I'll have a steak, please. • I'd like a chef's salad, please. • Could I have the spaghetti, please?

6. **Specifying an Option in a Restaurant**

Waiter/Waitress	Customer
• What kind of dressing would you like?	• I'll have Russian, please.

7. **Completing the Order in a Restaurant**

Waiter/Waitress	Customer
• Would you care for anything to drink? • Can I get you something to drink? • I'm afraid we don't. • I'm sorry, we're all out. • I'm sorry, we've run out.	• Do you have any hot tea?

8. Offering Service in a Restaurant

Waiter/Waitress	Customer
• Shall I bring your coffee now?	• Yes, please.
• Would you like me to get your coffee now?	• No, thanks.

9. At Someone's House for Dinner

Host/Hostess	Guest
• Can I offer you another cup of coffee?	• No, thanks. I've had plenty.
• Would you like some steak?	• Yes, please. I'm starving.
• How about some more milk?	• Yes, please. I'd love some.
• Would you like anything else?	• No, thanks. It was delicious, but I've already eaten too much. (I'm full. / I'm stuffed.) • Yes, please. Could I have some more turkey?
• Is there anything else I can get you?	• Yes, please. I'd love another helping of potatoes.

10. Menu Items

Main Course

Beef (牛肉)
Lobster tails (龙虾)
Salmon teriyaki (红烧马哈鱼)
Chicken nuggets (鸡块)
Chicken wings (鸡翅)
Fried egg (煎鸡蛋)
Scrambled egg (炒鸡蛋)
Pork chop (猪排)
Squirrel-shaped mandarin fish
 (松鼠桂鱼)
Shredded pork with Beijing bean
 sauce (京酱肉丝)
Lamb chop (羊排)

Pork (猪肉)
Mutton (羊肉)
Steak (牛排按熟的程度可分为以下几种)
(1) well done (全熟,但有时可能太老)
(2) medium (半熟,比较适合一般的口味)
(3) medium rare (半生,但略微有点儿生)
Boiled egg (煮鸡蛋)
Poached egg (荷包蛋)
Home style spareribs (红烧排骨)
Steamed mandarin fish (清蒸桂鱼)
Sweet-and-sour carp (糖醋鲤鱼)
Stewed fish with soy sauce, braised
 fish in brown sauce (红烧鱼)

Unit Two

Beef stew (红烧牛肉)
Steamed fish with black bean sauce (豉汁蒸鱼)
Roast mutton (烤羊肉)
Instant boiled sliced mutton (涮羊肉)
Fried shredded pork with sweet-and-sour sauce (鱼香肉丝)
Kung pao chicken (宫爆鸡丁)
Bean curd in chili sauce (麻婆豆腐)

Soup
Cream of mushroom (蘑菇奶油汤)
Cream of clam chowder (蛤蜊海鲜汤)

Vegetable
Baked potato (烤土豆)
Boiled potato /mashed potato (土豆泥)
French fries (炸薯条)
Broccoli (西兰花)
Asparagus (芦笋)
Peas and carrots (豌豆和胡萝卜)

Breakfast Items
Muffin (松饼)
Pancake (煎饼)
Waffles (华夫饼)
Toast (面包片)
Croissant (羊角面包)

III. Exercises

1. **Dialogue Completion**

    (1) Man: Well, I was wondering if you'd like to go to lunch this Friday?
    Woman: Oh, I'd love to, but I'm afraid I can't this Friday. I have to work.
    Man: _____

    A. Oh, that's a terrific idea.

    B. Oh, that's too bad. Well, could we make it some other time then?

    C. Just fine, thanks.

    D. That sounds very nice.

    (2) Waitress: Are you ready to order, sir?
    Man: _____

47

A. No, thank you.
B. Could I have some extra cream for the coffee?
C. Could I have a few more minutes, please?
D. Just the bill, please.

2. **Dialogue Comprehension**
   (1) Woman: Would you like a starter?
   Man: Yes, that would be nice. Can you help me with the menu?
   Woman: Yes, of course. Now these are soups here.
   Question: What does the man try to do?
   A. He tries to get a new copy of the menu.
   B. He asks the woman to help him decide what to have for his main course.
   C. He tries to decide on a soup as the starter.
   D. He doesn't need any starter.
   (2) Woman: What would you like for your main course?
   Man: What can you recommend?
   Woman: Well, the caldeirada is usually very good here. It's a kind of fish stew, with lots of different fish.
   Question: What is the caldeirada?
   A. A starter.
   B. A main course.
   C. A dessert.
   D. A salad.
   (3) Man: How about a dessert? I'm going to have phal mave. It's a fruit salad with melon, bananas, oranges, grapes, and mango. Would you like to try it? Or something else?
   Woman: Er... I think I'll just have a coffee.
   Question: What will the woman have for dessert?
   A. She will have coffee for dessert.
   B. She hasn't decided yet.
   C. She will try that fruit salad.
   D. She will not have any dessert.

Unit Two

Key to Part Three and Part Four

Part Three:

I. Vocabulary: 1. C   2. A   3. D   4. A   5. B
                6. C   7. A   8. A   9. D   10. C
                11. D   12. B   13. A   14. C   15. C

II. Expression: 1. C   2. C   3. B   4. A   5. A
                6. B   7. A   8. C   9. A   10. B
                11. D   12. B   13. A   14. A   15. B

III. Cloze: 1. C   2. A   3. B   4. B   5. C
                6. B   7. A   8. B   9. D   10. B

IV. Reading: 1. D   2. C   3. A   4. D   5. B

V. Reading: 1. F   2. F   3. F   4. T   5. T

Part Four:

1. Dialogue Completion: (1) B   (2) C
2. Dialogue Comprehension: (1) C   (2) B   (3) D

49

Unit Three

Text A

Selling Our Innocence Abroad

Part One: Language Points

I. Vocabulary

1. The largest debtor nation in the world, where ten million blacks live in poverty and whose capital, run by a cocaine addict, had a murder rate during the Eighties higher than that of Sri Lanka or Beirut, seems an unlikely model for <u>emulation</u>. (Para. 1)

   译文: 这一世界上最大的债务国(美国)里尚有一千万黑人生活在贫困之中, 可卡因瘾君子掌管下的首都在80年代的谋杀犯罪率比斯里兰卡或贝鲁特还高,(因此美国)似乎不大应当作为仿效的典范。

   emulation: *n.* trying to do sth. or behave in the same way as sb. because you admire them 仿效 *v.* emulate

   e.g. Sons are traditionally expected to <u>emulate</u> their fathers.
   传统上总期望儿子能仿效父亲。

2. A visitor today in Vietnam, one of the last of America's official enemies, will find crowds in Hue, in waterside cafes, <u>desperate</u> to get a glimpse of Meryl Streep on video. (Para. 2)

   译文: 假使如今有访客来到越南——它是美国仅剩的几个正式敌国之一——那么他会发现顺化市河边的小饭馆里挤满了人,他们想方设法只为一睹录像里梅丽尔·斯特里普的芳容。

Unit Three

desperate: *adj.* feeling that you have no hope and are ready to do anything to change the bad situation you are in 情急拼命的,极度渴望的

e.g. *The doctors made one last desperate attempt to save the boy's life.*
医生们奋力作了最后一搏,试图挽救男孩的生命。

3. The pirated version of Eddie Murphy's *Coming to America* went on sale well before the video had ever come to America. (Para. 2)

译文:埃迪·墨菲主演的《来去美国》在美国上映之前,其盗版影碟就已在不丹热卖了。

pirate: *v.* to copy and use or sell sb's work or a product without permission and without having the right to do so 非法翻印,盗版

e.g. *Pirated copies of music tapes are flooding the market.*
盗版音乐磁带泛滥市场。

4. By now, indeed, such products represent the largest single source of America's export earnings, even as America remains the single most popular destination for immigrants. (Para. 3)

译文:到目前为止,这样的产品(流行文化产品)确实是美国出口收入的最大一个来源,尽管美国仍然是唯一一个最受欢迎的移民迁居目的地。

represent: *v.* to be the result of something, or to be something 代表,意味着,相当于

e.g. *This book represents ten years of thought and research.*
这本书代表了10年的思索和研究。

5. The Europeans may have a stronger and more self-conscious sense of their aesthetic heritage. (Para. 3)

译文:欧洲人可能对本国的艺术遗产有一种更为强烈和自觉的意识。

heritage: *n.* all the qualities, traditions, or features of life there that have continued over many years and have been passed on from one generation to another 继承物,遗留物,传统

e.g. *These monuments are a vital part of the cultural heritage of South America.*
这些纪念碑是南美洲文化遗产的重要组成部分。

6. And however much America suffers an internal loss of faith, it will continue to enjoy, abroad, some of the immunity that attaches to all things in the realm of myth. (Para. 3)

译文:不管美国国内遭受多么严重的信仰缺失病,在国外它却将继续享有某种免疫力,而这种免疫力是和神话世界内的种种事物联系在一起的。(美国流行文化善于造梦,因此通过流行文化来了解美国的外国人仍会

51

将美国看作是一个完美的神话世界,从而对美国的信仰仍将继续。)

immunity: *n.* the state of being protected from sth.　免疫力,免疫性

e.g. *The vaccination gives you immunity against the disease for up to six months.*
这种疫苗可使你在 6 个月内对这种疾病免疫。

7. The suspicion will continue that Americans make the best dreams. (Para. 3)

　　译文: 人们仍将设想美国人是最善造梦的。

　　suspicion: *n.* a belief or idea that something may be true　猜想,疑心

　　e.g. *I have a suspicion that he only asked me out because my brother persuaded him to.*
我疑心他只是由于我哥哥的劝说才约我出去的。

8. As borders crumble and cultures mingle, more and more of us are becoming hyphenated. (Para. 4)

　　译文: 随着国界的消亡和文化的混合,我们中越来越多的人正成为双重公民。

　　crumble: *v.* to break or break sth. into very small pieces　崩溃,粉碎

　　e.g. *Under the pressure, the flint crumbled into fragments.*
火石在压力作用下碎裂成片状。

9. So efficient is her command of all the media. (Para. 5)

　　译文: 她对所有媒体的操控是如此地驾轻就熟。

　　efficient: *adj.* working or operating quickly and effectively in an organized way　效率高的

　　e.g. *The city's transport system is one of the most efficient in Europe.*
这个城市的运输系统是欧洲最高效的运输系统之一。

10. Madonna's global appeal is not unlike that of the Kentucky Fried Chicken parlor in Tian'anmen Square. (Para. 6)

　　译文: 麦当娜的全球感召力与天安门广场上开设的肯德基店的吸引力并无二致。

　　appeal: *n.* the quality in sb. or sth. that makes them attractive or interesting　吸引力,感染力

　　e.g. *Parties on river-boats have lost their appeal since one sank last year killing thirty-three people.*
自从去年一艘沉船事故导致 33 人死亡之后,在船上举行聚会已经失去了吸引力。

11. Both provide a way for people to align themselves, however fleetingly, with a world that is—in imagination at least—quick and flashy and rich. (Para. 6)

　　译文: 两者都使人们得以哪怕短暂地和那个世界结为一体——这个世界至少

存在于人们的想象中,节奏匆忙、艳丽而又富饶。

align: *v.* If you align yourself with an organization or person, you agree with and support their aims. 使结盟

e.g. There are signs that the prime minister is <u>aligning</u> himself with the liberals.
有迹象表明首相正与自由派站在一边。

12. One night, trying to <u>convey</u> his desperation to escape, he pulled out what was clearly his most precious possession. (Para. 7)

译文:一天晚上,为了表达自己对逃跑的极度渴望,他拿出显然是他最珍贵的财产。

convey: *v.* to express a thought, feeling or idea so that it is understood by other people 传达,传递,表达

e.g. I tried to <u>convey</u> in my speech how grateful we all were for his help.
我试图在讲话中表达我们大家对他帮助的谢意。

13. He did not, I suspect, know that Jackson was <u>reclusive</u>, eccentric, and about as likely to respond to political appeals as Donald Duck. (Para. 7)

译文:我疑心他并不知道杰克逊是一个离群索居、性格怪癖的人,对他政治诉求做出回应的可能性就和唐老鸭做出回应的可能性一样。(杰克逊和虚拟的动画人物唐老鸭一样,都不可能对这个人的政治诉求做出回应。)

reclusive: *adj.* living alone and liking to avoid other people 隐遁的

e.g. She had been living a <u>reclusive</u> life in Los Angeles since her marriage broke up.
自婚姻破裂后她就一直孤身一人住在洛杉矶。

14. What he did know was that Jackson was black, rich, and sexually <u>ambiguous</u>—all things that it is not good to be in Castro's Cuba. (Para. 7)

译文:他所知道的就是杰克逊是一个富裕的黑人,并且性取向不明——在卡斯特罗统治下的古巴内拥有这些特征可不是什么好事儿。

ambiguous: *adj.* that can be understood in more than one way; having different meanings 含糊不清的,引起歧义的

e.g. The government has been <u>ambiguous</u> on this issue.
政府在这个问题上的态度模棱两可。

15. Since the America that he <u>coveted</u> does not quite exist, it is immutable, a talisman that will fail him only if he comes here. (Para. 7)

译文:既然他所渴望的那个美国形象实际并不存在,那么这个形象(对他来说)就永远只是一个护身符,只有他来到美国才会大失所望。

covet: *v.* to want sth. very much, especially sth. that belongs to sb. else　垂涎，渴望

e.g.　*The Booker Prize is the most coveted British literary award.*
　　　在英国布克奖是最让人梦寐以求的文学奖项。

II. Expressions

1. There is a genuine sense in many parts of the world that America is <u>being left behind</u> by the rise of a unified Europe and the new East Asian powers. (Para. 1)

   译文：世界上的很多地方都确实出现了这样一种观念，那就是美国正在被崛起的欧洲联盟和东亚新势力甩在身后。

   be left behind: not to make as much progress as sb. else　落在后面

   a) *We're going to be left behind by the rest of the world.*
   我们将要落在世界其他国家的后边。

   b) *If executives fail to exploit the opportunities of networking, they risk being left behind.*
   如果主管们不能利用人际关系提供的机会，那么他们就会面临被人赶超的风险。

2. A visitor today in Vietnam, one of the last of America's official enemies, will find crowds in Hue, in waterside cafes, desperate to <u>get a glimpse of</u> Meryl Streep on video. (Para. 2)

   译文：假使如今有访客来到越南——它是美国仅剩的几个正式敌国之一——那么他会发现顺化市河边的小饭馆里挤满了人，他们想方设法只为一睹录像里梅丽尔·斯特里普的芳容。

   get/catch a glimpse of: to see sth. very briefly and not very well　瞥见

   a) *Some of the fans had waited 24 hours outside the Hyde Park Hotel to get a glimpse of their heroine.*
   一些仰慕者们 24 小时守候在海德公园酒店外，只为一睹女主角的芳容。

   b) *I came up on deck to get my first glimpse of the island.*
   我来到甲板上，第一次瞥见了小岛。

3. And however much America suffers an internal loss of faith, it will continue to enjoy, abroad, some of the immunity that <u>attaches to</u> all things in the realm of myth. (Para. 3)

   译文：不管美国国内遭受多么严重的信仰缺失病，在国外它却将继续享有某种免疫力，而这种免疫力是和神话世界内的种种事物联系在一起的。

attach to: to be connected with sb./sth.; to connect sth. to sth.   伴随，联系

a) *The high turnout was an affirmation of the importance that the voters attached to the election.*
如此高的出席人数是选民对选举重要性的一种肯定。

b) *No one is suggesting that any health risks attach to this product.*
没人认为这种产品有健康风险。

4. The French may rail against cultural imperialism and try to enforce a kind of aesthetic protectionism by striving to keep out *le burger* and *le video*. (Para. 5)

   译文：法国人会抱怨（美国的）文化帝国主义，并且竭力抵制美国汉堡和影视的入侵，以实行法国的那种审美保护主义。

   rail against: to complain about sth./sb. in a very angry way   愤恨地抱怨

   a) *He rails against the iniquities of capitalism.*
   他痛斥资本主义制度的不公。

   b) *He is always railing at his bad luck.*
   他总是抱怨自己的运气不佳。

   strive to do/for sth.: to make a great effort to do sth.   努力做某事

   a) *You should always strive to achieve more, however well you have done before.*
   不管你以前做得有多好，你总应当努力取得更大的成绩。

   b) *Mr. Annan said the region must now strive for economic development as well as peace.*
   安南先生说，这个地区现在应当在谋求和平的同时努力发展经济。

   keep out: to avoid sth.; to prevent sb. from being involved in sth. or affected by sth.   避免，防止，使……不进入

   a) *The blue-blooded homeowners in Beverly Hills once considered building a wall around their exclusive area to keep out the lowly people of surrounding Los Angeles.*
   贝弗利山庄的高贵户主们曾经考虑在他们的高档住宅区周围建造一堵墙，防止周围的洛杉矶下等人进入。

   b) *The bank is also investing heavily in a security system to keep out robbers.*
   银行也花重金打造安全系统以防盗贼。

5. Madonna shows up in Cannes. (Para. 5)

   译文：麦当娜在戛纳露面。

   show up: to arrive where you have arranged to meet sb. or do sth.   露面

   a) *The big-name players did not show up in the match.*
   知名球员并没有在比赛中出现。

b) *My friend Kara and I were planning to meet at 2:00, but heavy traffic prevented her from showing up until 3:00.*
我的朋友卡拉和我约好2点见面，但是由于交通堵塞她3点才露面。

6. She <u>sets off</u> the biggest stir in thirty years. (Para. 5)
   译文：她引发了30年来最大的轰动。
   set off: to start a process or series of events　引发，导致
   a) *The arrival of the charity van <u>set off</u> a minor excitement as villagers came for a share of the aid.*
   慈善车的抵达引起了一阵小小的骚动，因为村民们都拥上来要救助物资。
   b) *The crisis has <u>set off</u> a wave of nationalist feelings in Quebec.*
   这次危机在魁北克激起了一股民族主义浪潮。

7. What he also knew was that Jackson had succeeded <u>on his own terms</u>. (Para. 7)
   译文：他还知道杰克逊是靠自己取得成功的。
   on sb's own terms:　If you do something on your terms, you do it under conditions that you decide because you are in a position of power.　根据某人自己的主张
   a) *Wim Jansen has told Celtic that any return to Glasgow as head coach will only be <u>on his terms</u>.*
   维姆·扬森告诉凯尔特人足球俱乐部说，如果想要他回格拉斯高当主教练，一切都得按他的条件来做。
   b) *I'm not doing it <u>on your terms</u>.*　这件事我不会按你的意思来做的。

8. Somehow the moguls of Hollywood and Broadway and Nashville—perhaps because they were immigrants themselves, with half a heart on the streets they left—have never lost their <u>common touch</u>. (Para. 8)
   译文：从某种程度上来说，好莱坞、百老汇和纳什维尔的(娱乐业)巨头们——也许因为他们本身就是移民，心头还萦绕着故国的大街小巷——从来没有失去他们那种理解普通人的能力。
   the common touch: the ability of a powerful or famous person has to talk to and understand ordinary people　平易近人的特性
   a) *It was always said of the Princess that she had <u>the common touch</u> and that was why she was so well loved by the people.*
   人们都说王妃平易近人，这也是她深受热爱的原因。
   b) *In my hometown of Milwaukee, as in many of your neighborhoods and newsrooms, there's respect for leaders with a <u>common touch</u>.*

在我密尔沃基市的家乡,就好像在你们的很多街坊和报社里一样,人们很尊重那些平易近人的领导者。

III. Grammar

1. The more straitened or shut off a culture, the more urgent its hunger for the qualities it associates with America: freedom, wealth, and modernity. (Para. 3)

    译文:一个国家越是贫困或越是闭塞,就越渴求它在美国身上所看到的种种特质:自由、财富和现代。

    句型"越……越……":the+ 形容词 / 副词比较级……the+ 形容词 / 副词比较级

    e.g. The fatter one is, the slower one runs.

2. And however much America suffers an internal loss of faith... (Para. 3)

    译文:不管美国国内遭受多么严重的信仰缺失……

    however 用作连接副词,引导让步状语从句,意思是"不管,无论……",句型为 however+ 形容词 / 副词 + 主语 + 谓语

    e.g. However hard I work, there is more to be done.

3. ...so efficient is her command of all the media and so self-perpetuating her allure— (that) she sets off the biggest stir in thirty years. (Para. 5)

    译文:她对所有媒体的操控是如此地驾轻就熟,她的魅力又是如此地持久不衰,以至于她引发了(法国)三十年来最大的轰动。

    (1) so...that 句型中的 so 位于句首时,句子需要倒装:so+ 形容词 / 副词 + 谓语 + 主语

    e.g. So frightened was he that he didn't dare to move an inch.

    (2) so self-perpetuating her allure 为省略句,省略了谓语动词 is,因为前面已经出现过,后面不必重复。

4. One night, trying to convey his desperation to escape, he pulled out what was clearly his most precious possession... (Para. 7)

    译文:一天晚上,为了表达自己对逃跑的极度渴望,他拿出了自己最珍贵的财产……

    分词在句子中作状语,可以表示时间、条件、原因、结果、让步、伴随等。分词做状语时,它的逻辑主语与句子的主语应一致。本句的分词短语相当丁一个状语从句:as he tried to convey his desperation to escape...

Part Two: Key to Exercises

I. Suggested Answers to *Topics for Discussion*

1. How do you understand the title of the text?

    America sells its pop culture products such as movies and music to other countries. "Innocence" refers to the innocent dreams that America creates through these products. While America suffers an internal loss of faith, American values exert a pervasive influence in places outside of America.

    The title is an allusion to Mark Twain's *Innocents Abroad,* in which he describes his travels through Europe and the Near East and gives a nineteenth-century American's perspective on these older, more established cultures.

2. What dreams and myths does America represent to people around the world (Paragraph 3)?

    America represents freedom, wealth, and modernity. These qualities are foreign and forbidden, especially in some shut-off societies, and thus become dreams and myths alluring to the people there.

3. In what way is America "the center of internationalism" (Paragraph 5) and Hollywood "the capital of the world" (Paragraph 3)?

    The powerful promise of freedom, wealth, and other attractive qualities conveyed in American pop culture has a global appeal. Besides, America projects itself as the spiritual home of integration. More and more people immigrate to America and revive the notion of America. Both the collision and integration of different cultures make America "the center of internationalism."

    As the center of America's entertainment industry, the almost universal appeal of Hollywood lies in that it has kept its "common touch," that ability to speak to and on behalf of the dreams of the masses. Hollywood's command of global audiences is so pervasive that it has become "the capital of the world."

4. In what way or ways do the films mentioned in the last paragraph "speak to our most innocent dreams"? What recent films are examples of the kind of innocence to which the author is referring?

    E.T., Back to the Future, Gone with the Wind and *Casablanca* are famous Hollywood films. Whether they are science fiction films or romances, with their extraordinary stories and vivid presentation on the screen, they quicken people's thirst for friendship, imagination, equality, justice, and peace.

II. Key to Exercises
Text A
A.
1. With the example of his Cuban friend, the author wants to illustrate two points: (1) "The lure of the foreign is quickened by the lure of the forbidden" and (2) people may be disappointed if they come to America. In Castro's Cuba, as an intellectual dissident, the author's friend was not allowed freedom, individualism, and wealth. These deprivations left him open to the abstract influence of the symbolic power of the American pop star Michael Jackson. The author suggests that if one day the Cuban really would come to America and learn more about Michael Jackson and America's internal loss of faith, he would be disillusioned.
2. Home is a place where you feel comfortable and where you are always welcome. For many people abroad, America is a realm of myth associated with universal desires of the human heart, such as freedom, wealth, and modernity. Also, America has a history of opening its arms to welcome newcomers, and thus it has become a popular destination for immigrants and their descendants.

    However, the dreams about America held dear by those people are created through pop culture and sometimes turn out to be illusory when people actually come to America. Besides, home should also be a place you feel you belong in, but when immigrants come into contact with mainstream American society, they encounter differences in language, ethnic cultures, and religions. Integration into American society, the "melting pot," is another dream hard to realize.
3. Both qualities are part of America, a land of freedom, equality and democracy, as well as a land of quick rhythm, great wealth, and modern life style. This image of America is "innocent" and "forbidden," especially to people in cultures that are otherwise enclosed or opposed to these values—"innocent" because this image strikes universal chords and speaks to people's innocent and sometimes simple and naïve dreams, "forbidden" because it is disapproved of by the authorities.
4. B 5. D 6. B 7. A
8. (1) F (2) T (3) T (4) F (5) F (6) F (7) T (8) F (9) T (10) T

B.

1. last ... enemies ... waterside ... desperate ... glimpse ... floating
2. immigrants ... spiritual ... integration ... domination ... subside ... increasingly ... attracts ... revive ... refresh
3. convey ... desperation ... pulled ... precious ... album ... scrawled ... heartfelt ... appeals ... rescue ... suspect ... reclusive ... eccentric ... Donald Duck

C.

1. debtor   2. heritage   3. internalized   4. quickened   5. desperation
6. A   7. D   8. C   9. A   10. D

D.

1. straitened   2. perpetuate   3. Hyphenated   4. proliferate   5. genuine
6. fleetingly   7. subside   8. aesthetic   9. integration   10. renounce

E.

1. left behind   2. set off   3. attach to   4. the common touch
5. catching a glimpse of   6. on his own terms   7. railed against
8. keep out   9. show up   10. striving to

F.

1. struck a chord   2. in part   3. makes the world go around   4. maintain a hold on
5. draw from   6. failed me   7. appeal to   8. make a living   9. scrawled ... on
10. go on sale

G.

1. B   2. A   3. D   4. A   5. A   6. C   7. B   8. D   9. C   10. B   11. C   12. A
13. D   14. B   15. C

H.

1. In his diary, he always rails against the hypocrisy and greed of the people around.
2. The court's initial verdict in the police officer's trial set off serious riots.
3. In her writing she strove for a balance between innovation and familiar prose forms.
4. It is her courage in coming out, on her own terms, and speaking up in defense of lesbian and gay rights that makes her loved by fans all over the world.
5. Uncle George didn't show up for our wedding because he was knocked down by a car on his way.
6. The more he insisted he was innocent, the less other people seemed to believe him.
7. I only caught a fleeting glimpse of the driver of the getaway car, but I doubt I would recognize her if I saw her again.

Unit Three

8. They sandbagged their homes to keep out floods.
9. Those are advantages that attach to the profession.
10. Many observers contrasted Diana's common touch with the more formal approach of other members of the royal family.

I.
　　虽然巴黎、东京和悉尼都以各自的方式自然而然地成为这一多极文化的会合地，但是美国作为传统的移民之乡仍然是"融合"这一概念的精神家园。Milos Forman 说过，只有两个地方能给人以家的感觉，一个是家里，一个就是美国。这也能解释为什么美国在其(超级大国)势力渐成明日黄花的情况下，它对流行文化的掌控却没有松懈之势。美国这个词本身就吸引了越来越多的人到来，其定义又得到这些人的恢复和更新。某一文化越具有国际性，它也就越具有美国这一国际主义中心的特征。法国人会抱怨(美国的)文化帝国主义，并且竭力抵制美国汉堡和影视的入侵以实行法国人的那种审美保护主义。但是，麦当娜在戛纳的露面——她吸引媒体眼球的功夫是如此游刃有余，她个人的魅力又是如此地持久不衰——成为 (法国)三十年来最轰动的事件。

Text B
B.
1. C　2. A　3. A　4. C　5. D

Part Three: Self-check

I. Choose the word that is closest in meaning to the underlined word in each sentence.

1. America is the largest debtor nation in the world, and it seems an unlikely model for <u>emulation</u>.
　　A. imitation　　B. invention　　C. creation　　D. solution
2. Crowds in Hue, in waterside cafes, are <u>desperate</u> to get a glimpse of Meryl Streep on video.
　　A. decided　　B. looking　　C. disappointed　　D. urgent

3. The pirated version of Eddie Murphy's *Coming to America* went on sale well before the video had ever come to America.
   A. robbed   B. guilty   C. illegal   D. legal
4. Such products represent the largest single source of America's export earnings.
   A. exhibit in   B. are considered to be
   C. present as   D. display in
5. The Europeans may have a stronger and more self-conscious sense of their aesthetic heritage.
   A. property   B. possession   C. tradition   D. fortune
6. America will continue to enjoy, abroad, some of the immunity that attaches to all things in the realm of myth.
   A. protection   B. effect   C. infection   D. influence
7. ...the suspicion will continue that Americans make the best dreams.
   A. decision   B. notion   C. plan   D. meaning
8. As borders crumble and cultures mingle, more and more of us are becoming hyphenated.
   A. fall   B. shiver   C. shake   D. disintegrate
9. ...so efficient is her command of all the media....
   A. diligent   B. effective   C. easygoing   D. enough
10. Madonna's global appeal is not unlike that of the Kentucky Fried Chicken parlor in Tiananmen Square.
    A. action   B. attraction   C. ability   D. agility
11. Both provide a way for people to align themselves with a world that is quick and flashy and rich.
    A. keep up   B. set up   C. associate   D. make up
12. One night, trying to convey his desperation to escape, he pulled out what was clearly his most precious possession.
    A. carry   B. express   C. pass   D. send
13. He did not, I suspect, know that Jackson was reclusive, eccentric, and about as likely to respond to political appeals as Donald Duck.
    A. solitary   B. sad   C. helpless   D. strange
14. What he did know was that Jackson was black, rich, and sexually ambiguous.
    A. definite   B. ambitious   C. indeterminate   D. certain
15. The America that he coveted does not quite exist.
    A. dreamed   B. imagined   C. thought   D. craved

Unit Three

II. Choose the expression that best completes each sentence.

1. There is a genuine sense in many parts of the world that America is being _____ by the rise of a unified Europe and the new East Asian powers.
   A. caught out   B. left behind   C. made up   D. left out

2. A visitor today in Vietnam will find crowds in Hue, in waterside cafes, desperate to _____ Meryl Streep on video.
   A. keep an eye on   B. have an eye for
   C. get a glimpse of   D. take a peep at

3. And however much America suffers an internal loss of faith, it will continue to enjoy, abroad, some of the immunity that _____ all things in the realm of myth.
   A. attaches from   B. attaches on
   C. attaches in   D. attaches to

4. The French may _____ cultural imperialism and try to enforce a kind of aesthetic protectionism.
   A. approve of   B. agree with   C. rail against   D. rail to

5. The French are _____ protect themselves from the influence of American pop culture.
   A. striving to   B. striving for   C. striven to   D. striven for

6. The French are making a great effort to _____ American fast food and movies.
   A. keep out   B. keep on   C. keep back   D. keep up

7. A lot of fans waited until five o'clock, and finally Madonna _____.
   A. showed around   B. showed off
   C. showed for   D. showed up

8. Madonna's arrival in Cannes _____ the biggest stir in thirty years.
   A. sets up   B. sets off   C. sets down   D. sets on

9. What he also knew was that Jackson had succeeded _____.
   A. in his own terms   B. to his own terms
   C. by his own terms   D. on his own terms

10. Somehow the moguls of Hollywood have never lost their _____, so that the movies they produce speak to the most innocent dreams of the masses.
    A. common touch   B. common sense
    C. common cold   D. common ground

III. Read the following passage and fill in each blank with one of the words or expressions given.

The vast majority of people in Pakistan or Peru or Poland may never visit the United States or ever meet an American face to face. But they encounter images of L.A. and New York in the movies, television programs, and popular songs exported ___1___ by the American entertainment industry.

Those images inevitably exert a ___2___ powerful influence on overseas consumers than they do on the American domestic audience. If you live in Seattle or Cincinnati, you understand that the feverish media fantasies provided by a DMX music video or a Dark Angel TV episode do ___3___ represent everyday reality for you or your neighbors. If you live in Indonesia or Nigeria, ___4___, you will have little or no first-hand experience to balance the ___5___ impressions provided by American pop culture, with its intense emphasis on violence, sexual adventurism, and every inventive variety of anti-social behavior. No wonder so many Islamic extremists ___6___ America as a cruel, godless, vulgar society—a "Great ___7___," indeed.

The disproportionate emphasis on violent behavior only intensifies with the export of American entertainment. For many years, so-called action movies have traveled more effectively than other genres, since explosions and car crashes do not require ___8___. This leads to the widespread assumption abroad that the United States, ___9___ the dramatically declining crime rate of the last decade, remains a dangerous and insecure society. On a recent trip to rural Indonesia, an American traveler met a ten-year-old boy who asked to see her gun. When she insisted that she didn't carry any firearms, the child ___10___ to believe her: he knew that all Americans carried guns because he had seen them perpetually armed on TV and at the movies.

1. A. somewhere   B. everywhere   C. nowhere   D. elsewhere
2. A. less   B. least   C. more   D. most
3. A. not   B. sure   C. only   D. indeed
4. A. however   B. therefore   C. because   D. moreover
5. A. positive   B. negative   C. optimistic   D. pleasant
6. A. look for   B. look up   C. look upon   D. look after
7. A. God   B. Angel   C. Creator   D. Satan
8. A. definition   B. instruction   C. action   D. translation

Unit Three

9. A. though   B. because of   C. despite   D. in spite
10. A. refused   B. decided   C. agreed   D. preferred

IV. Read the following passage and choose the best answer for each question.

Crime today in New York is still high by any standards—though everyone knows that it is, comparatively speaking, well down these days. But it is still rash to go into Central Park at night—and one reason why apartments are preferred to houses is that you can walk straight in with a doorman to help you and not be caught on the doorstep fumbling with a key. However, people do feel safer than they did when we arrived in New York fourteen years ago. New York is largely filled with people like us who were born somewhere else and came here willing to be lucky.

Those days, most of the newcomers were European. Now, thanks to a change in the immigration laws in 1965, 85% percent of the 16.7 million legal immigrants between 1968 and 1992 were from the Third World. In the Fifties, the cab drivers all spoke like Jackie Gleason (a New York film actor). Now instead of Brooklynese, they speak Afghan-English, Punjab(印度旁遮普邦)-English, Russian-English, Haiti-English—languages that do not adapt to the natural inflections of English-English. It takes time to discover that most of the longwinded English preambles(序文) —Excuse me, but I wonder if you would mind taking me to— float on empty air. Everybody is in too much of a hurry to wait for the payoff.

As I discuss in my book, *The American Century*, many people worry that the ethnic differences will make this the Disunited States. But the cosmopolitan influx refreshes the uniformity of American culture. On a morning stroll in a few blocks of New York, I can buy a paper from a Sikh running a newsstand, a bagel (面包圈) from an Egyptian working in a Jewish delicatessen (熟食店), an apple from a Mexican working in a Korean market, a paperback book from an African running a street-corner bookstall.

America is above all a good place for working, one of the principal reasons for staying here. If you can do something they want done, they don't care at all where you come from, whom you know, how old you are, what color you are. Just show up. Everyone expects to change jobs frequently. I have enjoyed working at universities, magazines, book publishing, and newspapers. I find very little negativism. There are no arguments about who does what. Work is highly organized.

Every process is analyzed, and people are trained to be efficient cogs (齿轮), producing the most units of satisfaction for a given amount of time and motion.

1. According to the author, _____.
   A. the crime rate remains very high in New York
   B. crime is still a problem, but is much less pervasive than it was
   C. crime is so serious that people do not like living in New York
   D. crime is no longer a problem in New York.
2. When did large-scale immigration from countries other than Europe begin?
   A. The Fifties.
   B. The mid-sixties.
   C. 1976.
   D. 1992.
3. The writer is _____.
   A. in favor of immigration from all over the world
   B. against immigration from all over the world
   C. in favor of immigration, providing that it is controlled
   D. against immigration because of the rising crime figures
4. The writer believes that immigration will _____.
   A. improve American culture
   B. enrich American culture
   C. result in the destruction of English in the U.S.
   D. result in ethnic differences
5. The main reason why the writer likes being in America is that _____.
   A. it is a good place to study ethnic differences
   B. it is culturally enriching
   C. it is a good place to work
   D. you get very good service

V. Read the following passage and decide whether each statement is TRUE or FALSE.

Growing up in a Mexican-American family was not easy. I am the daughter of a father who wanted us to speak Spanish and prepare for a return to the old country and a mother who wanted us to learn English and be all that we could be in the United States.

Unit Three

Mom was very American. She came here when she was eighteen months old, after the Mexican Revolution had taken the lives of her grandfather and father, and became an American citizen in 1950 at age thirty-two, a day she remembers with great pride. She had a fourth-grade education because her hard-driving stepfather was always taking her and her brothers and sisters out of school to work in the fields. But even those few scattered years in school taught her that America offered more than just survival and that there was actually hope of getting ahead, of making a better life, and that education was the key. Mom sent us to school scrubbed and combed with our clothes clean and mended. There was never to be an unkind word spoken about the teachers. And she asked about everything that went on at school, especially our conversations with teachers.

My father was totally different. He came to America in his mid-twenties, during a severe economic depression in Mexico. His intention was to work hard for a couple of years and return to his beloved Mexico. He was a proud, nationalistic Mexican who had an excellent education, through the eighth grade. He knew and loved Mexican history, literature, drama, music, and dance. For every birthday and Mexican national holiday, he wrote poems for my sisters and me to recite. With him as director and star, we put on plays in our bedroom. The most glorious event was the masked ball he staged in the camp courtyard at summer's end, under an indigo blue sky of twinkling stars and a full moon.

My father was as sweet and gentle as my mother was resourceful and practical. And to him, proper social "etiquette" was important. When we were introduced to adults, we always had to respond in a formal, antiquated Mexican style. Dinner was a class in discipline, with Dad as professor. We had to sit very straight, be totally quiet, and try not to need anything once we were seated. Most important of all, we had to chew with our mouths closed. At bedtime Dad would bless us and give us his hand to kiss. I thought that was another strange custom from Mexico. Mom, always thinking that Dad was the authority on proper customs, followed him in his bedtime ritual.

Many traditions have been lost on my own children, but the love for literature and drama has not. The traditions I grew up with gave me a security greater than money could ever buy.

1. The writer's mother wanted her family to speak English and become American.
2. The writer's father was an uneducated farm laborer.

3. The writer's father believed in strong discipline, but was very loving.
4. The writer's mother didn't allow the children to follow proper Mexican customs.
5. The writer loves Mexican cultural traditions, but is not passing them on to her own children.

Part Four: Oral Expression: Going Shopping

I. Dialogues

Dialogue 1
Saleswoman: Do you need any help?
Customer: Yes. I am looking for an overcoat, size 40.
Saleswoman: How do you like this one? It's made of exceptionally good quality, pure wool, very soft.
Customer: Very good. May I try this on?
Saleswoman: Please come with me to the fitting room (更衣室).

Dialogue 2
Customer: These Nikes are so beautiful. I'll take them. How much?
Salesman: They are $100.
Customer: Don't you think that's expensive for a pair of shoes?
Salesman: Not at all. That's the best price in town.
Customer: All right, I'll take them. I expect they're worth it. Can I pay by Visa?
Salesman: We don't accept Visa. You have to pay cash. Please go to the cash counter and pay. I'll wrap them up for you.
Customer: All right. Thank you.

Dialogue 3
Salesperson: May I help you?
Customer: Yes, I would like to return these slacks (宽松长裤).
Salesperson: All right. Do you have your receipt?

Customer:	Yes. Here it is. I bought them last week.
Salesperson:	And what seems to be the problem?
Customer:	I bought them to go (相配) with a blouse of mine. But they don't really match.
Salesperson:	I see. Oh, wait. Ma'am, I'm sorry. These slacks were on sale (甩卖).
Customer:	Yes, they were thirty percent off.
Salesperson:	I'm sorry, but we usually don't allow returns of sale items. It is our policy.
Customer:	I just bought these slacks a week ago. And I am a regular customer (常客) here. Can you make an exception this time?
Salesperson:	Well. Let me talk to the manager for a moment... Ma'am, the manager says I can do it this time.
Customer:	Good. I am glad you can make an exception for me.

II. Useful Expressions

1. Getting Information

Salesperson	Customer
• Do you need any help? • Looking for something in particular? • What size shoes do you wear? • That suit looks very good on you.	• Excuse me, would you tell me where I can get some butter? • May I have a look at the watch? • This dress is made of silk, isn't it? • May I try it on? • I'll take it.

2. Asking Prices

Salesperson	Customer
• Here's your change. • They are on sale for $18.98. • These are fifty-nine each.	• What's the price of that electric iron? • How much is this rug? • Is this toothpaste on sale today? • How much do I owe you? • Do you have change for a twenty-dollar bill?

3. **Paying**

Salesperson	Customer
• You'd better take it to the next register. • Do you want to pay for it with cash or with a check? • Will you wait a moment, please? I'll have it wrapped.	• Where do I pay for this shirt? • Is it possible to use a credit card? • It's too expensive. I can't afford it. • Could you give me a discount? • How about buy one and get one free?

4. **Returning Items**

Salesperson	Customer
• What's the matter with them? • We can't give you a cash return. • I'm sorry. Purchases of sale items are final. • We can replace it for you. Do you have your receipt? • We can't refund or replace DVDs.	• Could I return these gloves? • I'd like to return this radio. • Let me talk to the manager.

III. Exercises

1. **Dialogue Completion**

   (1) Man: These silver earrings are only sixteen dollars. The gold ones are twenty-four.

   Woman: _____

   A. There are several earrings over here. Could you come this way?

   B. Give me the gold ones. I've got a gold necklace that would look very nice with them.

   C. There's one jewelry counter next to the suit rack.

   D. I'll put your packages behind the cash register. They'll be safe.

   (2) Man: I'm trying to find a green sweater in extra large.

   Woman: We have your size, but not in that color.

   Man: Can you order one for me?

   Woman: _____

A. Certainly. Just give me your name and address.

B. This is too small for me. Do you have a bigger one?

C. What's your size?

D. No, it seems too old fashioned to me.

2. **Dialogue Comprehension**

   (1) Woman: Excuse me, I am looking for the textbooks for Professor Wink's course.

   Man: I'm afraid they are out of stock. You'll have to order them, and it will take the publisher three weeks to ship them to us.

   Question: Where did this conversation probably take place?

   A. In a laundry.

   B. In a shipping company office.

   C. In a restaurant.

   D. In a university bookstore.

   (2) Man: I'd like to return this jacket. I bought it for my brother yesterday, but he doesn't like the color.

   Woman: We can't give you a refund, but you can exchange it.

   Question: What does the woman mean?

   A. The man can return the jacket.

   B. The man has to show the receipt.

   C. The jacket can be exchanged.

   D. The man can get a refund.

Notes:

Clothing sizes are measured differently in the United States from the way they are measured in countries where the metric system is used. 美国服装尺寸的量法和使用公制单位的国家不一样。

Key to Part Three and Part Four

Part Three:

I. Vocabulary: 1. A   2. D   3. C   4. B   5. C

               6. A   7. B   8. D   9. B   10. B

               11. C   12. B   13. A   14. C   15. D

II. Expression: 1. B   2. C   3. D   4. C   5. A

		6. A	7. D	8. B	9. D	10. A

III. Cloze:　　1. B　　2. C　　3. A　　4. A　　5. B
　　　　　　　6. C　　7. D　　8. D　　9. C　　10. A
IV. Reading:　1. B　　2. B　　3. A　　4. B　　5. C
V. Reading:　 1. T　　2. F　　3. T　　4. F　　5. T

Part Four:
1. Dialogue Completion:　　(1) B　　(2) A
2. Dialogue Comprehension: (1) D　　(2) C

Unit Four

Text A

The Right to Fail

Part One: Language Points

I. Vocabulary

1. I like "dropout" as an addition to the American language because it's brief and it's clear. (Para. 1)

   译文:"退出者"作为美国语言的补充词语深得我心,因为它简单而又明了。

   dropout: *n.* a person who leaves school, college or university before finishing a course, or a person who lives in an unusual way   中途退学的人;退出社会主流的人

   e.g. The dropout rate among students is currently one in three.
   目前学生的退学率是三分之一。

2. A boy or girl who leaves college is branded a failure—and the right to fail is one of the few freedoms that this country does not grant its citizens. (Para. 3)

   译文:退学的男孩或女孩会被人们冠以失败者的名号——失败的权利是这个国家不允许其公民拥有的少数自由权之一。

   grant: *v.* to give or allow someone something, usually in an official way   给予,授予

   e.g. France has agreed to grant him political asylum.
   法国已经同意授予他政治避难权。

3. Our advertisement and TV <u>commercials</u> are a hymn to material success. (Para. 3)

   译文：我们的(纸上)广告和电视商业广告都对物质成功大唱赞歌。

   commercial: *n.* an advertisement which is broadcast on television or radio (电视、广播中的)商业广告

   e.g. *The TV show was interrupted by too many <u>commercials</u>.*
   那档电视节目插进的商业广告太多了。

4. Yet in the fluid years of youth, the only way for boys and girls to find their proper road is often to take a hundred side trips, poking out in different directions, <u>faltering</u>, drawing back, and starting again. (Para. 4)

   译文：然而在青春的变迁岁月中，男孩女孩们找到正确出路的唯一方法往往是走千百次弯路、四处摸索、跌跌撞撞、屡屡退缩而后重新上路。

   falter: *v.* to stop walking or to walk in an unsteady way because you suddenly feel weak or afraid 蹒跚，踉跄

   e.g. *She <u>faltered</u> toward the door in the dark.*
   她在黑暗中向门口摇摇晃晃地走去。

5. Countless people have had a <u>bout</u> with it and come out stronger as a result. (Para. 6)

   译文：无数人都经历过次次失败，但最后都变得愈加优秀。

   bout: *n.* a short period of time during which you do something a lot, especially something that is bad for you 一阵，一次

   e.g. *A half-hour daily walk can be more beneficial than one hard <u>bout</u> of exercise a week.*
   每天散步半小时要比每周猛劲儿锻炼一次更有益。

6. Luckily, such rebels still turn up often enough to prove that individualism, though badly threatened, is not <u>extinct</u>. (Para. 7)

   译文：幸运的是，这样的叛逆者仍然层出不穷，证明特立独行之举虽遭遏止，却生生不息。

   extinct: *adj.* not now existing 灭绝的，绝种的

   e.g. *There is concern that the giant panda will soon become <u>extinct</u>.*
   有人担心大熊猫不久就会绝种。

7. Much has been written, for instance, about the <u>fitful</u> scholastic career of Thomas P. F. Hoving, New York's former Parks Commissioner and now director of the Metropolitan Museum of Art. (Para. 7)

   译文：例如，关于托马斯·P.F.霍文时断时续的学术生涯就多有著述，他曾是纽约公园管理部门负责人，现在是纽约大都会艺术博物馆馆长。

fitful: *adj.* often stopping and starting and not happening in a regular or continuous way   断续的，不规则的

e.g.   *I worried half the night and had a fitful sleep.*
我半个晚上都一直在担心，故而时醒时睡。

8. There is nothing accidental about the grip that this dropout continues to hold on the affections of an entire American generation. (Para. 8)

译文： 这位退学生（指 Holden Caulfield）继续深受美国一整代人的喜爱，决非偶然。

grip: *n.* control over something or someone   掌握，控制

e.g.   *The home team took a firm grip on the game.*
主队牢牢掌控了比赛的局势。

9. Nobody else, real or invented, has made such an engaging shambles of our "goal-oriented society," so gratified our secret belief that the "phonies" are in power and the good guys up the creek. (Para. 8)

译文： 没有任何其他真实或虚构的人物能（像霍尔顿·考尔菲尔德那样）把我们这个"以目标为导向的社会"搅成如此迷人的混乱场面，并如此满足了我们暗地里那种坏孩子掌大权、乖孩子吃苦头的信念。

shambles: *n.* If something is a shambles, it is very disorganized and there is a lot of confusion.   凌乱，杂乱无章

e.g.   *After the party, the house was a total shambles.*
派对过后，屋子里一片狼藉。

10. Holden Caulfield, incidentally, is now thirty-six. (Para. 8)

译文： 顺便说一句，霍尔顿·考尔菲尔德现在也该 36 岁了。

incidentally: *adv.*   used before saying something that is not as important as the main subject of conversation, but is connected to it in some way   顺便提一句

e.g.   *We had a marvellous meal at that restaurant you recommended—incidentally, I must give you the number of a similar one I know.*
我们在你推荐的那个饭店美餐了一顿——对了，我也知道一个和这差不多的好饭店，电话号码得给你。

11. Brooks told me that he learned more about his craft from this considerable failure than from his many earlier hits. (Para. 10)

译文： 布鲁克斯告诉我说，比起他早先的许多叫座大片来说，（《吉姆老爷》一片）这次的惨败却令他学到更多的行业知识。

considerable: *adj.* great in amount or degree   相当大的，相当重要的

  e.g. *The fire caused <u>considerable</u> damage to the church.*
    火灾给教堂带来相当大的损失。

12. It could also mean, however, that they just don't <u>buy</u> the old standards of success and are rapidly writing new ones. (Para. 12)

  译文： 然而,这也可以意味着他们(退学生和嬉皮士)就是不接受老一套的衡量成功的标准,而是在迅速书写自己的新标准。

  buy: *v.* to believe that something is true　　(俚语)接受,同意,相信

  e.g. *She'll never <u>buy</u> that story about you getting lost!*
    她永远都不会相信你迷路那回事儿!

13. Yet I have met many of these young volunteers, and they are not <u>pining</u> for traditional success. (Para. 13)

  译文： 但是我遇到过很多这样的年轻志愿者,他们并不渴求传统意义上的成功。

  pine: *v.* If you pine for something, you want it very much, especially when it is unlikely that you will be able to have it.　　渴望,十分盼望

  e.g. *The little girl was <u>pining</u> for her mother's return.*
    小女孩渴望母亲回来。

14. The <u>dawning</u> awareness of this fact seems to me one of the best things happening in America today. (Para. 15)

  译文： 对我来说,(人们)对这一事实的开始觉悟是如今发生在美国的最好的事情之一。

  dawn: *v.* If something is dawning, it is beginning to develop or come into existence.　　开始出现,渐露端倪

  e.g. *Throughout Europe a new railway age, that of the high-speed train, has <u>dawned</u>.*
    在全欧洲,一个新的铁路时代即高速列车时代已经初露端倪。

II. Expressions

1. The American dream is a dream of "<u>getting ahead</u>", painted in strokes of gold wherever we look. (Para. 3)

  译文： 美国梦就是"成功"梦,遍地都可以看到这两个金色铸就的字眼。

  get ahead:　to be successful and do better than other people in a job or work　　成功,领先

  a) *Which just goes to prove, you do have to be a somebody to <u>get ahead</u> in this town!*

这说明，要想在这城里干出番事业，你必须得是个人物！

b) *The flattening of organizations means that all employees have to learn that old-fashioned promotion is not the only way of getting ahead.*
组织结构的扁平化意味着所有员工都得明白像过去一样等待被提升不是唯一的成功途径。

2. I want to put in a good word for the fink, especially the teen-age fink. (Para. 4)
译文：我想替讨厌鬼尤其是十几岁的讨厌鬼说几句好话。

put in a (good) word for: to try to help someone get or achieve something by saying good things about them to someone else 为某人说情，替某人美言

a) *I'll put in a good word for you with the management.*
我会在领导面前说你好话的。

b) *He put in a good word for him at meetings of the Jockey Club.*
他在赛马俱乐部的会议上替他说情。

3. Yet in the fluid years of youth, the only way for boys and girls to find their proper road is often to take a hundred side trips, poking out in different directions, faltering, drawing back, and starting again. (Para. 4)
译文：然而在青春的变迁岁月中，男孩女孩们找到正确出路的唯一方法往往是走千百次弯路、四处摸索、跌跌撞撞、屡屡退缩而后重新上路。

poke out: If something is poking through or out of something else, you can see part of it but not all of it. 伸出，突出；伸手摸索着走

a) *Ella looked at the tiny face poking out of the blanket.*
艾拉看着从毯子中钻出的小脸蛋。

b) *A young doctor poked his head out, and called me into the examination room.*
一位年轻的医生探出头来，叫我进体检室。

draw back: to move backwards, especially because you are frightened or surprised 退缩

a) *She peeped into the box and drew back in horror.*
她朝盒子里偷看了一眼，吓得直往后退。

b) *In the end the government drew back from their extreme standpoint.*
最后政府的极端立场有了让步。

4. History is strewn with eminent dropouts. (Para. 6)
译文：历史上卓越的退学生比比皆是。

be strewn with: to contain a lot of something 散播，点缀，撒满

a) *The street was strewn with broken glass.*
街道上到处撒满了碎玻璃。

b) *Lafayette Square <u>was strewn with</u> the stuff of deconstruction: moving vans, cherry pickers, lumber and paper.*

拉法耶特广场上充斥着支离破碎的景象：搬家汽车、动臂装卸机、木料和纸。

5. Luckily, such rebels still <u>turn up</u> often enough to prove that individualism, though badly threatened, is not extinct. (Para. 7)

   译文：幸运的是，这样的叛逆者仍然层出不穷，证明特立独行之举虽遭遏止，却生生不息。

   turn up: to be found, especially by chance, after having been lost or searched for 出现；找到

   a) *Eventually my watch <u>turned up</u> in a coat pocket.*

   最终我的手表在外衣口袋里找到了。

   b) *After seven months on the case, the police failed to <u>turn up</u> any real clues.*

   在这个案子上耗费了7个月之后，警察没有发现任何真正的线索。

6. Nobody else, real or invented, has made such an engaging shambles of our "goal-oriented society," so gratified our secret belief that the "phonies" are in power and the good guys <u>up the creek</u>. (Para. 8)

   译文：没有任何其他真实或虚构的人物能（像霍尔顿·考尔菲尔德那样）把我们这个"以目标为导向的社会"搅成如此迷人的混乱场面，并如此满足了我们暗地里那种坏孩子掌大权、乖孩子吃苦头的信念。

   be up the creek: to be in a very difficult situation 处于困境

   a) *I'll really <u>be up the creek</u> if I don't get paid this week.*

   如果这周拿不到工资的话我的情况就真的不妙了。

   b) *Chairmen of football clubs are only in the papers and on the radio when the team <u>is up the creek</u>.*

   球队处于困境时，足球俱乐部主席只会在报纸或电台发表声明。

7. I only mean that failure isn't bad <u>in itself</u>, or success automatically good. (Para. 9)

   译文：我只是说失败本身并不那么糟糕，成功也并非必然就是好的。

   in itself: considered separately from any other facts 以其本身而言；本质上

   a) *This awareness, <u>in itself</u>, is believed to generate sufficient grief to restore and ensure cooperation.*

   据信这种觉悟本身能够引发充分的悲伤之情来恢复和保证合作。

   b) *The planning becomes an end <u>in itself</u>.*

   这一规划过程本身就是目的。

8. Writers, playwrights, painters and composers work <u>in the expectation of</u> periodic defeat, but they wouldn't keep going back into the arena if they thought it was the end of the world. (Para. 11)

   译文：作家、剧作家、画家和作曲家们心里明白失败会随时降临，但他们仍一如既往地工作。如果他们认为一次失败就是世界末日的话就不会一再重返自己的领域。

   in the expectation of: in the hope that something will happen 期待（某事会发生）

   a) *Anne left Germany <u>in the expectation of</u> seeing her family again before very long.*
      安妮离开了德国，期待不久就能再见到家人。

   b) *He spent money lavishly <u>in the expectation of</u> receiving a large inheritance.*
      他以为能得到一大笔遗产，因此花钱大手大脚。

9. Today's younger generation seems to know that this is true, seems willing to <u>take the risks</u> in life that artists take in art. (Para. 12)

   译文：如今的年轻一代似乎知道事实确实如此（即失败助人成长这一事实），似乎愿意在生活中冒险，就如艺术家在艺术上冒险一样。

   take the risk(s): to decide to do something even though you know it may have bad results 冒险做某事

   a) *I couldn't <u>take the risk</u> of leaving him alone even for a short time.*
      即使把他单独留下一小会儿，我也担不了这样的风险。

   b) *Now he saw his chance and desperation forced him to <u>take the risk</u> of climbing down on to the line in the darkness.*
      现在他看到有机可乘，黑暗中情急之下，他冒险爬到绳子上。

10. This is hardly <u>the road to</u> riches or to an executive suite. (Para. 13)

    译文：这可不是赚大钱或成为企业高管人员的必经之路。

    the road to: if you are on the road to something, you will achieve it soon, or it will happen to you soon 通往……的途径

    a) *It was the first step along <u>the road to</u> democracy.*
       这是沿着民主之路迈出的第一步。

    b) *Now is the time for tonics to help us forget the pain and step out on <u>the road to</u> recovery.*
       现在是该用良药来帮助我们止痛和痊愈了。

11. Obviously business does not have the answer—otherwise the young would not be so <u>scornful of</u> its call to be an organization man. (Para. 14)

译文：显然商业界对于这个问题也没有答案——不然年轻人就不会对商业界呼吁大家做企业人的作法嗤之以鼻了。

be scornful of: feeling or showing scorn　对……轻蔑、嘲笑

a) He *was scornful of* the women's movement.

他对妇女运动不屑一顾。

b) Once *scornful of* cable companies, telephone firms have learnt that they can be useful.

电话公司曾经瞧不起电缆公司，但现在知道它们挺有用的。

III. Grammar

1. More than 3 million American college students would serve VISTA in some capacity <u>if given</u> the opportunity (Para. 13)

   译文：如果有机会的话，超过300万的美国大学生会以某种方式参加服务志愿总队。

   if 从句补充完整应为 if they were given the opportunity。以 if, when, though, as if 等连词引导的从句中，如从句中的主要动词是 be，且从句主语与主句主语为同一个，常将从句主语和动词 be 省略。

   e.g.　No matter how frequently performed, the works of Beethoven always attract large audiences.

   　　While cycling, don't forget the traffic lights.

2. Obviously the colleges don't have <u>more than</u> a partial answer (Para. 14)

   译文：很显然，大学也只不过提供了一个有失偏颇的答案而已。

   not more than：不超过，仅仅

Part Two: Key to Exercises

I. Suggested Answers to *Topics for Discussion*

1. What two sides of society are pitted against each other in this essay? On whose side is the author?

   　　One side is the older generation which cherishes the American dream of "getting ahead" and cultivates a "goal-oriented society." The other side is the group of dropouts who rebel against the traditional system, learn from their failures, and follow their own paths. The author is on the dropouts' side.

2. What is Zinsser's definition of "dropout"? How is it different from the Establishment's definition?

   Zinsser defines dropouts as loners and rebels who follow their own trail, not worrying about its odd twists and turns because they have faith in their own sense of direction. But the Establishment condemns dropouts as failures because they do not accept the conventional standards of success or play by conventional rules.

3. What does the title mean?

   America has a national admiration for material success and does not grant its citizens the right to fail. But the author wants to tell us there is no one right path to the top. Everyone has the right to succeed on his or her own terms and to fail as often as necessary because failure is not the end of the world, but a way to grow.

II. Key to Exercises

Text A

A.

1. Dropping out is often a way of dropping in.
2. In his opinion failure isn't fatal and we can find a lot of distinguished people who have experienced failure before or after they came to the top.
3. Paragraph 9.
4. That they both went through considerable failure in directing films makes it important to mention them. The purpose is to illustrate that people can learn a great deal from failures and come out successful.
5. Actually, the author doesn't believe there is a right path to success. He maintains that the only way to find a proper road is to go through difficulties, experience failures, face challenges and start again.
6. B   7. C   8. A   9. D
10. (1) T   (2) F   (3) F   (4) F   (5) T

B.

1. treason ... branded ... fail ... strokes of gold ... hymn ... toast
2. fink ... attaining ... chance ... idol ... a mind of his own
3. Generation Gap ... "middle-class values" ... "goal-oriented society"

C.

1. B   2. A   3. C   4. D   5. B   6. C

D.

1. therapy   2. dissenter   3. befallen   4. paralyzed   5. treason   6. unorthodox
7. vapid   8. swoon   9. disaffected   10. fluid   11. exhilarating

E.

1. was strewn with   2. be up the creek   3. in itself   4. in the expectation of
5. take the risk   6. turned up   7. poking out   8. the road to   9. get ahead
10. put in a good word for

F.

1. addition to   2. a good chance of   3. upper hand   4. twists and turns
5. far more than   6. have faith in   7. dropout   8. in power   9. follow the trail
10. on ... terms   11. who's to say

G.

1. A   2. B   3. C   4. A   5. D   6. D   7. B   8. A   9. C   10. A   11. C   12. D   13. B   14. C   15. D   16. B   17. B   18. A   19. D

H.

1. The horse began to get ahead halfway through the race.

2. If she hadn't put in a good word for me, the company wouldn't have recruited me.

3. He poked out his tongue and looked at it carefully in the mirror.

4. The crowd drew back in terror as the building crashed to the ground.

5. The streets were strewn with rubbish.

6. The missing bag turned up, completely empty, in the lake.

7. I would be really up the creek if I lost my car key.

8. The problem is unimportant in itself, but its long-term effects could be very serious.

9. They closed the windows in the expectation of rain.

10. You have to take the risk if you want to succeed in business.

11. He finally felt he was on the road to success after years of hard work.

12. He used to be scornful of religion and its influence over people.

I.

　　最近公布有超过20万美国人询问过加入美国服务志愿队（美国国内维和警队）的事宜，同时据盖洛普民意调查显示"超过300万美国大学生愿意在机会允许的情况下参加美国服务志愿队"。这几乎不是赚大钱或成为企管人员的必经之路。然而我遇到过很多这样的年轻志愿者，他们不寄希望于传统的成功。相反，与拥有游泳池的平庸的副总裁们相比，他们显得更充实。

Unit Four

Text B

1. C 2. B 3. A 4. C 5. A 6. B

Part Three: Self-check

I. **Choose the word closest in meaning to the underlined word in each sentence.**

1. But the <u>dropouts</u> and the hippies are not as afraid of failure as their parents and grandparents.
   A. people who quit college
   B. people who hate college
   C. people who are successful at college
   D. people who fail many courses at college

2. A boy or girl who leaves college is branded a failure—and the right to fail is one of the few freedoms that this country does not <u>grant</u> its citizens.
   A. refuse   B. accept   C. give   D. take

3. Our advertisements and TV <u>commercials</u> are a hymn to material success.
   A. businesses   B. movies   C. shows   D. advertisements

4. The only way for boys and girls to find their proper road is often to take a hundred side trips, poking out in different directions, <u>faltering</u>, drawing back, and starting again.
   A. stammering   B. stumbling   C. flattering   D. flattening

5. Countless people have had a <u>bout</u> with it and come out stronger as a result.
   A. long period   B. short struggle
   C. boxing match   D. wrestling match

6. Luckily, such rebels still turn up often enough to prove that individualism, though badly threatened, is not <u>extinct</u>.
   A. non-existent   B. existing   C. distinct   D. instinct

7. Much has been written, for instance, about the <u>fitful</u> scholastic career of Thomas P. F. Hoving.
   A. suitable   B. appropriate   C. irregular   D. regular

8. There is nothing accidental about the grip that this dropout continues to hold on the affections of an entire American generation.
   A. operation
   B. understanding
   C. grief
   D. control
9. Nobody else has made such an engaging shambles of our "goal-oriented society."
   A. shadows
   B. disorder
   C. disconnection
   D. shaking
10. Holden Caulfield, incidentally, is now thirty-six.
    A. by the way   B. on the way   C. however   D. accidentally
11. Brooks told me that he learned more about his craft from this considerable failure than from his many earlier hits.
    A. considerate
    B. considering
    C. serious
    D. slight
12. It could also mean, however, that they just don't buy the old standards of success and are rapidly writing new ones.
    A. purchase   B. pay   C. accept   D. trade
13. Yet I have met many of these young volunteers, and they are not pining for traditional success.
    A. yearning   B. looking   C. chopping   D. searching
14. The dawning awareness of this fact seems to me one of the best things happening in America today.
    A. drowning   B. developing   C. drawing   D. happening

II. Choose the expression that best completes each sentence.

1. The American dream is a dream of "_____," painted in strokes of gold wherever we look.
   A. getting up
   B. getting along
   C. getting about
   D. getting ahead
2. I want to _____ for the fink, especially the teen-age fink.
   A. put in a good word
   B. put on a good word
   C. put up a good word
   D. put down a good word
3. The only way for boys and girls to find their proper road is often to take a hundred side trips, _____ in different directions, faltering....
   A. poking around
   B. poking away
   C. poking out
   D. poking aside

Unit Four

4. Only by _____ and starting again can boys and girls find their proper road.
   A. taking back   B. drawing back
   C. giving back   D. getting back
5. Luckily, such rebels still _____ often enough to prove that individualism, though badly threatened, is not extinct.
   A. turn out   B. turn down   C. turn up   D. turn off
6. Nobody else has made such an engaging shambles of our "goal-oriented society," so gratified our secret belief that the "phonies" are in power and the good guys _____.
   A. up the creek   B. off the creek
   C. in the creek   D. over the creek
7. I only mean that failure isn't bad _____, or success automatically good.
   A. inside itself   B. behind itself
   C. on itself   D. in itself
8. Writers, playwrights, painters, and composers work _____ periodic defeat.
   A. in the expectation of   B. to the expectation of
   C. on the expectation of   D. by the expectation of
9. Today's younger generation seems to know that this is true, seems willing to _____ in life.
   A. give the risks   B. grant the risks
   C. have the risks   D. take the risks
10. This is hardly _____ riches or to an executive suite.
    A. the road to   B. the road into
    C. the way into   D. the way on
11. Obviously business does not have the answer—otherwise the young would not be so _____ its call to be an organization man.
    A. satisfied with   B. scornful of   C. satisfied to   D. scornful to
12. History _____ eminent dropouts.
    A. is strewing with   B. is strewn with
    C. strews with   D. strewed with

III. Read the following passage and fill in each blank with the best word or expression.

The problem is that the students do more than they are expected to. A professor will __1__ a five-page paper. Several students will start writing ten-page papers to __2__ him. Then more students will write ten-page papers, and a few will raise the ante to fifteen. Pity the poor student who is still just doing the assignment.

Why can't the professor just cut back and not accept the longer papers? He can, and he probably will. But by then the term will be half over and the damage done. Grade fever is highly contagious and not easily reversed. __3__, the professor's main __4__ is with his course. He knows his students only in relation to the course and does not know that they are also over-exerting in their other courses. Not that it is really his business. He did not __5__ dealing with the student as a whole person and with all the emotional baggage the student brought __6__ from home. That is what deans, masters, chaplains, and psychiatrists are for.

To some extent this is nothing new: a certain number of professors have always been self-contained islands of scholarship and shyness, more __7__ with books than with people. But the new pauperism has widened the gap still __8__, for professors who actually like to spend time with students do not have as much time to spend. They are also over-exerting. If they are young, they are busy trying to publish in order not to perish, hanging by their fingernails onto a shrinking profession. If they are old and tenured, they are __9__ under the duties of administering departments—as departmental chairmen or members of committees—which have been __10__ by the budgetary ax.

1. A. examine   B. assign   C. test   D. arrange
2. A. impress   B. surprise   C. amuse   D. entertain
3. A. However   B. Besides   C. Nevertheless   D. Except
4. A. thought   B. worry   C. care   D. concern
5. A. sign on for   B. sign in for   C. sign up for   D. sign away for
6. A. up   B. alone   C. along   D. away
7. A. glad   B. sad   C. gloomy   D. comfortable
8. A. further   B. distant   C. more   D. less
9. A. covered   B. buried   C. pressed   D. pushed
10. A. chopped down B. expanded upon   C. thinned out   D. enlarged on

IV. Read the following passage and choose the best answer for each question.

A feature of U.S. education is continuous classroom interaction between teacher and students. From Los Angeles to New York, and from Chicago to Houston, educators believe that students master information by discovering it for themselves. They believe that teachers do not actually teach, but simply help students learn. In this view, learning takes place through a process of challenging old ideas and asking questions. Because the formal lecture permits little questioning, it is less common in the United States than in many countries; the faculty member aims to exchange ideas with students, rather than simply tell them what they should know.

The concept of constantly exchanging ideas may seem strange to you at first. Perhaps you come from a country where people believe that whatever is written in a book must be true and that teachers are always right in matters of learning. If so, you will probably find the United States system disquieting. Of course, American students know that their textbooks are mostly right and that their teachers are better informed than they are. But they think for themselves—and their teachers expect them to ask questions and challenge ideas. The point, again, is not that Americans have the "right" approach to learning, but that the interactive classroom is a strong feature of U.S. education. You will need to adjust to it—and in time, take advantage of it.

The course in which a professor lectures steadily to hundreds of silent students is relatively rare in the United States. Enrollments are often limited (many classes will have fewer than thirty students), so that all students have a chance to participate. Where the lecture format is necessary, as in a freshman chemistry course, the large class meets once or twice a week, then divides into "recitation" sections, or small group meetings. The lecture is used to present information efficiently—for example, through slides and demonstrations as well as actual lecturing—but recitations provide important sessions where homework can be reviewed and questions answered.

You may believe that it is impolite to ask a teacher a question and that it is offensive to challenge a teacher's presentation (for example, to ask, "But how can we solve the equation if we are not given the value of 'y'?"). In North American culture, however, it is only impolite to interrupt the teacher with a question and only offensive to attack the teacher's presentation (for example, to say, "How can we solve the problem if you don't present it clearly?"). Questioning—particularly that which shows students trying to learn for themselves—is appropriate and encouraged. By contrast, memorization is considered a poor way to learn. Rewards in the form of good grades will come if you have an inquiring mind and think for yourself.

1. According to the article, new approaches to learning in American universities _____.

   A. are happening only in certain parts of the country
   B. are particularly popular in New York, Los Angeles, Chicago, and Houston
   C. have swept through the whole United States
   D. are popular only in certain large cities

2. The writer thinks that the characteristic feature of U.S. education is that _____.

   A. whatever is written in a book must be true
   B. teachers are always right in matters of learning
   C. textbooks are better informed than most teachers
   D. teachers expect students to ask questions and challenge ideas

3. "Disquieting" in Paragraph 2 means _____.

   A. disturbing   B. exciting   C. stimulating   D. pleasing

4. What is the main value of the recitation class?

   A. It is used to present information efficiently.
   B. It gives an opportunity for doing homework.
   C. It is a good time to review the work done and ask questions.
   D. It gives the lecturer a chance to test whether the work has been learned.

5. In the U.S., it is _____.

   A. impolite to ask a teacher a question
   B. offensive to ask a teacher a question
   C. impolite to attack a teacher's presentation
   D. polite to challenge a teacher's presentation

V. Read the following passage and decide whether each statement is TRUE or FALSE.

Campus watchers everywhere know what I mean when I say students are sad, but they don't agree on the reason for it. During the Vietnam War some ascribed the sadness to the draft. Now others blame affluence, or say it has something to do with permissive upbringing. Not satisfied with any of these explanations, I looked for some answers by using journalistic tools—scholarly studies, economic analyses, the historical record, conversations with parents, professors, college administrators, and employers. Mostly, I learned from my interviews with hundreds of young people on and off campuses all over the country.

My conclusion is that students are sad because they are not needed. Somewhere between the nursery and the employment office, they become unwanted adults. No one has anything in particular against them. But no one knows what to do with them either. We already have too many people in the world of the 1970s, and there is no room for so many newly minted (刚刚生产出来的) eighteen-year-olds. So we temporarily get them out of the way by sending them to college where in fact only a few belong.

To make it more palatable (令人愉快的), we fool ourselves into believing that we are sending them there for their own best interests and that it's good for them. Some students talk about their time in college as if it were a sentence to be served. I listened to a 1970 Mount Holyoke graduate: "For two years I was really interested in science, but in my junior and senior years I just kept saying, 'I've done two years; I am going to finish.' When I got out, I made up my mind that I wasn't going to school anymore because so many of my courses had been bullshit."

But bad as it is, college is often preferable to a far worse fate. It is better than the drudgery of an uninspiring nine-to-five job and better than doing nothing when no jobs are available. For some young people, it is a graceful way to get away from home and become independent without losing the financial support of their parents. And sometimes it is the only alternative to an intolerable home situation.

It is difficult to assess how many students are in college reluctantly. A survey found that "a significant number were not happy with their college experience because they felt they were there only in order to get the 'ticket to a big show' rather than to spend the years as productively as they otherwise could." Older alumni (校友) will identify with Richard Baloga, a policeman's son, who stayed in school even though he "hated it" because he thought it would do him some good. But fewer students each year feel this way. Daniel Yankelovich has surveyed undergraduate attitudes for a number of years, and reported in 1971 that 74% thought education was "very important." But just two years earlier, 80% thought so.

1. According to the writer, the students are sad because they are not wanted by society.

2. The writer believes that it is in the young people's best interests to send them to college.
3. For some students, going to college is only a way to leave their parents and live on their own.
4. In Paragraph 3, the 1970 Mount Holyoke graduate was so interested in science that he would probably further his study after his graduation.
5. According to the last paragraph, in the United States more undergraduates thought education was "very important" in 1971 than in 1969.

Part Four: Oral Expression: At the Bank

I. Dialogues

Dialogue 1

Woman: I'd like to open a savings account and a checking account.
Teller: Our minimum deposit (存款) for a savings account is $25.
Woman: What is the interest rate?
Teller: It's 1.7%.
Woman: Do you charge for checks?
Teller: Each check that you write will cost twenty cents.

Dialogue 2

Man: I'd like to withdraw (取钱) some money from my savings account.
Teller: First you have to fill out one of these withdrawal forms.
Man: Oh, no. It asks for my account number. I forgot my bank book (银行存折).
Teller: I'm afraid you'll need that first.

Dialogue 3

Man: Can I cash a check here?
Teller: Do you have an account with us?
Man: Yes, I have a checking account here.
Teller: Please write your account number on the back of the check.

Man:	Is that all you need?
Teller:	Could I see one more piece of identification?
Man:	Will a driver's license do?
Teller:	Yes, that'd be fine.
Man:	Oh, one more thing, I would like to ask about taking out a loan (办理贷款).
Teller:	How much do you want to borrow?
Man:	Three thousand dollars.

II. Useful Expressions

the balance of the account 账户余额

open an account 开账户

a checking/current account 活期存款账户

a savings account 储蓄存款账户

a deposit account 定期存款账户

annual interest rate 年息率

draw money/make a withdrawal 取钱

deposit in one's account 存钱

cash a check 兑换支票

endorse 在(支票)背面签字

sign a withdrawal slip 在取款单上签名

change foreign currency 兑换一些外币

Bank Employee	Bank Client
• Your account is overdrawn.	• Could you tell me my balance?
• It's 800 yuan for 100 dollars.	• I'd like to know the exchange rate (汇率) for U.S. dollars.
• How much cash do you plan to deposit in your account?	• Do you pay interest on this account?
• Will five tens (五张十元面值) be all right?	• What's the interest rate for a savings account?
• Could I see your I.D.?	• Will a hundred dollars be enough for a minimum deposit?
• Please fill in the receipt in duplicate (一式两份).	• Please give me sixty dollars in tens and twenty dollars in fives.
• Do you have any outstanding (未偿付的) loans?	• Could you cash this traveler's check,

• How much debt do you have on your credit card?	please? • I'm interested in applying for a credit card/taking out a mortgage/taking out a loan.

III. Exercises

1. **Dialogue Completion**

   (1) Man: Excuse me, the ATM has swallowed my bank card!

   Woman: _____

   A. You'd better go to the ATM, as the bank is closed.

   B. They deal with foreign currency at the next counter.

   C. I'm afraid that it's faulty—there have been quite a few complaints about it.

   D. Certainly. How much do you require?

   (2) Man: I think we should stop at the bank.

   Woman: _____

   A. Oh, you forgot to sign the deposit slip.

   B. Why? Are we running out of cash?

   C. I'm afraid that you can't see the manager without an appointment.

   D. I'm sorry. You have to ask at another counter in the bank.

   (3) Man: I'd like to cash a check. Would you please tell me which window to go to?

   Woman: _____

   A. Yes, May I help you?

   B. Do you have an account with us?

   C. What kind of account would you like to open?

   D. You can cash checks over there at Window 5.

2. **Dialogue Comprehension**

   (1) Woman: I can't cash your traveler's check without some identification like a driver's license.

   Man: Since I have only just arrived in the United States, I only have my passport. Will that do?

   Question: Why does the man offer the woman his passport?

A. To apply for a driver's license.

B. As identification to cash a check.

C. The woman is an immigration official.

D. To check in at the airport.

(2) Woman: Will that be cash or credit?

Man: Can I write a check?

Question: What will the man do?

A. He'll pay by cash.

B. He'll pay by check.

C. He'll pay later.

D. He'll have the goods charged to his credit card.

Key to Part Three and Part Four

Part Three:

I. Vocabulary:	1. A	2. C	3. D	4. B	5. B
	6. A	7. C	8. D	9. B	10. A
	11. C	12. C	13. A	14. B	
II. Expression:	1. D	2. A	3. C	4. B	5. C
	6. A	7. D	8. A	9. D	10. A
	11. B	12. B			
III. Cloze:	1. B	2. A	3. B	4. D	5. C
	6. C	7. D	8. A	9. B	10. C
IV. Reading:	1. C	2. D	3. A	4. C	5. C
V. Reading:	1. T	2. F	3. T	4. F	5. F

Part Four:

1. Dialogue Completion: (1) C   (2) B   (3) D
2. Dialogue Comprehension: (1) B   (2) B

Unit Five

Text A

A Granddaughter's Fear

Part One: Language Points

I. Vocabulary

1. Now I really did hurry, <u>racing</u> out the door and grabbing a cab. But the moment I arrived at her apartment I wanted to run the other way again. (Para. 10)

   译文：现在我真得赶紧了。我冲出房门,匆忙拦了一辆出租车。但一到她的公寓我却想掉头就走。

   race: *v.* to go very fast   疾走,迅跑

   e.g.   *He jumped into his car and <u>raced</u> back home.*
   他跳进汽车,开足马力赶回家。

2. The apartment smelled <u>stale</u>. I threw open a window and sat down stiffly on the couch. (Para. 10)

   译文：公寓里空气污浊。我推开窗户,僵坐在沙发上。

   stale: *adj.* no longer fresh (used of food or air)   不新鲜的(指食物或空气)

   e.g.   *These old peanuts taste <u>stale</u>.*
   这些陈花生变味了。

3. She talked madly about how they were trying to steal her money, how they'd taken away her keys,   how they never spent more than ten minutes at a time with her—although I knew only too well that both her children <u>structured</u> their days and nights around her needs. (Para. 11)

Unit Five

译文：她非常生气地数落他们如何想方设法偷她的钱。她说他们拿走了她的钥匙，却从来都不愿陪她超过10分钟——但我非常清楚她的两个孩子从来都是根据她的需要来安排他们的时间的。

structure: *v.* to arrange the different parts of something into a pattern or system in which each part is connected to the others 组织，安排

e.g. Software helps users structure their work and data.
软件可以帮助用户组织工作、整理数据。

4. I told her that nobody and nothing could help her. "The only person who could help you is you!" I said in righteous fury. "Do you understand me? You've got to stop being so damned dependent on everybody!" (Para. 12)

译文：我告诉她没有人也没有任何东西能帮得了她。"你只能自己帮自己！"我义愤填膺地说："你懂不懂？你不能老依赖我们！"

fury: *n.* very great anger 狂怒；暴怒

e.g. He stormed out of the meeting in a fury.
他怒气冲冲地退出会议。

5. At which point she let out a piercing shriek of agony and hurled herself on her bed. (Para. 13)

译文：听到这些她发出了一声痛苦的尖叫，扑倒在床。

agony: *n.* very great pain or suffering in your mind or body （身心的）极度痛苦

e.g. He lay in agony until the doctor arrived.
他十分痛苦地躺在那里，直到医生来。

6. The only thing I'd accomplished with my idiotic lecture was to heighten both her hysteria and my sense of impotence. (Para. 13)

译文：我那番愚蠢的说教只是让她更歇斯底里，让我更觉得自己无能。

impotence: *n.* the state of being unable to take effective action because you do not have enough power, strength, or control 无能，无能为力

e.g. The speech delivered by the representative on the meeting only showed the government's impotence on the human-rights issues.
代表在会议上的发言只能表明政府在人权问题上的无能为力。

7. What is clear is that she hates being old, she can't stand being left alone for even minutes at a time, and she'll do anything to surround herself with people. (Para. 14)

译文：很明显，她痛恨变老，让她独自呆几分钟她都受不了，她总是想方设法找人陪着她。

stand: *v.* to be good enough or strong enough to bear something 承受，经得起

e.g. *This work will hardly stand close examination.*
  这项工作经不起仔细的检查。

8. By far the most debilitating consequence of the ordeal is the guilt. (Para. 16)

   译文：这种煎熬所带来的最令人痛苦的结果就是内疚。

   ordeal: *n.* a difficult or painful experience 苦难的经历；严峻的考验

   e.g. *Being lost in the wilderness for a week was an ordeal for the campers.*
   在荒野里迷路一周对露营者来说是一场磨难。

9. The result is that my mother visits and calls my grandmother constantly, but then ends up lashing out in senseless indignation. My uncle usually represses his emotions, but he's starting to gain weight and to look his 56 years. (Para. 16)

   译文：结果是我妈妈经常去看我外婆，不断给她打电话，但最后都是以互相指责而不欢而散。我舅舅通常会克制自己的情绪，但他开始渐渐发胖，已显示出 56 岁人的老态。

   indignation: *n.* feelings of surprised anger about something which you think is not right 愤慨，气愤

   e.g. *I expressed my indignation at such rudeness.*
   我对如此的粗鲁无礼表示了愤慨。

   repress: *v.* to control or hold back natural feelings 抑制；压制

   e.g. *I could hardly repress my laughter.*
   我忍不住要大笑起来。

10. She told stories about her past with the narrative panache of Isaac Bashevis Singer. Wherever she went, she made flocks of friends—a trait that I, a lonely and sullen girl, particularly admired. (Para. 18)

    译文：她在讲述自己过去的事情时，说话的文采不亚于艾萨克·巴什维斯·辛格。无论走到哪，她都能结交上很多朋友——我是个孤独而又沉闷的女孩，于是特别崇拜她的这种本事。

    sullen: *adj.* angry and silent, especially because you feel life has been unfair to you 闷闷不乐的，愠怒的

    e.g. *She's a rather sullen-looking woman.*
    她是个样子总有点闷闷不乐的女人。

11. As my grandmother has worsened, so too has my response to her. My mother implores me to be decent and stay in touch, and I launch into all the reasons why I don't. But my excuses sound shallow and glib, even to myself. The truth is that my grandmother terrifies me. (Para. 20)

译文：随着外婆越来越不像话，我对她的态度也越来越差。妈妈央求我不要失礼，不要(对外婆)不闻不问。我却找出各种理由为自己辩护。但这些理由甚至连我自己都觉得听起来肤浅、油滑。事实是外婆让我感到恐惧。

implore: *v.* (formal) to ask someone for something or to do something with great eagerness and anxiety　恳求，乞求

e.g.　I <u>implore</u> you to go now.
　　　我求求你现在就走吧。

shallow: *adj.* lacking deep or serious thinking　浅薄的

e.g.　His arguments seemed <u>shallow</u> and tedious.
　　　他的论点显得肤浅乏味。

12. Or she is a less <u>celebrated</u> woman, who reads, listens to Bach, and threads together the scattered days into a private whole. (Para. 21)

译文：或者她是位不太出名的妇人，她读书，听巴赫的音乐，把过去零散的日子串成一个整体，独自品味。

celebrated: *adj.* famous　著名的

e.g.　Venice is <u>celebrated</u> for its beautiful buildings.
　　　威尼斯以其美丽的建筑而闻名。

13. When I look at my grandmother, <u>fragile</u>, frightened, unhappy, wanting to die but clinging desperately to life, I see myself—and I cannot stand the sight. (Para. 24)

译文：我的外婆身体纤弱、忧心忡忡、闷闷不乐、有心去死却又留恋生命，当我看到她时，我仿佛也看到了自己——这一幕真让我不忍目睹。

fragile: *adj.* weak in health　虚弱的

e.g.　She looks <u>fragile</u>.　她显得纤弱。

II. Expressions

1. "Please, darling, <u>come over</u>! Can't you come here? Please Natalie! I'm ALL ALONE!" (Para. 6)

译文："亲爱的，快来！你不能来吗？求求你了纳塔利！我太寂寞了！"

come over: 1) to come after traveling a long distance　从远方过来
　　　　　　2) to make a short informal visit　短暂造访，顺便来访

a) Please <u>come over</u>. I have something to talk with you.
　　请过来一趟，我有话跟你谈。

b) When did you first <u>come over</u> to China?
　　你第一次来访中国是什么时候？

c) *Come over and see us when you come back to Beijing sometime.*
要是回北京的话请过来看看我们。

2. I hung up and told my colleague that I'd have to leave in a few minutes. (Para. 8)

   译文：我挂上电话，告诉我的同事几分钟后我得离开。

   hang up: to finish a telephone conversation by putting the receiver back   挂断电话

   a) *It's a bad line; hang up and I'll call you back.*
   这条线说话听不清楚，请挂上电话，我重新打给你。

   b) *Don't hang up on me—I need to talk with you.*
   请别挂断电话，我需要跟你谈谈。

   c) *I was so angry that I hung up on him.*
   我一气之下挂断了他的电话。

3. Her face was a gray blur of tears and her thin white hair stood up in wild peaks. (Para. 10)

   译文：她满脸泪痕，脸上灰一道白一道，稀疏的白发盘成了一个散乱的高髻。

   stand up: to stand   站，站立

   a) *I've been standing up all day.*
   我已站了一整天。

   b) *He stood up when I came into the room.*
   我走进房间时，他站了起来。

4. At which point she let out a piercing shriek of agony and hurled herself on her bed. (Para. 13)

   译文：听到这些她发出了一声痛苦的尖叫，扑倒在床。

   let out: to express loudly and violently   大声(强烈)地表达……

   a) *Hearing the good news, the boy let out a cry of joy.*
   听到这个好消息，小男孩高兴地大叫了一声。

   b) *Henry let out a long and slow breath and stared up at the brilliant blue sky.*
   亨利长长地、慢慢地叹了一口气，凝望着阳光灿烂的蓝天。

   c) *He let out a deep breath to show his disappointment.*
   他深深地叹了口气表达他的失望之情。

5. These days, much of the family conversation centers on her. What are we going to do about Grandma? (Para. 15)

   译文：这些日子，家里的话题大多都集中在她身上。我们该拿外婆怎么办？

   center on: to (cause to) have as a main subject or area of concern   (使)集中于……

Unit Five

a) *His interests are <u>centered on</u> seeking fame and money.*
他的全部兴趣都在追名逐利上。

b) *The he disputes <u>centers on</u> how to pay for the overtime work.*
争论集中在如何支付加班费这个问题上。

c) *The topic <u>centers on</u> the crisis in these two countries.*
话题以那两个国家的危机为中心。

6. So another question my family <u>grapples with</u> is: whose turn is it to sleep over on Grandmother's sofa bed? (Para. 15)

   译文：所以我们家要解决的另外一个问题是：该轮到谁在外婆家的沙发床上过夜了？

   grapple with: to work hard to deal with something difficult　努力设法解决

   a) *Don't interrupt me; I'm <u>grappling with</u> accounts.*
   别打扰我，我正在专心计算账目。

   b) *The newly elected prime minister has a grave economic crisis to <u>grapple with</u>.*
   新当选的总理要应对一场严重的经济危机。

   c) *The government has to <u>grapple with</u> the problem of escalating crime rates.*
   政府必须要设法解决犯罪率日益增长的问题。

7. The result is that my mother visits and calls my grandmother constantly, but then <u>ends up</u> <u>lashing out</u> in senseless indignation. (Para. 16)

   译文：结果是我母亲经常探望外婆，不断地给她打电话，但却总是以毫无意义的指责而告终。

   end up: to be in a particular situation, state, or place after a series of events, especially when you did not plan it　结束，以……告终

   a) *I <u>ended up</u> having to pay for everyone's dinner.*
   最后我不得不给大家的晚餐买单。

   b) *After swimming at night, we all <u>ended up</u> with colds.*
   那天晚上游泳后，我们都得了感冒。

   c) *Somewhat to her own surprise she <u>ended up</u> designing the whole car and putting it into production.*
   连她自己也有点惊讶，她最终竟设计了整辆汽车并把它投入生产。

   lash out (at): to make a sudden violent attacking movement　攻击，猛击

   a) *In his speech the judge <u>lashes out</u> against those drug dealers.*
   在演讲中法官猛烈地抨击了那些毒品贩子。

   b) *On Tuesday China <u>lashed out at</u> a US decision to limit imports of socks made in China.*

星期二中国(政府)严厉谴责了美国限制进口中国制造的袜类产品的决定。

c) *Some Arabs lash out at terror groups for the bomb blast which killed many innocent people.*
一些阿拉伯人猛烈抨击恐怖组织制造了这起导致很多人无辜死亡的爆炸事件。

8. I neglect to call my grandmother for weeks at a stretch. When I do visit, I lapse into the role of boot-camp sergeant. (Para. 17)

    译文：我一连几周都不给外婆打电话。当我终于去看她时,我对她就像新兵训练营的中士(对待新兵)一样。

    at a stretch: without stopping 连续

    a) *She has been working for hours at a stretch.*
    她一连工作了好几个小时。

    b) *There's no way I could work for ten hours at a stretch.*
    我不可能连续不断地工作十个小时。

    c) *A lion can lie in the same spot without moving for 12 hours at a stretch.*
    狮子能在同一地点一动不动地趴12个小时。

    lapse into: to pass gradually into a less active or less desirable state 退步,陷入,倒退,衰退

    a) *No one could think of anything more to say, and the meeting lapsed into silence.*
    谁也想不出还有什么话要说,因此会议陷入一片沉默。

    b) *After a year of fame the singer lapsed back into obscurity.*
    这歌手红了一年,之后又被遗忘了。

    c) *He has lapsed once again into his old smoking habits.*
    他又犯抽烟的老毛病了。

9. My mother accuses me of being heartless; she's right. (Para. 17)

    译文：妈妈说我没心没肺;她说得没错。

    accuse sb. of: to charge with doing wrong or breaking the law 指责,谴责

    a) *No one in this department has ever accused the governor of taking advantage of his position; he is hard-working and considerate.*
    这个部门没有人指责过主管以权谋私。他工作勤奋而且肯替人着想。

    b) *Critics accused the writer of a lack of originality.*
    评论家指责这位作家缺少独创性。

    c) *I was accused of stealing money from her but in fact it was the other way round.*
    说我偷了她的钱,其实正相反是她偷了我的钱。

Unit Five

10. But then hard times began to <u>pile up</u> around her like layers of choking silt. (Para. 19)

    译文：但是她的日子越来越艰难，痛苦就像层层淤泥一般压得人透不过气来。

    pile up: to put (one thing) on top of another, to form a pile; to move in a mass or in masses　把(东西)堆成堆；堆叠

    a) *The work has been <u>piling up</u> for days. I'm beginning to wonder if it will ever stop!*

    这些天来工作越堆越多，我开始想知道这样的状态是否还有个头！

    b) *People are dying one after another, and their dead bodies are <u>piling up</u>.*

    人们一个接一个地死去，死尸越堆越多。

    c) *The clouds are <u>piling up</u>. It's going to rain.*

    云越聚越多，天要下雨了。

11. My mother implores me to be decent and stay in touch, and I <u>launch into</u> all the reasons why I don't. (Para. 20)

    译文：妈妈央求我不要失礼，不要(对外婆)不闻不问。我却寻找各种理由为自己辩护。

    launch into: to suddenly start doing something　开始

    a) *He tried his best to keep her from <u>launching into</u> topics that might betray that he didn't know her.*

    他竭力阻止她开始谈论某些话题，这些话题可能会暴露他不认识她的事实。

    b) *I sat down at the piano and <u>launched into</u> Bach's Toccata in C major.*

    我在钢琴前坐了下来，开始弹奏巴赫的托卡塔 C 大调。

    c) *The opposition <u>launched into</u> a violent attack on the government.*

    反对党猛烈地攻击政府。

12. Of course, there are many things my fantasy doyenne is not. She's not <u>strapped for</u> money. Her joints don't ache, her breath doesn't rattle. She isn't losing her memory, her reason, her eyesight. Above all, she is not the old woman I know best. (Para. 22)

    译文：当然，也有很多缺点是我想象中的老太太不应具备的。她不为金钱所困，没有关节痛，没有呼吸困难。她不应该记性差、不讲道理、眼神糟糕。最重要的是，她应该不是我最熟知的那位老太太的样子。

    strapped for: to be in need of　短缺

    a) *He is always <u>strapped for</u> cash the week before pay day; he cannot make his money last from one pay day to the next.*

发工资前的那周他总是缺钱；他总不能让钱维持到下一个发薪日。

b) *At the end of the semester, everyone is <u>strapped for</u> time.*
学期末,大家都缺时间。

c) *Can you lend me one hundred dollars? I'm a little <u>strapped for</u> money.*
你能借给我100美元吗？我现在有点缺钱花。

13. When I look at my grandmother, fragile, frightened, unhappy, wanting to die but <u>clinging</u> desperately <u>to</u> life, I see myself—and I cannot stand the sight. (Para. 24)

    译文: 我的外婆身体纤弱、忧心忡忡、闷闷不乐、有心去死却又留恋生命,当我看到她时,我仿佛也看到了自己——这一幕真让我不忍目睹。

    cling to: to hold tightly; to refuse to go or let go; to stick firmly 紧握（紧抱）住；牢牢粘着

    a) *He <u>clung to</u> the hope that he would succeed.*
    他坚信自己将会成功。

    b) *They <u>clung to</u> each other for support.*
    他们互相依赖,互相支持。（他们紧紧抱住对方,以互相支撑。）

    c) *He has been watching for every mail as he <u>clings to</u> a hope that one day his missing brother will contact him.*
    他一直留心着自己收到的每一封信,因为他坚信有一天他失踪的弟弟会跟他联系。

III. Grammar

1. The voice on the other end was loud and panicked; my colleague looked over at me, <u>horrified</u>. (Para. 1)

    译文: 电话那头的声音非常响亮而且惊惶；我的同事看着我,很震惊。

    过去分词短语做状语：主语与分词所表示的动作是被动关系,分词短语用来修饰谓语,说明动作发生的背景或情况。

    e.g. *Delighted with her work, they made her the general manager.*
    他们很欣赏她的工作,让她当了总经理。

    Built in 1100, the bridge is over 900 years old.
    这座桥是1100年修的,已经有九百多年的历史了。

    Frustrated, he went back to his home village.
    他大失所望,回到家乡去。

2. She started to cry, <u>her voice heaving and gasping</u>. (Para. 4)

    译文: 她开始哭起来,声音哽咽,时高时低。

独立结构(Absolute Construction): 在用分词短语作状语时,它逻辑上的主语一般必须与句子的主语一致。但有时它也有自己独立的逻辑上的主语,这种结构就称为"独立结构"。在很多情况下它都表示一种伴随的动作或情况。

e.g. *He rushed into the room, his face covered with sweat.*
他满脸是汗跑进屋来。

The shower being over, we continued to march.
阵雨过后我们继续行进。

Late that autumn, his work finished, he prepared to return to his institute.
深秋时,他工作结束了,就准备回学院去。

Part Two: Key to Exercises

I. Suggested Answers to *Topics for Discussion*

1. What is the thesis of the story? If the author does not state the thesis explicitly, express it in your own words.

    The thesis of the story is how to age magnificently. Angier has conflicted feelings as she watches her grandmother growing old. She hopes she will not be like her grandmother when she gets old. She wants to be a wise and dignified old woman who is quietly proud of the world she has forged.

2. Why does Angier choose the title "A Granddaughter's Fear" instead of, say, "My Fear"?

    The title "A Granddaughter's Fear" is more representative, implying that such fear is not specific to the author herself but common among granddaughters like her whose grandmothers become more and more unreasonable as they get old.

3. How does Angier react to her grandmother? Why does she respond as she does?

    Angier feels quite bitter and angry about her grandmother, but at the same time she feels guilty for not being able to make her grandmother happy. Such reaction lies in that she cannot put up with her grandmother's unrelenting unfair complaints and annoying requests for company.

II. Key to Exercises
Text A
A.

1. C 2. C 3. B 4. C 5. A

6. According to Angier, a perfect old woman should be quiet, wise, and dignified. She should be contented with her own life. However, her grandmother is always finding fault with her children and grandchildren. She always doubts their love and never feels satisfied with what they do.

7. What Angier explores first is the effects of the grandmother's decline on the family. The decline of Angier's grandmother is the cause of her fear. Angier depicts a negative image of an old woman to better convey her idea of how to age magnificently.

8. There are conflicts between Angier's grandmother and other family members and emotional conflicts within the family members themselves. To be specific, Angier's grandmother is unhappy with her children and grandchildren, and they are unhappy with the grandmother. They grapple with guilt and annoyance for not being able to make her happy.

9. First, the actual dialogues are short, so it is convenient to quote them directly. The paraphrased dialogues are too long in their original state to be quoted directly and would make for tedious reading. Second, the author's words are few compared with the amount of her grandmother's nagging.

    There are several comments quoted in capitals, and we can imagine that those words must have been said in a loud and impatient voice. In this way, the author vividly presents to us an anxious, desperate grandmother and an impatient granddaughter.

10. (1) F (2) F (3) F (4) T (5) F

B.

1. hung up ... immediate crisis ... raced out ... grabbed
2. shuffled around ... ranting against ... blur ... standing up
3. sputtered on ... helpless and resentful ... overwhelmed ... let out ... shriek ... hurled
4. a host of ... hates ... stand ... at a time ... nursing home ... live-in
5. explode ... out of sight ... at a stretch ... lapses into ... accuses of

C.

1. B 2. A 3. C 4. C 5. A 6. C 7. A 8. B 9. A 10. D

Unit Five

D.

1. indignation 2. implored 3. shuffled 4. celebrated 5. stale 6. live-in
7. sullen 8. fragile 9. mouthpiece 10. tantrum

E.

1. clung to 2. lashed out 3. launched into 4. came over 5. let out 6. hung up
7. was accused of 8. has been grappling with 9. at a stretch 10. piling up

F.

1. stay in touch 2. working at her craft 3. turned away from 4. by far
5. hair-trigger 6. terminal illness 7. lost his mind 8. gaining weight
9. strapped for 10. end up

G.

1. B 2. A 3. A 4. C 5. B 6. D 7. C 8. A 9. B 10. D 11. A 12. A
13. C 14. C 15. A

H.

1. She was so angry with her son that she hung up on him.
2. At the news of being dismissed, he let out a cry of anger.
3. Public interest centers on the outcome of the next week's presidential election.
4. He grappled with the problem for an hour before solving it.
5. It seemed that she was going to lash out at him, but she controlled herself.
6. They had to remain standing for hours at a stretch.
7. After taking the medicine, she lapsed into a state of deep sleep.
8. She still clings to the belief that her husband is alive and will come back one day.
9. We were late for the live show and ended up watching it on a TV screen.
10. The manager had so much work piling up on her desk that she knew she was going to have to burn the midnight oil to finish it.

I.

1. 她开始哭起来，声音哽咽，时高时低。她告诉我从12点开始就只有她一个人在家——已经有5个小时了！——根据安排到今晚10点才会有人来陪她。她无法忍受，快要发疯了。没人陪她，她感到很害怕。她一直给大家打电话——所有的人，她的儿子(我的舅舅)、继子、孙子。现在轮到了我。

2. 接下来的几分钟，我一语不发，任凭外婆在客厅里一边乱转，一边高声咒骂。她埋怨我舅舅今天一大早就撇下她(他不得不去工作)；怪我母亲——她的女儿——跑到澳大利亚去度假。她非常生气地数落他们如何想方设法偷她的钱，如何拿了她的钥匙，每次却连10分钟也不愿意陪她——尽管我非常清楚她的两个孩子无时无刻不在根据她的需要来安排他们的时间。
3. 她噼里啪啦地不停地抱怨,这让我不由自主地越来越生气。最后愤怒压倒了理智,我站起来,开始冲她大吼。我告诉她没有人、也没有任何东西能帮得了她。"能帮助你的人只有你自己!"我义愤填膺地说:"你懂不懂?你不能老这样依赖我们!"
4. 我想庄严地老去,就像奥基夫和穆尔那样。我希望自己 50 年后能比现在 31 岁时更好;但我不知道是否能够实现。我的外婆虚弱多病、忧心忡忡、闷闷不乐、有心死去却又留恋生命,当我看到她时,我仿佛也看到了自己——我真不忍看到这一幕。

Text B
B.
1. C 2. A 3. D 4. A 5. D 6. D

Part Three: Self-check

I. Choose the word closest in meaning to the underlined word in each sentence.

1. Now I really did hurry, racing out the door and grabbing a cab.
   A. driving   B. walking   C. jogging   D. rushing

2. The apartment smelled stale. I threw open a window and sat down stiffly on the couch.
   A. fresh   B. musty   C. dirty   D. fragrant

3. I knew only too well that both her children structured their days and nights around her needs.
   A. scheduled   B. checked   C. established   D. set

4. "The only person who could help you is you!" I said in righteous fury.
   A. anger   B. voice   C. pleasure   D. anguish

5. At which point she let out a piercing shriek of agony and hurled herself on her bed.
   A. cry   B. pain   C. joy   D. surprise

6. The only thing I'd accomplished with my idiotic lecture was to heighten both her hysteria and my sense of impotence.
   A. power   B. ambition   C. powerlessness   D. fragility

7. She can't stand being left alone for even minutes at a time, and she'll do anything to surround herself with people.

   A. bear   B. build   C. set   D. support

8. By far the most debilitating consequence of the ordeal is the guilt.

   A. suffering   B. contract   C. threat   D. order

9. The result is that my mother ends up lashing out in senseless indignation.

   A. nonsense   B. explosion   C. anger   D. argument

10. My uncle usually represses his emotions, but he's starting to gain weight and to look his fifty-six years.

    A. hides   B. controls   C. expresses   D. relieves

11. Wherever she went, she made flocks of friends—a trait that I, a lonely and sullen girl, particularly admired.

    A. cheerful   B. moody   C. isolated   D. arrogant

12. My mother implores me to be decent and stay in touch.

    A. advises   B. begs   C. blames   D. warns

13. But my excuses sound shallow and glib, even to myself.

    A. considerate   B. serious
    C. superficial   D. light

14. Or she is a less celebrated woman, who reads, listens to Bach, and threads together the scattered days into a private whole.

    A. dressy   B. showy   C. acclaimed   D. ostentatious

15. When I look at my grandmother, fragile, frightened, unhappy, wanting to die but clinging desperately to life, I see myself—and I cannot stand the sight.

    A. broken   B. crispy
    C. handicapped   D. weak

II. Choose the expression that best completes each sentence.

1. "Please, darling, _____ ! Can't you come here? Please Natalie! I'm ALL ALONE!"

   A. come at   B. come by   C. come up   D. come over

2. I _____ and told my colleague that I'd have to leave in a few minutes.

   A. hanged up   B. hanged on   C. hung up   D. hung on

3. Her face was a gray blur of tears and her thin white hair _____ in wild peaks.

   A. stood up   B. stood on   C. stood   D. stood high

4. At which point she _____ a piercing shriek of agony and hurled herself on her bed.
   A. turn out   B. let out   C. speak out   D. give out
5. These days, much of the family conversation _____ her. What are we going to do about Grandma?
   A. talks about   B. centers on   C. speaks of   D. converses with
6. So another question my family _____ is: whose turn is it to sleep over on Grandmother's sofa bed?
   A. gropes for   B. deals with   C. grapples with   D. give out
7. The result is that my mother _____ lashing out in senseless indignation.
   A. results in   B. ends up   C. ends in   D. comes out
8. The result is that my mother visits and calls my grandmother constantly, but then ends up _____ in senseless indignation.
   A. lashing at   B. lashing out   C. lashing against   D. lashing on
9. I neglect to call my grandmother for weeks _____.
   A. from time to time   B. at intervals
   C. at a time   D. at a stretch
10. When I do visit, I _____ the role of boot-camp sergeant.
    A. leap into   B. drop into   C. bounce into   D. lapse into
11. My mother _____ me _____ being heartless; she's right.
    A. accuses ... of   B. charges ... with   C. indicts ... for   D. convicts ... of
12. But then hard times began to _____ around her like layers of choking silt.
    A. show up   B. pop up   C. come up   D. pile up
13. My mother implores me to be decent and stay in touch, and I _____ all the reasons why I don't.
    A. lapse into   B. launch into   C. run into   D. get into
14. My fantasy doyenne is a woman who is not _____ money.
    A. strapped for   B. tied for   C. stripped of   D. excepted from
15. When I look at my grandmother, wanting to die but _____ desperately _____ life, I see myself—and I cannot stand the sight.
    A. looking ... for   B. waiting ... for   C. clinging ... to   D. longing ... for

III. Read the following passage and fill in each blank with one of the words or expressions given.

   Being a mother of two very active boys, ages seven and one, I am sometimes worried about their making a shambles (混乱场面) of my carefully __1__ home. In their innocence and play, they occasionally __2__ my favorite lamp or upset my well-designed arrangements. In these moments I remember the __3__ I learned from my wise mother-in-law, Ruby.

Ruby is the mother of six and grandmother of thirteen. She is the __4__ of gentleness, patience, and love.

One Christmas, all the children and grandchildren were gathered __5__ at Ruby's home. Just the month __6__, Ruby had bought beautiful white carpeting after living with the "same old carpet" for __7__ twenty-five years. She was overjoyed with the new look it gave her home.

My brother-in-law, Arnie, had just distributed his gifts for all the nieces and nephews—prized homemade honey from his beehives (蜂房). They were excited. But as fate would have it, eight-year-old Sheena __8__ her tub of honey on Grandma's new carpeting and trailed it throughout the entire downstairs of the house.

__9__, Sheena ran into the kitchen and into Grandma Ruby's arms. "Grandma, I've spilled my honey all over your brand new carpet."

Grandma knelt down, looked tenderly __10__ Sheena's tearful eyes and said, "Don't worry, sweetheart, we can get you more honey."

1. A. decorated   B. decorating   C. decorate   D. decoration
2. A. knock down   B. knock over   C. knock at   D. knock against
3. A. lesson   B. class   C. word   D. behavior
4. A. embodiment   B. expression   C. represent   D. body
5. A. in practice B. as usual   C. as custom   D. in order
6. A. ago   B. before   C. later   D. old
7. A. more   B. less   C. over   D. fewer
8. A. spurred   B. spread   C. spoiled   D. spilled
9. A. Cried   B. Cry   C. Crying   D. Having Cried
10. A. onto   B. against   C. in   D. into

IV. Read the following passage and choose the best answer for each question.

Like many middle-aged people these days, Edie Stern, who lives in New York, often finds herself worrying about an aging parent. Her father, Aaron, is eighty-seven years old and lives on his own in Florida, hundreds of miles away. "He's a very independent soul," she says. Many people in Ms. Stern's position feel torn: they want their parents to continue to live in their own homes and pursue their own lives, but are concerned about their parents' growing frailties (虚弱). Unlike others, however, Ms. Stern can at least feel she is doing something to help resolve this dilemma (进退两难的窘境). As a researcher at IBM, a big computer firm, she is one of many people developing new technologies intended to make it easier, less stressful, and even healthier for older folks to continue living at home.

At IBM's research lab in Zurich, researchers are working on mobile health networks. Called mHealth, the kit could, for example, work with Bang & Olufsen's Helping Hand so that a forgotten pill triggers (引发) a mobile-phone call. HP (美国惠普公司), meanwhile, is working on wearable wireless sensors (传感器), the size of sticking plasters, that could be used for remote monitoring of heart activity and other information. The idea behind all of these monitoring systems is to allow old people to remain in their own homes for as long as possible, even when they are being treated for chronic illnesses (慢性病), rather than moving into a nursing home.

Another category of devices monitors non-medical activities: Has Mum got up today? Did Dad have any breakfast? Lance Larivee, who works in the software industry and lives in Portland, Oregon, is testing a new system from Lusora, a start-up (新兴公司) based in San Francisco. The Lusora Intelligent Sensory Architecture, which will go on sale later this year, is a collection of wireless devices, including a wearable panic alarm (紧急警报装置) and various monitoring devices that are placed around the home and detect motion, sound, and temperature. Data from these devices can be accessed securely via the Internet. So Mr. Larivee can, for example, check online to see if his eighty-seven-year-old grandmother—who lives alone in Los Altos, California—has opened the refrigerator yet today.

While the demand for all these technologies seems certain to grow, this kind of monitoring inevitably raises the question of privacy—a prickly (棘手的) issue that has derailed (干扰) other technologies in the past. Will the elderly tolerate a barrage of devices monitoring and tracking them, revealing everything down to when they had breakfast or last had a cup of tea? Richard Jones, the boss of Lusora, responds with a question of his own: "What's a greater loss of privacy than moving out of your own house?" He has a good point.

1. Which word in the following is closest in meaning to the word "torn" (Line 4, Paragraph 1)?

A. helpless   B. desperate   C. angry   D. conflicted

2. According to the passage, which of the following statements is true?

   A. People in the position of Ms Stern prefer not to live with their parents.

   B. HP is marketing a wearable wireless sensor for remote monitoring of heart activity and other information.

   C. Many middle-aged people in America are not concerned about their aging parents.

   D. All the devices and systems monitor medical activities.

3. What problem will the technologies mentioned in this passage bring to the elderly?

   A. They violate their privacy.

   B. They put their lives in disorder.

   C. They are a threat to other technologies.

   D. They cost too much money.

4. What is "Lusora"?

   A. A person's name.

   B. A technology company.

   C. An architecture company.

   D. A place in San Francisco.

5. What is the author's attitude towards the technologies aimed to help older folks to live at home?

   A. Negative.   B. Positive.   C. Critical.   D. Uncertain.

V. Read the following passage and decide whether each statement is TRUE or FALSE.

Squinting (眯着眼看, 窥看) through the myopic (近视的, 目光短浅的) eyes of a youth-obsessed culture, we Americans have tended to regard each successive birthday after thirty as a harbinger (前兆) of loss. But as the bulge (暂时或突然增大、增多) of the baby boom (二战后 1947—1961 年间的生育高峰) pushes into middle-age—thirty to thirty-nine-year-olds are now the largest age group in this country—our outlook on getting older is changing. In fact, experts are finding today that getting older is getting better in very real ways. Here is how.

Gray hair doesn't mean fuzzy thinking. Sigmund Freud published his first great work, The Interpretation of Dreams, at forty-four. Rachel Carson completed her classic, Silent Spring, at fifty-five. "If you continue reading, thinking, and creating all your life, the knowledge you gain improves your intelligence," says Robin Henig, author of *How Women Get Old*. "Given enough time, you'll score better and better on intelligence tests as you age. The speed of reasoning and remembering may decrease but not the quality." We do lose some brain cells with age. But neuro-scientists now know we grow more connecting branches between brain cells—increasing our depth of knowledge—through our seventies, if we live a stimulating (使人感到振奋的) life.

Studies by psychiatry professor Dr. George E. Vaillant show that our psychological defense mechanisms—ways of coping with difficult feelings—become healthier as we grow older. The young protect themselves with strategies such as denial and impulsive acting out. The middle-aged rely far more on defenses such as humor, altruism (利他主义，无私), and creativity. Older people rate the same event as less stressful than younger people. "With age, we really do cope better with life's upsets," says Philip L. Berman, author of The Courage to Grow Old. That's because "you've been fired once, gone through a divorce, or lost a loved one—and you've survived. Psychologically you're tougher."

"Most people in their middle years are at the peak of their working lives," says psychoanalyst Elizabeth Auchincloss. "This is the time of competence when people get a great deal of satisfaction and security out of realizing they have something to offer to others."

"As you get older, you're more secure in your relationships," says Henig. "The longer you've been married, the more likely it is that you are going to stay married." "And if you have a good marriage," adds psychologist Belsky, "the chances are it will be even better after the children leave the house."

One of the things we fear about growing older is increasing isolation. "If you let it, your world can shrink," says Monsignor Fahe. "But if you make the effort, midlife can be a time of more personal relationships." "If you nourish your relationships," agrees gerontologist (老年学家) Dr. Robert, "by the time you have reached midlife, you have a rich network—lifelong friends, acquaintances, colleagues, and extended family."

"You can't run as fast as you once could, but the spiritual side of you becomes much stronger," says Berman. "You have time to reflect and make sense of your life experience. The result may be a deepening of religious faith or simply a much greater development of interior life."

Another word for it is wisdom.

1. According to the passage, as people grow older, their thinking ability decreases.
2. As people grow older, they tend to protect themselves with strategies such as denial, humor, altruism, and creativity.
3. People become tougher psychologically because they have gone through many frustrations.
4. The older you are, the more secure you are in your relationship with your spouse.
5. According to the author, people can become stronger both spiritually and physically as they grow older.

Part Four: Oral Expression: Transportation

I. Dialogues

Dialogue 1

A: Excuse me. Is this the right bus for Tian'anmen Square?
B: No, sir. I'm afraid you've gotten on the wrong bus.
A: Oh, my God! What shall I do?
B: You'll have to get off at the next stop and change to Bus No. 5.
A: I really appreciate your help.
B: My pleasure.

Dialogue 2

A: I'm lost. Could you tell me where I am now?
B: You've just traveled through the loop line (环线). You're now in the subway interchange station. Where are you going?
A: I'm going to the Beijing West Railway Station. How can I get to the station from here?
B: You can transfer to Line 1 until you get to the Military Museum. Then take Bus No. 320 and get off at the last stop.
A: Thank you very much.

Dialogue 3

A: I'd like a ticket to Chicago. How much is the fare?
B: Would you like a one way (单程) or a round trip (回程)?

A: A round-trip ticket, please.

B: $524 for first class and $ 310 for economy.

A: I want to go economy.

B: That'll be $ 310.

    (After paying the ticket)

B: Here are your ticket and your change.

A: Thank you.

II. Useful Expressions

By Taxi/Bus	By Train	By Plane
• Driver, take me to the airport. • Step in and shut the door, please. • I'm afraid I might be late for the appointment. • I'm sorry. There's a speed limit. • We can make it if the lights are with us. • How much is the fare? • Let's call it fifty yuan. • You're overcharging me. • Excuse me. Is this the right bus for Beihai Park? • I'm afraid you've got on the wrong bus.	• I want to buy two one-way tickets to Shanghai, please. • I want two return tickets to Beijing, please. • That's $58 in all. • What time does the train reach Shanghai? • You should be there at 11:30. • How long will the journey take? • It takes three hours. • Is it necessary to change (需要换车吗)？ • Excuse me. Would you mind trading seats with me? • I prefer a window seat.	• Would you like one-way or round-trip tickets? • A round-trip ticket, please. • I want to go economy. • Please be at the airport twenty minutes before your flight time for check-in. • Is this the right counter to check in for this flight? • Is the plane on schedule? • Would you like me to check your baggage through to your destination? • Would you please put your baggage on this scale? • Here are your ticket, passport, and boarding pass. • Have a pleasant flight.

Unit Five

III. Exercises

1. **Dialogue Completion**

    (1) Man: Can you drive faster? I'm afraid I might be late for the appointment. It's at ten o'clock.

    Driver: _____

    A. No, I was driving at the fastest speed.

    B. I'll drive as fast as I can, but there's a speed limit.

    C. I'm sorry. The policeman might stop us.

    D. Could you give me more money?

    (2) Man: To the Friendship Hotel. Do you know where it is?

    Driver: _____

    A. Sure I do. I've taken a lot of people there.

    B. No, I've no idea where this place is. Please ask someone else.

    C. I'm afraid you are asking the wrong person.

    D. It's far away from here. I'm afraid I can't take you.

    (3) Man: Excuse me. Where can I get a limited express ticket to Tianjin?

    Woman: _____

    A. I don't know.

    B. Go this way, please.

    C. Can I help you?

    D. Right here, at this window.

2. **Dialogue Comprehension**

    (1) Man: Excuse me. Where is the ticket office?

    Woman: It's in the west wing of this building. Go that way and you'll find it.

    Man: Thank you very much.

    Woman: You're welcome.

    Question: Where does this conversation most likely take place?

    A. At a travel agency.

    B. At a supermarket.

    C. At a railroad station.

    D. At a bank.

(2) Man: Hello. May I have your ticket and your passport please?
Woman: Here you are.
Man: Do you have any luggage?
Woman: One piece, right here.
Man: Any hand luggage?
Woman: Just a carry-on bag.
Question: What is the most probable relationship between the speakers?
A. Bus driver and passenger.
B. Doctor and patient.
C. Bank teller and customer.
D. Airport clerk and passenger.

Key to Part Three and Part Four

Part Three:
I. Vocabulary: 1. D   2. B   3. A   4. A   5. B
                6. C   7. A   8. A   9. C   10. B
                11. B   12. B   13. C   14. C   15. D
II. Expression: 1. D   2. C   3. A   4. B   5. B
                6. C   7. B   8. B   9. D   10. D
                11. A   12. D   13. B   14. A   15. C
III. Cloze: 1. A   2. B   3. A   4. A   5. B
                6. B   7. C   8. D   9. C   10. D
IV. Reading: 1. D   2. A   3. A   4. B   5. B
V. Reading: 1. F   2. F   3. T   4. T   5. F

Part Four:
1. Dialogue completion: (1) B   (2) A   (3) D
2. Dialogue comprehension: (1) C   (2) D

Unit Six

Text A

The Generation Lap

Part One: Language Points

I. Vocabulary

1. I love <u>troubleshooting</u> computer problems for teachers, and it's quite unfortunate that some of them see me as a negative. (Introduction)

   译文：我喜欢为老师们解决计算机方面的问题，可很不幸的是有些老师视我为捣乱分子（把我看得一无是处）。

   troubleshoot: *v.* to find and eliminate problems 检修（机器）；排解纠纷或解决困难 troubleshooter *n.* 解决困难者

   e.g. Old John is quite a <u>troubleshooter</u> although he has had little education.
   老约翰尽管没受过什么教育，却是个解决困难的高手。

2. I think I am a little less <u>patient</u> with her than with my teachers (it's a normal family thing I guess). (Introduction)

   译文：我觉得自己对待她（我妈妈）比对待我的老师们要差点耐心（我想这是家庭里常见的）。

   patient: *adj.* having or showing patience 有耐心的，克制的
   (*opposite*) impatient

   e.g. She's too <u>impatient</u> with kids to be a kindergarten teacher.
   她对小孩子太没耐心，不适合做幼儿园老师。

117

3. Children are more adept at using computers. (Para. 1)

   译文：孩子们(比大人们)使用电脑更在行些。

   adept: *adj.* highly skilled　熟练的,内行的

   e.g.　He was very adept at making up excuses for his lateness.
   　　　他非常善于为自己的迟到编造借口。

4. Society has never before experienced this phenomenon of the knowledge hierarchy being so effectively flipped on its head. (Para. 2)

   译文：社会从未经历过如此知识等级被彻底颠覆的现象。

   hierarchy: *n.* formally ranked group, formal grading of group from top to bottom　等级

   e.g.　There's a very rigid hierarchy in the Civil Service.
   　　　政府文职(行政)部门有一套十分严格的等级制度。

5. But it is definitely happening and the situation is magnified with each new technology. (Para. 2)

   译文：但是它确确实实在发生，而且每种新技术的出现都使形势越来越严峻。

   magnify: *v.* to make something appear larger than it really is; to overstate　放大,夸大

   e.g.　The importance of his remark has been magnified out of all proportion.
   　　　他的话的重要性被过分夸大了。

6. The challenge in these episodes was not only how to explain the new technology, but how to convince their parents they needed something they'd never even heard of. (Para. 2)

   译文：这些故事里的挑战不仅在于如何解释新技术,而且在于如何使他们的父母相信他们需要这些父母们从未听说过的东西。

   convince: *v.* to make someone completely certain about something; to persuade　使确信,使信服

   e.g.　They failed to convince the directors that their proposals would work.
   　　　他们未能使董事们相信他们的建议是切实可行的。

7. Researchers introduced computers and the Internet into forty-eight demographically diverse families. (Para. 3)

   译文：研究者将计算机和互联网介绍到四十八个人员构成各不相同的家庭中去。

   diverse: *adj.* different; showing variety　各不相同的,各种各样的

   e.g.　The program deals with subjects as diverse as pop music and ancient Greek *drama.*

节目涉及从流行音乐到古代希腊戏剧这样形形色色的题材。

8. They often provide the motivation for parents to invest in a computer. (Para. 3)

    译文: 他们经常为父母提供投资购买计算机的理由。

    motivation: *n.* the state of being motivated; need or purpose 动力,动机,诱因

    e.g. *His parents give him so much money that he's got no motivation to get a job.*
    他的父母给他的钱太多,以致他不想找工作做。

9. Two-thirds of the kids in the Growing Up Digital survey on FreeZone said they were more proficient at the computer than their parents. (Para. 5)

    译文: "自由地带"的"数字化成长"调查发现,三分之二的孩子说他们比父母更精通计算机。

    proficient: *adj.* thoroughly skilled, well-practised 熟练的,精通的

    e.g. *She is a proficient typist.* 她是个熟练的打字员。

10. This is a unique period in history in that the role of the child in the home is changing. (Para. 6)

    译文: 这是一个不同寻常的历史时期,因为孩子在家中的角色正在改变。

    unique: *adj.* being the only one of its type; unusual; greater or better than any other 独一无二的,独特的,无与伦比的

    e.g. *The town is fairly unique in the wide range of leisure facilities it offers.*
    该城市在提供广泛的闲暇活动设施方面是独特的。

11. The notion of the child being able to do anything new, novel, or really useful for the parent was bogus. (Para. 6)

    译文: 认为孩子能为父母做任何新生、新奇或真正有用的事情的观念是矫情的。

    notion: *n.* an idea, belief, or opinion in someone's mind; concept 概念,观念,看法

    e.g. *The education system was based on the old-fashioned notion of women as home-makers.*
    这种教育体制的基础是认为妇女只应操持家务的过时观念。

12. This insight can be extended to other social institutions as well. (Para. 9)

    译文: 这种见识也可以延伸到其他社会制度中。

    insight: *n.* the power of using one's mind to see or understand the true nature of a situation; a sudden, clear, but not always complete understanding 洞察力;领悟,顿悟,猛省

  e.g. *Although she lives in the countryside all her life, she is a woman of great insight.*

   虽然一辈子生活在农村,她却是个极有见识的女人。

13. The power dynamic between students and teachers will be forever <u>altered</u>. (Para. 9)

  译文: 学生和教师之间的权势关系将永远被改变。

  alter: *v.* to make or become different but without changing into something else (使)改动,更改

  e.g. *The village hasn't really <u>altered</u> much since the last time I was there.*

   自从我上次来这里以后,这个村子并没有多大变化。

14. Harr notes that parents who are not <u>threatened</u> by the lap can benefit. (Para. 14)

  译文: 哈尔指出,那些没有被代差吓倒的父母将从中会受益。

  threaten: *v.* to express a threat against someone; to seem likely to harm, spoil or ruin 威胁,威吓;危及

  e.g. *Noisy traffic <u>threatens</u> the peace of the village.*

   来往车辆的喧闹声会破坏乡村的宁静。

15. Some adults have difficulty accepting the generation lap and seeing the <u>potential</u> for growth. (Para. 15)

  译文: 有些成年人很难接受这样的代差,也很难看到它还有扩大的可能。

  potential: *n.* possibility for developing 潜力,潜能,潜势,可能性

  e.g. *This new invention has (an) enormous sales <u>potential</u>.*

   这项新发明有巨大的销售潜力。

II. Expressions

1. Outside of school I <u>help out</u> my mom with computer-related projects. (Para. 0)

  译文: 放学后我帮妈妈做一些与计算机相关的事情。

  help out: to give somebody some help, e.g., by doing some work or giving money 给某人提供帮助

  a) *He's always willing to <u>help (us) out</u> when we're short of staff.*

   在我们缺人手时,他总是很愿意帮忙。

  b) *Outside of school she <u>helped out</u> her mom by cooking, washing, sewing, and looking after her little brother.*

   放学后她帮妈妈做饭、洗涮、缝补并照看小弟弟。

2. <u>When it comes to</u> understanding and using the new media and technology, ... (Para. 1)

  译文: 说到理解和使用新媒介和新技术,……

Unit Six

when it comes to (doing) something: when it is a case, question, or matter of (doing) something 说到,涉及

a) *I'm as good a cook as she is except <u>when it comes</u> to (making) pastry.*
除非是做糕点,我的厨艺和她不相上下。

b) *<u>When it comes</u> to using multimedia, my daughter knows more than I do.*
谈到运用多媒体,我女儿比我懂得多。

3. ...many parents <u>are falling</u> woefully <u>behind</u> their children. (Para. 1)
译文:……很多父母正可怜地被孩子们甩在身后。

fall behind: to fail to keep up with somebody or something; to be late in doing something 落后(于);拖欠

a) *The major world powers are afraid of <u>falling behind</u> in the arms race.*
那些超级大国唯恐在军备竞赛中落后。

b) *France has <u>fallen behind</u> Germany in coal production.*
法国在煤炭生产上已落后于德国。

c) *He <u>fell behind</u> with the car payments.* 他拖欠了汽车款。

4. Austin Locke, fifteen, <u>sums</u> it up perfectly... (Para. 1)
译文:15岁的奥斯丁·洛克概括得好极了……

sum up: to present the main points or substance of something concisely; to describe or evaluate somebody or something concisely 总结,概括;评价,评估

a) *Now <u>sum up</u> your views in a few words.*
现在用几句话概括你的观点。

b) *I <u>summed</u> her <u>up</u> as a competent manager.*
我认为她是个有能力的经理。

c) *He <u>summed up</u> the situation at a glance.*
他一眼就把形势看了个明白。

5. ...and other adults <u>are looking to</u> children <u>for</u> information and help with computers and other computer-related stuff. (Para. 1)
译文:另外有些成人正求助于孩子们,获得计算机方面以及与计算机有关的信息和帮助。

look to someone for (to do) something: to hope or expect somebody to do something 希望某人做某事

a) *She's regularly <u>looked to for</u> advice.*
经常有人请她出主意。

b) *Many people <u>are looking to</u> the new government <u>to reduce</u> unemployment.*

121

许多人正期盼新政府能降低失业率。

6. Teenagers are central to Internet use at home. (Para. 3)

   译文：十几岁的孩子是家中计算机的主要使用者。

   be central to: to be a major part of 是……的核心

   a) *Reducing inflation is central to the government's economic policy.*
      降低通货膨胀是政府经济政策的核心。

   b) *Central to the argument is the availability of such an effective tool.*
      此争论的核心是有无这样一个有效的工具。

7. Of course, her parents are oblivious to the fact that if she sets up the system, she then controls it. (Para. 4)

   译文：当然，她的父母忽略了一个事实，那就是既然她安装了这个系统，她也就能操控它。

   be oblivious to/of: to be unaware of or have no memory of 忽略，忘记

   a) *He was oblivious of his surroundings when immersed in reading.*
      他沉浸于读书时完全忘记了周围环境的存在。

   b) *The kids were playing merrily along the rail track, totally oblivious to danger.*
      孩子们正沿着铁路轨道快乐地玩耍，完全不知危险。

   set up: to make (an apparatus, a machine) ready for use 设置

   a) *How long will it take to set up the projector?*
      把投影仪设置好需要多长时间？

   b) *He always helped the foreign professors with setting up their computers when they arrived.*
      外教们到达后的时候，总是他去帮忙设置好计算机。

8. We must be prepared to learn major things from our subordinates and vice versa. (Para. 11)

   译文：我们必须做好向下级学习一些重要知识的准备，反之亦然。

   vice versa: conversely, the other way around 反之亦然

   a) *We gossip about them and vice versa.*
      我们聊他们，他们也聊我们。

   b) *He likes her but doesn't know if it's vice versa.*
      他喜欢她，但不知她是否也喜欢他。

9. Peer interaction in homes and schools is setting the stage for the kind of experiences that prepare us to move into the postmodern world. (Para. 11)

   译文：在家里和学校里与同龄人的交流有助于我们获得以后进入后现代社会所需的一些经历。

Unit Six

set the stage for: to prepare for, make possible or easy 为……做准备，促成

a) *The president's recent death set the stage for a military coup.*
  总统最近的去世引发了一场军事政变。

b) *His ideas set the stage for China's economic reforms over the past thirty years.*
  他的思想促成了中国过去三十年来的经济改革。

10. Seventeen-year-old Andy speaks wistfully of the Apple IIs of his early childhood, much as his grandparents probably spoke of their favorite stuffed toys. (Para. 12)

  译文：十七岁的安迪怅惘地说起他幼年的苹果二代计算机时，可能就像他的祖父母提起他们当年最爱的毛绒玩具。

  speak of: to indicate, suggest; to talk about, mention 提到，说到；透露

  a) *His behavior speaks of suffering bravely borne.*
    他的表现透露出他曾经勇敢经历的磨难。

  b) *My classmates often speak of the "good old days" when we get together.*
    我的同学们聚会时常常谈论那些"过去的好时光"。

11. Andy experiences the generation lap every day in his high school classes where he lends a hand to his fellow students and rescues his teachers. (Para. 12)

  译文：安迪在他就读的高中每天都体验着这种代差，在班里他常常（在电脑方面）帮助同学、援救老师。

  lend a hand to: to give help to 帮助，伸出援手

  a) *Lend me a hand with putting up the tent, will you?*
    帮我支起帐篷，好吗？

  b) *They decided to lend a hand to the kindergarten by teaching the kids how to make kites.*
    他们决定给幼儿园提供援助，教孩子们如何制作风筝。

12. The child headed for the computer equipped with a CD-ROM encyclopedia, and the mother went to the reference shelf. (Para. 13)

  译文：那个孩子径直朝装有百科全书光盘的计算机走去，而他的妈妈却走向参考书的书架。

  head for: to move towards (a place) 向……走去

  a) *The boat was heading for some rocks.* 船正驶向一些岩石。

  b) *He headed straight for the bar.* 他径直走向酒吧台。

  c) *Is the world heading for disaster?* 世界是否正走向灾难？

13. It is a totally different experience, and there is a comfort level that is established early on. (Para. 14)

译文：这是一种完全不同的体验,而且是一种年龄很小的时候就建立的一种(使用计算机的)自信。

early on: at the beginning or start of something such as a chain of events or a period of time 在早期

a) *We should have realized early on that financing would be a major problem.*
我们一开始就应当意识到财政会是个大问题。

b) *I knew early on that I was not going to enjoy the film.*
我一开始就知道我不会喜欢这个电影。

14. Needless to say, some adults have difficulty accepting the generation lap and seeing the potential for growth. (Para. 15)

    译文：无庸赘言,有些成年人很难接受这种代差,也很难看到它还有扩大的可能。

    needless to say: as you already know or would expect 无庸赘言

    a) *Needless to say, I survived.* 不用说,我活了下来。

    b) *Needless to say, he kept his promise.* 不用说,他恪守了诺言。

III. Grammar

1. I love troubleshooting computer problems for teachers.

    译文：我喜欢为老师们解决计算机方面的问题。

    love 后跟动名词的宾语表示习惯性、经常性喜欢做的事,后跟动词不定式的宾语则表示一次性想做的事。类似的动词还有 like 和 hate。

2. My mom used to ask me why I was always on the Internet or playing with the computer.

    译文：我妈妈过去老爱问我为什么总是在上互联网或总是在玩电脑。(她现在不问了)

    used to do something 意指过去常常做某事,而现在不做了。其否定式是 didn't use to do something。

3. The mother insisted that they use the book.

    译文：那位妈妈坚持认为他们应该用书本(百科全书)。

    insist 意为"坚持认为"时表达了一种意愿,其宾语从句因此常常采用虚拟语气,以减少强加意味,形式上表现为 should + 原形动词,should 常被省略。类似的动词还有 suggest, advise, demand, request, require, command 等。

4. Some adults have difficulty accepting the generation lap and seeing the potential for growth.

译文：有些成年人很难接受这样的代差，也很难看到它还有扩大的可能。
have difficulty (in) doing something: 做某事有困难

5. I also find it funny when a teacher won't let me help and then gets the computer specialist at the school to do it.

译文：我还觉得老师有时候很滑稽，不让我帮忙而宁可去找学校的计算机专家。

it 在句中的作用是充当形式宾语，真正的宾语是 when 引导的从句。

Part Two: Key to Exercises

I. Suggested Answers to *Topics for Discussion*

1. How does the opening quotation relate to the discussion that follows?

    It provides a case in which a teenager is more skilled at using the computer than both his teachers and his mother, is willing to help them with the new technology, and is proud of his authority role and the influence he exerts on adults. His experience illustrates the author's point regarding the generation lap in the digital era and how adults adapt to the changes.

2. What implications does Tapscott see in children's knowing more than their parents about new technology?

    Parents are no longer authority figures on everything. Children can be authorities on certain subjects. Family members have to respect each other for their areas of expertise. Families will become more open and more democratic.

3. What are the implications for other social institutions besides the family when young people know more about technology than older people?

    The power dynamic between students and teachers, or between managers and subordinates, may also change. Both teenagers and adults can benefit from sharing knowledge.

4. How does Tapscott illustrate his statement that "some adults have difficulty accepting the generation lap and seeing the potential for growth"? To what extent does your own experience support that statement?

    He quotes a teenager's account of his own experience with his teachers at school. He sees two types of teachers: those willing to learn from kids and those reluctant to accept that kids know more about something than they do.

II. Key to Exercises
Text A
A.
1. D
2. "Gap" is the difference in ideas, feelings, and interests that causes lack of understanding, usually between the older, as authority figures, and the younger generations.
   "Lap" is the difference in mastery of new technologies, with the younger generation as authority figures for the first time in history.
3. C
4. At home, kids are the motivation for buying a computer, they are the main and expert users of computers and the Internet, and they often teach other family members how to use computers and the Internet.
5. A
6. The power dynamic between students and teachers, or between managers and subordinates, may also change.
7. The examples illustrate that the generation lap is being experienced every day by children and adults, although adults are often not aware of it.
8. Listen to them more and learn from them, instead of feeling offended by their authority on technology.
9. (1) F (2) T (3) F (4) T (5) F (6) F

B.
1. comes to ... falling behind ... shifted ... outpacing ... overtaking ... lapping
2. central to ... provide the motivation ... invest ... sources of expertise ... catalyze
3. impact ... fluent ... power ... respect ... crucial to ...
4. authority ... domain ... settings...satisfied ... hierarchy
5. wistfully ... favorite ...
6. experiences ... lends a hand to ... rescues ... episode ... entailed
7. surrounded ... virtually ... comfort ... early on ... compared to

C.
1. D 2. B 3. C 4. A 5. C 6. B 7. C 8. D 9. A 10. B

D.
1. magnified 2. novel 3. rude 4. proficient 5. adept 6. altered 7. bogus
8. manage 9. convinced 10. domain 11. entail 12. installed

Unit Six

E.

1. spoke of   2. (to be) oblivious to   3. headed (heading) for   4. help (me) out
5. lent a hand to   6. looked to   7. set up   8. summed up   9. when it comes to
10. fallen behind

F.

1. early on   2. with the exception of   3. firsthand experience   4. start up
5. in terms of   6. in that   7. Needless to say   8. shares memories of   9. in some way
10. vice versa

G.

1. A   2. A   3. B   4. B   5. D   6. B   7. B   8. C   9. C   10. A   11. C   12. C
13. D   14. D   15. B   16. D   17. D   18. A   19. A   20. C

H.

1. The bullet marks on the wall spoke of the fierce fighting that took place here.

2. He was totally oblivious to being laughed at by his neighbors.

3. He is fifty-nine this year and heading (headed) for retirement, though he is still healthy.

4. Most of the old people in China help out with their grandchildren.

5. Don't always look to others to structure your time. Learn to make your own schedule.

6. He set up the camera in the shade of a tree as soon as he got to the shooting scene.

7. At the end of the discussion, he summed it up and added a few points.

8. Tom is an outstanding surgeon and has conducted many operations successfully. However, when it comes to traditional Chinese medicine, he has little to say.

9. We learned a lesson from history that a country must be strong and will be bullied if it falls behind.

10. Parents' spoiling sets the stage for children's lack of understanding and respect for them when they grow up.

I.

Para. 2. 社会从未经历过这种知识等级被彻底扭转的现象，但是它确实在发生，并且随着每一种新技术的出现而加剧。二十多岁的大学生们都记得童年时不得不向父母解释鼠标或CD机为何物的情景。那一幕幕情景中最难的还不是解释新技术，而是如何让父母明白自己需要那个他们闻所未闻的东西。

Para. 4. 六岁的孩子们摆弄父母们摆弄不了的放像机的故事已经老掉牙了。新版故事讲的是最近一个十四岁女孩子的父母求她给家里的电脑装上"网络保姆"软件来防范互联网色情内容。显然她的父母忽略了一个事实，那就是，她如果能安装这系统,她当然也能控制这系统。

Para. 10. 当网络一代进入大学和劳动大军后,会有同样的情况。当今世界上的经理们个人对新技术的应用还非常有限。在发达国家中,欧洲和日本尤其如此。想象一下这些技术熟练的青年带来的冲击波吧!他们每一个人都通过了解对于公司成功至关重要的一方面而赢得了权利和尊重。进而,作为(家庭,学校或其他环境中)至少一个领域的权威,这些网络一代还会满意企业中旧有的等级模式吗?

Text B
B.
1. B   2. C   3. A   4. D   5. B   6. A   7. B   8. D   9. C   10. B

Part Three: Self-check

I. Choose the word closest in meaning to the underlined word in each sentence.

1. I love troubleshooting computer problems for teachers, and it's quite unfortunate that some of them see me as a negative.
   A. solving   B. creating   C. finding   D. leaving

2. I think I am a little less patient with her than with my teachers (it's a normal family thing I guess).
   A. uneasy   B. comfortable   C. satisfied   D. tolerant

3. Children are more adept at using computers.
   A. skilled   B. interested   C. talented   D. motivated

4. Society has never before experienced this phenomenon of the knowledge hierarchy being so effectively flipped on its head.
   A. gap   B. ranking system C. privilege   D. economy

5. But it is definitely happening and the situation is magnified with each new technology.
   A. clarified   B. eased   C. improved   D. amplified

6. The challenge in these episodes was not only how to explain the new technology, but how to convince their parents they needed something they'd never even heard of.
   A. cheat   B. trust   C. persuade   D. believe

128

Unit Six

7. Researchers introduced computers and the Internet into forty-eight demographically diverse families.
   A. different   B. similar   C. varied   D. identical
8. They often provide the motivation for parents to invest in a computer.
   A. evidence   B. reason   C. condition   D. support
9. Two-thirds of the kids in the Growing Up Digital survey on FreeZone said they were more proficient at the computer than their parents.
   A. enthusiastic   B. satisfied   C. skilled   D. familiar
10. This is a unique period in history in that the role of the child in the home is changing.
    A. horrible   B. inspiring   C. crucial   D. unusual
11. The notion of the child being able to do anything new, novel, or really useful for the parent was bogus.
    A. idea   B. ideology   C. notice   D. announcement
12. This insight can be extended to other social institutions as well.
    A. principle   B. definition   C. perception   D. argument
13. The power dynamic between students and teachers will be forever altered.
    A. kept   B. changed   C. valued   D. despised
14. Harr notes that parents who are not threatened by the lap can benefit.
    A. rejected   B. injured   C. accepted   D. intimidated
15. Some adults have difficulty accepting the generation lap and seeing the potential for growth.
    A. possibility   B. advantage   C. disadvantage   D. qualification

II. Choose the expression that best completes each sentence.

1. Outside of school I _____ my mom with computer-related projects.
   A. help out   B. put on   C. work out   D. take on
2. _____ understanding and using the new media and technology, young people have an advantage over old people.
   A. When it occurs to   B. When it comes to
   C. When it relates to   D. When it turns to
3. In some respects, many parents _____ woefully _____ their children.
   A. are falling ... off   B. are falling ... apart
   C. are falling ... behind   D. are falling ... down

4. Now _____ your views in a few words.
   A. break up   B. put up   C. end up   D. sum up
5. …and other adults _____ children _____ information and help with computers and other computer-related stuff.
   A. are looking to ... for
   B. are looking for ... to
   C. are looking up ... in
   D. are looking at ... for
6. Teenagers _____ Internet use at home.
   A. are blind to   B. are central to   C. are alien to   D. are oblivious to
7. The kids were playing merrily along the rail track, totally _____ danger.
   A. aware of   B. keen to   C. oblivious to   D. scared of
8. Of course, if she _____ the computer system, she then controls it.
   A. sets up   B. puts up   C. takes up   D. makes up
9. We gossip about them and _____, which means they also gossip about us.
   A. versa vice   B. vis-à-vis   C. vice versa   D. via
10. Peer interaction in homes and schools is _____ the kind of experiences that prepare us to move into the postmodern world.
    A. preparing the stage for
    B. setting the stage for
    C. setting the platform for
    D. preparing the platform for
11. My classmates often _____ the "good old days" when we get together.
    A. laugh at   B. consist in   C. admit to   D. speak of
12. _____ with putting up the tent, will you?
    A. Lend me a hand
    B. Pass me a hand
    C. Hold onto my hand
    D. Let go of my hand
13. The child _____ the computer equipped with a CD-ROM encyclopedia, and the mother went to the reference shelf.
    A. came across   B. headed for   C. left for   D. ran into
14. We should have realized _____ that financing would be a major problem.
    A. early in   B. early at   C. early on   D. early up
15. _____, some adults have difficulty accepting the generation lap and seeing the potential for growth.
    A. It goes without saying
    B. To name a few
    C. It's up to you
    D. Needless to say

Unit Six

III. Read the following passage and fill in each blank with one of the words or expressions given.

Of all the areas of learning, the most important is the development of attitudes. Emotional reactions as ___1___ as logical thought processes affect the behavior of most people.

"The burnt child fears the fire" is one instance; ___2___ is the rise of despots like Hitler. Both of these examples also point up the fact that attitudes ___3___ experiences. In one case the experience was direct and impressive, in the other it was indirect and cumulative. The Nazis were formed largely by the speeches they ___4___ and the books they read.

The classroom teachers in elementary schools are in a strategic position to influence attitudes. This is true partly because children ___5___ attitudes from those adults whose opinions they respect.

Another reason is that pupils often delve somewhat deeply into a subject in school that has only been touched ___6___ at home or has possibly never occurred to them before. To a child who had previously acquired little knowledge of Mexico, his teacher's method of ___7___ such a unit would greatly affect his attitude toward Mexicans.

The media through which the teacher can develop wholesome attitudes are innumerable. Social attitudes (with special ___8___ to races and nationalities), science matters of health and safety, the very atmosphere of the classroom—these are few of the fertile fields for the induction of proper emotional reactions.

However, ___9___ children come to school with undesirable attitudes, it is unwise for the teacher to attempt to change their feelings by scolding them. She can ___10___ the proper effect by helping them obtain constructive experiences. Finally, a teacher must ___11___ evaluate his or her own attitudes, because his or her influence can be ___12___ if he or she has personal prejudices. This is especially true with respect to controversial issues and questions on which children should be encouraged to reach their own decisions as a result of objective analysis of all the facts.

1. A. long   B. far   C. well   D. large
2. A. the other   B. one another   C. one other   D. another
3. A. stem from   B. spring from   C. result in   D. comprise of
4. A. attended   B. presented   C. delivered   D. heard

5. A. inquire   B. require   C. acquire   D. derive
6. A. at   B. upon   C. in   D. by
7. A. handling   B. lecturing   C. tackling   D. managing
8. A. regard   B. respect   C. mention   D. reference
9. A. since   B. even   C. when   D. unless
10. A. attain   B. obtain   C. achieve   D. reach
11. A. superficially B. subconsciously C. continually   D. constantly
12. A. harmful   B. beneficial   C. harmless   D. helpful

IV. Read the following passage and choose the best answer for each question.

Willie Soon, a climatologist (a climate scientist) at the Harvard-Smithsonian Center for Astrophysics, is increasing the heat within the global-warming community. In a recent paper, he challenges a much-quoted United Nations expert panel which concluded that the 1990s were the warmest decade on record and that Earth heated up more in the twentieth century than in any other century during the past thousand years. "All of these statements about twentieth-century climate change cannot be backed up with data," he says. Michael Mann, a climatologist at the University of Virginia who was one of the U.N. panel's lead authors, counters that Soon's paper is "a thinly disguised publicity stunt (噱头)" that is "not legitimate science."

The controversy stems from a meta-analysis in which Soon and his co-authors combed through hundreds of recent studies of long-term climate indicators, including tree rings, ice cores, fossils, and the movements of glaciers (冰川). The data affirm that atmospheric carbon dioxide levels have reached a record high, but Soon says that they reveal no clear consequences: "There aren't any bad effects. The climate is not responding as people have expected." In fact, temperatures around the world were higher from A.D.800 to 1300, a span known as the medieval warm period, than they are now. Soon theorizes that the present warm phase is part of an ongoing cycle driven by fluctuations in the sun's activity. "The natural variability in climate systems is very large and could have triggered the twentieth-century change," he says.

Most climate researchers are not buying it. Mann says Soon's analysis focuses on the early part of the twentieth century while it ignores unmistakable signals of warming in the latter part of the century. He also disputes Soon's claim that temperatures during the medieval (中世纪的) era topped today's. "His argument is based on the interpretation of evidence that often reflects precipitation (the amount of rain, snow, hail, etc.) rather than temperature," Mann says. Change the selection standards slightly and one could reclassify those years as a cold period. Soon refuses to accept the criticisms: "Our papers are strictly in the interest of making progress, however little that may come from a clarification of the geographic pattern of climate changes that operate on timescales of several decades to centuries."

1. With which of the following statements would Willie Soon probably disagree?
   A. The global warming debate is overheated.
   B. The United Nations experts are over-quoted.
   C. The 1990s was the warmest decade in the past thousand years.
   D. Temperatures around the world did not change in the twentieth century.
2. What is the major problem with the U.N. experts, according to Soon?
   A. Their statements about climate change are not legitimate.
   B. They refused to publish his research paper on the climate change.
   C. They do not take his opinions about the climate change seriously.
   D. Their conclusions about climate change are not supported by data.
3. In their research, Soon and his colleagues found _____.
   A. new indicators of long-term climate change
   B. bad effects of more atmospheric carbon dioxide
   C. clear consequences of twentieth-century climate change
   D. higher temperatures around the world in the medieval era
4. Which of the following is closest in meaning to "buying" (Line 1, Paragraph 3)?
   A. believing   B. ignoring   C. expecting   D. considering
5. Soon thinks his paper is significant because it has _____.
   A. changed the standards for data selection
   B. reclassified the medieval era as a cold period
   C. clarified the variability of climate change
   D. examined warming signals in the twentieth century

V. Read the following passage and decide whether each statement is TRUE or FALSE.

When Patricia Weathers' son Michael had problems in his first-grade class, a school psychologist told the mother he had attention deficit hyperactivity disorder, or ADHD, and needed to be medicated with stimulants. If not medicated, he would be sent to a special education facility near his school.

Confused and frightened, Weathers says she consented to put Michael on Ritalin, a commonly used stimulant that doctors prescribe to decrease the symptoms of ADHD—restlessness, disorganization, hyperactivity.

But Michael exhibited negative effects from the drug, such as social withdrawal. Instead of spotting the side effects, Weathers says, school officials again pressured her back to the psychiatrist's office, where Michael's diagnosis was changed to social anxiety disorder and an antidepressant prescribed.

Finally, says Weathers, "I saw that the medicines were making Michael psychotic, so I stopped giving them to him." When she stopped the medicine, the school reported her to state child protective services for child abuse.

Though charges were dropped, the Weathers case has become a symbol of the boiling controversy surrounding ADHD, treatment for it, and the subjective diagnostic tests that some critics say has led to an overuse of stimulants in schools.

According to testimony given before Congress in 2000, ADHD diagnoses in children grew from 150,000 in 1970 to six million in 2000, representing twelve to thirteen percent of U.S. schoolchildren.

On the one hand, a recent study by the National Institute of Mental Health, published in April, confirmed long-held assumptions that consistent use of stimulants mildly suppresses children's growth—at an average rate of about an inch over the course of two years—in addition to causing weight loss in some children.

At the same time, another part of the same study gave the use of medication a boost when it comes to the treatment of ADHD. The study showed that strict behavioral rules, used without drugs, were not as successful as treatments involving stimulants. They suppressed ADHD symptoms in thirty-four percent of the children tracked over a two-year period, while medication worked in fifty-six percent of cases.

Yet if the study was reassuring to some who work with children, it was alarming to others. "We know only half the story about ADHD," says William Frankenberger, a professor at the University of Wisconsin who has been studying ADHD for almost two decades. "If these medicines suppress growth, you have to ask what else they are doing that we can't measure."

1. Kids with ADHD are often anxious about seeing the doctor.
2. Patricia stopped giving the medicine to her son because she sensed the side effects of the medicine.

3. The figures in Paragraph 6 indicate the drastic increase of ADHD symptoms observed among children.
4. The study by the National Institute of Mental Health suggested that kids put on weight quickly after receiving medication.
5. The Wisconsin professor's concern was that the anti-ADHD medicines might have more serious side effects.

Part Four: Oral Expression: Getting Directions

I. Dialogues

Dialogue 1

Woman: Do you know how to get to Paul's house from here?
Man: Yes. Stay on this road until you get to Glenn Road. Then take a left.
Woman: Left on Glenn Road, OK....
Man: Stay on Glenn Road for about four blocks until you come to Washington Street. Then turn right.
Woman: Left on Glenn, right on Washington...
Man: He lives at 222 Washington. It's on the right side of the street.

Dialogue 2

Man: Should I turn right here?
Woman: No. Keep going straight and turn at the next light.
Man: Do you mean at Scott Road?
Woman: That's right. Turn right there.

Dialogue 3

Man: How far is it from here to L.A.?
Woman: Oh, about seven hours by car.
Man: What's the best way to get there?
Woman: I-10 is the fastest. (I-10: Interstate Highway #10, 美国 10 号州际高速公路)

II. Useful Expressions

When we ask for directions, we can say:	When we give directions, we can say:
• Do you know (Could you tell me) how to get to...? • How can I get to...? • What's the best way to get to...? • Should I (turn right here, go straight on, ...)? • Do you know where... is (located)?	• Stay on ... • Take (make) a left / right (turn) at (the next light, the drug store, Washington Street, ...) • Keep going straight until you come to ... • Go straight for... and then turn (left, right). • (I-10, Freeway, Chang'an Avenue,...) is the best/fastest (way). • It's on the right/left side of ... • It's right across (the street) from....

III. Exercises

1. **Dialogue Completion: Choose the best answer to complete the dialogue.**

    (1) Man:　　Do you know where the nearest hospital is?
    　　Woman: _____
    　　A. No. How could I?
    　　B. Sorry. I'm not sick.
    　　C. Sure. You can ask the cop over there.
    　　D. Yes. Go straight and turn left at the grocery store.

    (2) Man:　　Here you go, Ma'am. This is your boarding pass.
    　　Woman: _____
    　　Man:　　Gate 10. It's straight ahead past the security check area.
    　　A. What's it for?
    　　B. When's the boarding time?
    　　C. Where's the departure gate?
    　　D. Where's the security check area?

    (3) Man:　　Which gate does my plane leave from?
    　　Woman: It leaves from Gate 22.
    　　Man:　　Is that this way or that way?

Woman: _____

A. It's to your left.

B. It's been delayed.

C. You'd better hurry.

D. They're loading right now.

2. **Dialogue Comprehension: Choose the best answer to the question.**

(1) Woman: Excuse me, could you tell me how to get to the University Bookstore?

Man: Sure. Go straight for two blocks, then turn left and walk three more blocks until you get to the drugstore. It's right across the street.

Question: Where is the drugstore?

A. Next to the bookstore.   B. Behind the bookstore.

C. Opposite the bookstore.   D. In front of the bookstore.

(2) Woman: Excuse me. I'm trying to get to the Student Union.

Man: Sure. Just go down here to the corner and turn left. Then go straight for three blocks and turn left at the tower. It's two blocks from there.

Question: How far must the woman walk to get to the Student Union?

A. Five miles.   B. Five or six blocks.

C. Three blocks.   D. Two or three miles.

(3) Woman: This bus goes past the university, doesn't it?

Man: It goes near the university.

Woman: When should I get off?

Man: Get off at Fourth Street and walk two blocks east.

Question: Where is the woman going?

A. To Fourth Street.   B. To the university.

C. To the second block.   D. To the bus terminal.

(4) Woman: Is this taxi taken?

Man: No. Where are you going?

Woman: To the Lincoln Park Apartments. They are on 44th Street.

Man: I know where they are. Get in.

Question: Who is the woman speaking to?

A. A taxi driver.   B. A policeman.

C. A travel agent.   D. A passer-by.

Notes:

block: (AmE) the distance between two cross streets, in a city usually an eighth of a mile 街区

drugstore: (AmE) a pharmacy, esp. one which sells not only medicine, but also beauty products, film, and sometimes light snack foods 药房；(兼售药品、化妆品、胶卷和简易食品的)杂货店

Key to Part Three and Part Four

Part Three:
I. Vocabulary:	1. A	2. D	3. A	4. B	5. D
	6. C	7. A	8. B	9. C	10. D
	11. A	12. C	13. B	14. D	15. A
II. Expression:	1. A	2. B	3. C	4. D	5. A
	6. B	7. C	8. A	9. C	10. B
	11. D	12. A	13. B	14. C	15. D
III. Cloze:	1. C	2. D	3. A	4. D	5. C
	6. B	7. A	8. D	9. B	10. C
	11. D	12. A			
IV. Reading:	1. C	2. D	3. D	4. A	5. C
V. Reading:	1. F	2. T	3. T	4. F	5. T

Part Four:
1. Dialogue Completion: (1) D   (2) C   (3) A
2. Dialogue Comprehension: (1) C   (2) B   (3) B   (4) A

Unit Seven

Text A

Propaganda Techniques in Advertising

Part One: Language Points

I. Vocabulary

1. Advertisers often use subtle deceptions to <u>sway</u> people's opinions. (Para. 2)

    译文:广告商们总是使用巧妙的骗术来左右人们的想法。

    sway: *v.* to move from side to side; to have influence or change opinions 影响、改变(观点)

    e.g. Your arguments won't <u>sway</u> her: she's determined to leave.
    你讲的道理说服不了她,她已经下定决心离开。

2. Name-calling is a propaganda tactic in which a competitor is <u>referred</u> to with negatively charged names or comments. (Para. 4)

    译文:中伤是一种给竞争者冠以负面名称或评论的宣传手段。

    refer (to sb./ sth.): *v.* to mention or speak of sb./sth. 提到、说到或涉及到(某人或某事)

    e.g. In her autobiography she occasionally <u>refers</u> to her unhappy schooldays.
    她在自传里间或提起自己不愉快的学生时代。

3. For example, a political advertisement may <u>label</u> an opposing candidate a "loser," "fence-sitter," or "warmonger." (Para. 4)

    译文:例如,一则政治广告可能会称对方竞选者为"失败者"、"骑墙派"或"好战分子"。

label: *v.* to describe or classify sb./sth.　描述(某人或某事),将(某人或某事)归类

　　e.g. *She is usually labeled (as) an Impressionist.*
　　　　人们通常称她为印象派艺术家。

4. The label of foreignness will have unpleasant connotations in many people's minds. (Para. 4)

　　译文: 外来货这种称号对很多人来说具有贬义。

　　connotation: *n.* the implied or suggested meaning in addition to the simple or literal meaning, overtone　外延,言外之意,隐含之意

　　e.g. *The word "lady" has connotations of refinement and excessive femininity that some women find offensive.*
　　　　"淑女"这个词带有文雅和过度阴柔的意味,会令某些女性觉得反感。

5. Advertisers who use glittering generalities surround their products with attractive-and slippery-words and phrases. (Para. 5)

　　译文: 使用虚夸空谈手段的广告商们用诱人的但靠不住的词语来形容自己的产品。

　　slippery: *adj.* difficult to grasp, as in having a smooth surface; elusive and hard to catch　油滑的,不可靠的

　　e.g. *He's as slippery as an eel—you can never get a straight answer out of him.*
　　　　他很油滑——从他嘴里从来套不出一句实话。

6. This kind of language stirs positive feelings in people. (Para. 5)

　　译文: 这种语言激起了人们内心的积极感情。

　　stir: *v.* to excite or arouse (a person or his feelings, etc)　激发(某人的感情等)

　　e.g. *The story stirred the boy's imagination.*
　　　　那个故事引发了男孩的幻想。

7. The feelings may spill over to the product or idea being pitched. (Para. 5)

　　译文: 这种感情的洋溢可能会使人们对商家鼓吹的产品或理念也产生好感。

　　pitch: *v.* to present or advertise for sale especially in a high-pressure way　竭力推销

　　e.g. *The salesman stood at the door, pitching his products.*
　　　　推销员站在门口,极力推销他的产品。

8. As with name-calling, the emotional response may overwhelm logic. (Para. 5)

　　译文: 和中伤手段一样,(虚夸空谈宣传手段引发的这种)情感反应也会战胜逻辑思维能力。

　　overwhelm: *v.* to overcome completely, crush　压倒,制服

Unit Seven

  e.g. *Government troops have <u>overwhelmed</u> the rebels and seized control of the capital.*
  政府军战胜了叛军,夺得了首都控制权。

9. Product names, for instance, are often designed to <u>evoke</u> good feelings. (Para. 8)
   译文:例如,产品名称也往往是为了引发好感而设计出来的。

   evoke: *v.* to call forth, bring out 唤起,引起(感情或回忆)
   e.g. *The music <u>evoked</u> memories of her youth.*
   这乐曲勾起了她对青年时代的回忆。

10. Corporations also use the transfer technique when they sponsor <u>prestigious</u> shows on radio and television. (Para. 10)
    译文:商家赞助那些有影响力的电台或电视节目,也同样是使用了这种转移宣传技巧。

    prestigious: *adj.* having an excellent reputation, worthy of respect 享有声誉的,有名望的,有影响力的
    e.g. *It's one of the best equipped and most <u>prestigious</u> schools in the country.*
    它是全国配备最好、最富盛名的学校之一。

11. Such appeals to Americans' love of country surround the candidate with an aura of patriotism and <u>integrity</u>. (Para. 11)
    译文:这种对美国人爱国之心的迎合给候选人戴上了爱国和正直的光环。

    integrity: *n.* the quality of being honest, moral uprightness 正直,诚实(的品格)
    e.g. *He is a man of <u>integrity</u>; he won't break his promise.*
    他是一个诚实正直的人,决不食言。

12. Newspaper ads for films often <u>feature</u> favorable comments by well-known reviewers. (Para. 13)
    译文:报纸上的电影广告总是把知名评论家的好评文章放在显眼的位置。

    feature: *v.* to give prominence to, give special attention to 给(某人或某事)以显著地位;由某人主演
    e.g. *This week's broadcast <u>features</u> a report on victims of domestic violence.*
    本周的广播就家庭暴力受害者做了专题报道。

13. Applied to propaganda, card stacking means telling half-truths—misrepresenting the facts by <u>suppressing</u> relevant evidence. (Para. 17)
    译文:洗牌作弊法运用到宣传上就意味着说话半真半假——通过隐瞒相关证据来歪曲事实。

    suppress: *v.* to prevent sth. from being known or seen 防止(某事物)被人知道或

看到

    e.g.   *His feelings of resentment have been <u>suppressed</u> for years.*
          他的愤恨之情已经压抑了多年。

14. Again, the audience feels under pressure to <u>conform</u>. (Para. 19)

    译文：观众们又一次迫于压力而顺从了。

    conform (to sth.): *v.* to act according to law or rule, in agreement with generally accepted standards   遵循,依循,保持一致

    e.g. *The building does not <u>conform</u> to safety regulations.*
           这座建筑物不符合安全条例。

15. They tell us, for example, that "Nobody doesn't like Sara Lee" (the message is that you must be <u>weird</u> if you don't). (Para. 20)

    译文：例如,广告告诉我们"没人不喜欢莎拉·李"(意思是如果你不喜欢这个人的话你一定很怪异)。

    weird: *adj.* of strange or extraordinary character   怪异的

    e.g. *That's <u>weird</u>—I thought I'd left my keys on the table but they're not there.*
          真奇怪——我以为我把钥匙放在桌上了,但是那儿没有。

II. Expressions

1. One study reports that each of us, during an average day, is <u>exposed to</u> over *five hundred* advertising claims of various types. (Para. 1)

    译文：一项调查表明我们每人平均每天会接触到500多种各式各样的广告。

    expose ... to: to make liable to, be open to   使暴露于,使接触

    a) *The report showed that the workers had been <u>exposed to</u> a dangerous environment.*

    报告显示,工人们一直都在危险环境下工作。

    b) *The children were <u>exposed to</u> fever because one of their classmates was ill.*

    有一个同学生病了,其他孩子有可能(被传染而)发烧。

2. Advertisers <u>lean</u> heavily <u>on</u> propaganda to sell their products, whether the "product" is a brand of toothpaste, a candidate for office, or a political viewpoint. (Para. 2)

    译文：广告商们非常依赖宣传来销售自己的产品,不管其"产品"是某种品牌的牙膏、某一政府机关的候选人还是某种政治观念。

    lean on: to depend on, rely on   依靠

    a) *The family <u>leaned on</u> each other for support in this hard time.*

    家里人互相依赖、互相支持以共渡难关。

Unit Seven

b) *Some businessmen <u>lean</u> heavily <u>on</u> their social connections to promote their businesses.*

一些商人非常依赖自己的社会关系来做生意。

3. Propaganda is a systematic effort to influence people's opinions, to <u>win</u> them <u>over</u> to a certain view or side. (Para. 2)

译文：宣传是一种影响人们的想法、说服他们支持某一观点或某一立场的系统化努力手段。

win over: to get support or friendship （通过劝说）获得（某人的）支持或好感

a) *The candidate asked everybody in the team to work hard to <u>win over</u> those undecided votes.*

候选人要求小组里所有人都要努力去争取那些犹豫不决的投票人的选票。

b) *His excellent performance in this film helped to <u>win over</u> some audiences.*

他在电影里的精彩表演帮助他赢得了一些观众的支持。

4. They may even use what <u>amount to</u> outright lies. (Para. 2)

译文：他们甚至(在广告里)使用赤裸裸的谎言。

amount to: to be equal to, have the same effect 等于，相当于

a) *The measure the government took in the economic crisis <u>amounted to</u> nothing.*

政府在经济危机中采取的措施根本无济于事。

b) *If you do it in this way, it will only <u>amount to</u> doing it over again, which is useless.*

如果你用这种方式做事的话，只相当于又重新做了一遍，一点儿用都没有。

5. The advertisers hope that the trust and prestige <u>attached to</u> the symbol or image will carry over to the product. (Para. 9)

译文：广告商们希望与这一标志或形象联系在一起的信任和威望能够传递到产品身上。

attach ... to: to be part of, to work for a part of an organization; to connect sth. with sth. 依附于；相联系

a) *I used to work for the high school <u>attached to</u> the university.*

我过去曾在那所大学的附属中学工作。

b) *He was <u>attached to</u> a department in an American newspaper.*

他暂属于一家美国报纸的某个部门。

6. In transfer, advertisers try to improve the image of a product by <u>associating</u> it <u>with</u> a symbol or image most people respect and admire, like the American flag or Uncle Sam. (Para. 9)

译文:在转移宣传手段中,广告商们试图把某种产品和大众所尊敬仰慕的标志或形象(如美国国旗或美国政府)联系起来,从而提高该产品的形象。

associate ... with: to make a mental connection with 把(人或事物)联系起来,在头脑中联想

a) *In North America, some people associate turkey with Thanksgiving.*
在北美,有些人将火鸡和感恩节联系在一起。

b) *I don't think I can associate him with academic research.*
我认为他和学术研究不沾边。

7. American Express features a slew of well-known people who assure us that they never go anywhere without their American Express card. (Para. 13)

译文:美国运通信用卡的广告由许多名人主演,他们向观众保证说自己无论去哪里都会带着运通信用卡。

a slew of: (informal) a large number of 许多,大量

a) *On the two sides of the highway is a slew of cheap hotels.*
大路两边有很多便宜的旅馆。

b) *A slew of celebrities is present at today's press conference.*
很多名人出席了今天的新闻发布会。

8. The plain folks approach says, in effect, "Buy me or vote for me. I'm just like you." (Para. 15)

译文:亲民宣传法实际上是在说:"买我们产品或者给我投票吧。我就和你一样。"

in effect: in essence, in fact, for all purpose 实际上,事实上

a) *In effect, we will meet with more difficulties in our work this year than last year.*
实际上,我们今年在工作中遇到的困难将要比去年多。

b) *The two approaches to this problem are in effect the same.*
解决这个问题的两个方法实际上是一样的。

9. The idea is to convince voters that the candidates are at heart average people with the same values, goals, and needs as you and I have. (Para. 16)

译文:这个主意是要说服投票人其实候选人本质上也是普通人,就和你我一样,都拥有相同的价值观、目标和需求。

at heart: in nature, in fact 本质上,实际上

a) *She is already in her late sixties, but is young and romantic at heart.*
她已经快70了,但内心里还很年轻浪漫。

b) *At heart Tom may be a working class boy, but in fact he has become an executive.*
汤姆本质上也许是一个工人阶级的孩子,但事实上他已经成为一名企管人员了。

10. They work because they appeal to our emotions, not to our minds. (Para. 21)
    译文:这些宣传技巧之所以奏效是因为它们迎合的是我们的情感而非理智。

    appeal to: to have an attraction for; to earnestly ask for help 使(某人)感兴趣;恳求

    a) *Entertainment such as movies and popular songs always appeals to one's emotions rather than to one's reason.*
    电影和流行歌曲这些娱乐节目总是迎合我们的情感而非理性。

    b) *When I told my son "No," he would appeal to his mother.*
    当我跟儿子说"不"的时候,他就会向他母亲求助。

11. Similar to the transfer device, the testimonial capitalizes on the admiration people have for a celebrity—even though the celebrity is not an expert on the product being sold. (Para. 12)
    译文:证词宣传法和转移宣传法类似,也是利用了人们对名人的仰慕———即使该名人并非被售产品方面的专家。

    capitalize on: to take advantage of, to make use of 利用某事物,从某事物中获利

    a) *One suggestion is that the county should capitalize on its natural beauty to attract tourists.*
    有一种建议认为,本县应当利用自己的自然美景来吸引游客。

    b) *Why don't we capitalize on people's expectation for the "new" and the "free" to promote our product?*
    我们为什么不利用人们对"新颖"和"免费"的期待来推销我们的产品呢?

12. If we don't drink Pepsi, we're left out of "the Pepsi generation." (Para. 20)
    译文:如果我们不喝百事可乐,我们就会被排除出"百事可乐一代"。

    be left out (of) / leave out: to be excluded 不包括,排除在外,忽略掉

    a) *Jim has been left out of the team because he has not attended its practice times.*
    吉姆被队伍开除了,因为他没参加训练。

    b) *She has been very careful in organizing the party, hoping not to leave anything out.*
    她精心策划这次聚会,希望能做到万无一失。

13. Otherwise, we will have consented to handing over to others our independence of thought and action. (Para. 21)

译文: 不然的话,我们将自愿把自己思想和行动的自由拱手交给他人。

consent to: to give permission for something, to agree to do something 同意

a) *The father reluctantly consented to the daughter's marriage.*
父亲勉强同意了女儿的婚事。

b) *They rarely consent to do the homework assigned by their teacher.*
他们很少同意做老师布置的作业。

hand over / hand ... over (to): to transfer authority, to give over 交出

a) *The soldiers were ordered to hand over their guns after they lost the battle.*
战败后,士兵们被命令缴械投降。

b) *After my retirement, I will hand my business over to my son.*
退休后,我会把生意交给儿子来做。

14. Why do so many of us buy the products, viewpoints, and candidates urged on us by propaganda messages? (Para. 21)

译文: 为什么我们那么多人会接受那些通过宣传信息极力推荐给我们的产品、观点和候选人呢?

urge sth. on/upon sb. (urge on/upon sb. sth.): to recommend sth. strongly 向某人竭力推荐某事物

a) *I have urged upon him the need for extreme secrecy.*
我特别叮嘱他要绝对保密。

b) *The government urged on industry the importance of low pay settlements.*
政府向工业界强调解决低工资问题的重要性。

III. Grammar

1. They may even use what amount to outright lies. (Para. 2)

   译文: 他们甚至(在广告中)使用赤裸裸的谎言。

   what 引导的名词性从句在本句中充当 use 的宾语。what 只能引导名词性从句,用作连接代词,作从句的具体成分,且不能省略。

   在句子中起名词作用的句子叫名词从句(Noun Clauses)。名词从句的功能相当于名词词组,它在复合句中能担任主语、宾语、表语、同位语、介词宾语等。

   that, who, whom, whose, whoever, what, whatever, which, whichever, where, when, how, why 都可引导名词从句。

   e.g. *In one's own home one can do what one likes.*

Unit Seven

That depends on where we shall go.

I'm not sure why she refused their invitation.

2. Political advertisements make almost <u>as much use</u> of the "plain folks" appeal <u>as</u> they do of transfer devices. (Para. 16)

译文：政治广告中使用"亲民法"几乎和"转移法"一样多。

表示倍数的用法：

倍数 + as + 形容词 / 副词 + as + 被比较对象，译作"是……的多少倍"（如果表示"和……同样多"则前面不加倍数）。

e.g. *My room is five times as big as yours.*

若该结构中现出了名词，名词应放在形容词 / 副词之后：

倍数 + as + 形容词 / 副词 + 名词 + as + 被比较对象

e.g. *They have produced twice as many records as they did last year.*

I have spent twice as much money as I thought.

Part Two: Key to Exercises

I. Suggested Answers to *Topics for Discussion*

1. Some of the propaganda techniques listed in the selection have contrasting appeals. How do the "name-calling" and "glittering generalities" approaches contrast each other? How do the "testimonial" and "plain folks" strategies contrast each other?

   (1) By name-calling, advertisers associate their competitors with negative images or comments and therefore arouse feelings of mistrust, fear, and even hate in their audiences. Advertisers who use glittering generalities surround their products with attractive—and slippery—words and phrases. They use vague terms such as "great," "progress," "beautiful," and "super." This kind of language stirs up positive feelings in people, feelings that may spill over to the product or idea being pitched.

   (2) Testimonials capitalize on the admiration people have for a celebrity. We admire the celebrity so much that we like the product too. The "plain folks" approach uses ordinary people in folksy and warmhearted scenes to pitch the

products or ideas. This approach helps advertisers convince their audiences that they, and their ideas, are "of the people."

2. Why are ads with a bandwagon appeal so effective? What ads have you seen lately that use this technique?

The basic theme of the bandwagon appeal is that "everyone else is doing it, and so should you." Since few of us want to be left out, this technique can be quite successful.

3. McClintock states, "We are victims, seemingly content—even eager—to be victimized." Why does she says this, and do you agree? Will this article change how you view ads in the future?

Yes, I agree. In an age of information overload, every day we are bombarded with one persuasive communication after another. Many people respond to this pressure by processing messages more quickly and, when possible, by taking mental shortcuts. Propagandists encourage this by agitating emotions, by capitalizing on the ambiguity of language, and by bending the rules of logic. Many of us would rather let the propagandists do our thinking for us, since clear thinking requires hard work. We become victims of propaganda because we consent to handing over to advertisers our independence of thought and action.

4. What other propaganda techniques—in addition to those described in this essay—can you find in today's advertisements?

(1) Fear. When propagandists warn their audiences that disaster will result if they do not follow a particular course of action, they are using the fear appeal. For example, a television commercial portrays a terrible automobile accident (the fear appeal) and reminds viewers to wear their seat-belts (the fear-reducing behavior).

(2) Authority. Appealing to authority is a valid type of argument if the authority being appealed to is a noted expert in the area in question.

(3) Black-and-white fallacy. Presenting only two choices, with the product or idea being promoted as the better choice. (e.g., "You are either with us, or you are with the evil enemy.")

Unit Seven

II. Key to Exercises
Text A
A.

1. (1) Name-calling is a propaganda tactic in which a competitor is referred to with negatively charged names or comments.
   (2) A glittering generality is an important-sounding but general claim for which no explanation or proof is offered.
   (3) Transfer is a propaganda tactic in which advertisers try to improve the image of a product by associating it with a symbol or image most people respect and admire.
   (4) Testimonial capitalizes on the admiration people have for a celebrity—even though the celebrity is not an expert on the product being sold.
   (5) The plain folks approach uses ordinary language and mannerisms in attempting to equate the propagandist's point of view with that of the average person.
   (6) Card stacking means telling half-truths—misrepresenting the facts by suppressing relevant evidence.
   (7) Bandwagon appeals attempt to persuade the target audience to join in and take the course of action that "everyone else is taking."
2. The purpose of propaganda is to make people believe in the message without concern for what is true or false, good or bad.
3. Referring to a car as a "foreign car" may have unpleasant connotations while "imported car" may not.
4. *Loves Diapers, New Freedom* feminine hygiene products, *Joy* liquid detergent.
5. The purpose is to convince the voters that the candidates are at heart average people with the same values, goals, and needs as everyone else.
6. For example, the Honda motorcycle ad tells the customers: "Follow the Leader. He is on a Honda." He is the leader—everyone wants to be like a leader.
7. B   8. C   9. B   10. D   11. C   12. B
13. (1) F   (2) F   (3) F   (4) T   (5) T

B.

1. the seducers and the brainwashers ... invite into our homes ... read ... magazines ... watch ... alluring ... absorb ... subconscious.
2. great ... progress ... beautiful and super ... stirs ... spill over ... overwhelm ... audiences ... without ... about
3. folks ... line ... offices ... "everyday Joes" ... care

4. emotions ... minds ... thinking ... analyzing ... researching ... examining ... using ... flaws

C.
1. A   2. C   3. C   4. A   5. B   6. A

D.
1. consent   2. featuring   3. epithet   4. buzzword   5. sway   6. evoke
7. was overwhelmed   8. conform   9. sprinkle   10. label

E.
1. was left out   2. handed over   3. A slew of   4. exposes ... to   5. associate ... with
6. at heart   7. win over   8. leans on   9. appealing to   10. In effect   11. Urged on
12. consented to

F.
1. an average day   2. deep desire   3. ordinary folks   4. public image   5. clear thinking
6. average people   7. assembly line   8. target audiences   9. alluring images
10. important-sounding

G.
1. A   2. B   3. A   4. C   5. C   6. A   7. C   8. C   9. A   10. A   11. A   12. B
13. A   14. A   15. B   16. A   17. C   18. B   19. C   20. A   21. C   22. A

H.
1. The success of some ads lies in that they fully capitalize on people's psychology of worshipping celebrities.
2. I am really concerned that such a big company will be handed over to a young man in his twenties.
3. The purpose of this program is to tell the audience that these heroes are at heart ordinary people just like us.
4. One basic principle in solving conflict is to appeal to mind not emotion.
5. I still miss very much the days I spent in the high school attached to Peking University.
6. One may get skin cancer easily by exposing oneself to the sun for a long time. That is why I don't like to lie on the beach enjoying sunshine.
7. The harder the situation is, the more people should lean on each other. Only in this way can difficulties be eventually overcome.
8. Our strategy in this campaign is first to win over the trust of the public and then to get their support.
9. In this company what the manager says amounts to an order.

Unit Seven

10. The content of the report is extensive, but the scope is limited. Many details have to be left out.

I.

广告商们推出产品时,非常依赖于宣传手段,不管其"产品"是某一种牌子的牙膏,竞争某个职位的候选人还是一种政治观点。宣传手段指的是一种系统的影响人们观点的做法,将其争取到某一边或者让他们相信某一种观点。在进行宣传时,(广告商们)并不在意什么是真的或假的,什么是好的或坏的。那些宣传者们只是要让人们相信他们传送出去的信息。广告商们经常使用一些微妙的欺骗手法来左右人们的观点,甚至不惜使用谎言类的东西。

Text B
1. A   2. C   3. A   4. D   5. D   6. D   7. C   8. D   9. C   10. B

Part Three: Self-check

I. Choose the word that is closest in meaning to the underlined word in each sentence.

1. Advertisers often use subtle deceptions to sway people's opinions.
   A. influence   B. invent   C. include   D. inform
2. Name-calling is a propaganda tactic in which a competitor is referred to with negatively charged names or comments.
   A. remembered   B. alluded to   C. respected   D. memorized
3. For example, a political advertisement may label an opposing candidate as a "loser," "fence-sitter," or "warmonger."
   A. say   B. talk   C. speak   D. classify
4. The label of foreignness will have unpleasant connotations in many people's minds.
   A. associations   B. context   C. purpose   D. significance
5. Advertisers who use glittering generalities surround their products with attractive—and slippery—words and phrases.
   A. unimportant   B. unattractive   C. deceitful   D. unavailable
6. This kind of language stirs up positive feelings in people.
   A. mixes   B. enables   C. mingles   D. excites

7. The feelings may spill over to the product or idea being pitched.
   A. promoted   B. fixed   C. thrown   D. struck
8. As with name-calling, the emotional response may overwhelm logic.
   A. flood   B. overdo   C. defeat   D. succeed
9. Product names, for instance, are often designed to evoke good feelings.
   A. foster   B. arouse   C. develop   D. nurture
10. Corporations also use the transfer technique when they sponsor prestigious shows on radio and television.
    A. respecting   B. respective   C. respectful   D. respected
11. Such appeals to Americans' love of country surround the candidate with an aura of patriotism and integrity.
    A. completeness   B. honesty   C. integration   D. completion
12. Newspaper ads for films often feature favorable comments by well-known reviewers.
    A. characterize   B. express   C. emphasize   D. portray
13. Applied to propaganda, "card stacking" means telling half-truths—misrepresenting the facts by suppressing relevant evidence.
    A. concealing   B. oppressing   C. pressing   D. distressing
14. Again, the audience feels under pressure to conform.
    A. confirm   B. complain   C. commit   D. comply
15. They tell us, for example, that "Nobody doesn't like Sara Lee" (the message is that you must be weird if you don't).
    A. stupid   B. stable   C. strange   D. standard

II. Choose the expression that best completes each sentence.

1. One study reports that each of us, during an average day, is _____ over *five hundred* advertising claims of various types.
   A. occurred to   B. happened to   C. brought to   D. exposed to
2. Advertisers _____ heavily _____ propaganda to sell their products, whether the "product" is a brand of toothpaste, a candidate for office, or a political viewpoint.
   A. lean ... on   B. decide ... on C. give ... up   D. agree ... with
3. *Propaganda* is a systematic effort to influence people's opinions, to _____ them _____ to a certain view or side.
   A. ask ... out   B. win ... over   C. fight ... for   D. call ... in
4. They may even use what _____ outright lies.

A. pile up to   B. mount up to   C. add up to   D. amounts to
5. The advertisers hope that the trust and prestige _____ the symbol or image will carry over to the product.
   A. aside from   B. except for   C. in touch with   D. attached to
6. In "transfer," advertisers try to improve the image of a product by _____ it _____ a symbol or image most people respect and admire, like the American flag or Uncle Sam.
   A. acquainted ... with   B. protesting ... against
   C. associating ... with   D. preventing ... from
7. American Express features _____ well-known people who assure us that they never go anywhere without their American Express card.
   A. an amount of   B. a slew of   C. a little of   D. a bit of
8. The "plain folks" approach says, _____, "Buy me or vote for me. I'm just like you."
   A. in need   B. in want   C. in effect   D. in all
9. The idea is to convince voters that the candidates are _____ average people with the same values, goals, and needs as you and I have.
   A. at heart   B. at best   C. at once   D. at risk
10. They work because they _____ our emotions, not to our minds.
    A. appeal to   B. accuse of   C. approve of   D. agree with
11. Similar to the transfer device, the testimonial _____ the admiration people have for a celebrity—even though the celebrity is not an expert on the product being sold.
    A. consists of   B. capitalizes on   C. composes of   D. makes up for
12. If we don't drink Pepsi, we're _____ of "the Pepsi generation."
    A. left alone   B. left off   C. left out   D. left behind
13. Otherwise, we will have _____ giving to others our independence of thought and action.
    A. consistent with   B. consented to
    C. conformed to   D. confronted with
14. Otherwise, we will have consented to _____ to others our independence of thought and action.
    A. handing in   B. handing out   C. handing over   D. handing down
15. Why do so many of us buy the products, viewpoints, and candidates _____ us by propaganda messages?
    A. relied on   B. blamed on   C. depended on   D. urged on

III. Read the following passage and fill in each blank with one of the words or expressions given.

The word "doublespeak" was coined in the early 1950s. It is often __1__ attributed to George Orwell and his 1948 dystopian (反乌托邦的) novel *Nineteen Eighty-Four*. The word actually never appears in that novel. Orwell did, however, coin "newspeak," "oldspeak," and "doublethink." It was therefore just a matter of time before someone __2__ "doublespeak." Doublespeak may be defined as words __3__ constructed for political purposes: words, that is to say, which not only have in every case a political implication, but are intended to evoke a desirable mental attitude __4__ the person using them.

Doublespeak is most reminiscent of Orwell's newspeak when it is used by a government agency to __5__ something unpleasant. The government may need to talk about something that has negative __6__ for the public and avoids backlash (强烈反对) by __7__ the term with a new one that most people will not recognize as the same thing. Thus "area denial munitions" means "landmines," "physical persuasion" and "tough questioning" mean "__8__" and "operational exhaustion" means "shell shock."

A prominent example of doublespeak in the corporate world is the number of different phrases that __9__ describe the action of "firing lots of employees," usually obliquely (拐弯抹角地). These phrases include "layoffs," "downsizing," "right-sizing," "headcount adjustment," "RIF" (__10__ in force), and "realignment." Corporate doublespeak can also involve downplaying problems, such as calling a fix for a software bug a "reliability enhancement."

1. A. incorrectly   B. correctly   C. accurately   D. exactly
2. A. come in for   B. come into being C. come down with   D. came up with
3. A. obviously   B. carelessly   C. carefully   D. deliberately
4. A. in   B. to   C. upon   D. with
5. A. show off   B. cover up   C. find out   D. run after
6. A. symbols   B. connotations   C. remarks   D. marks
7. A. changing   B. replacing   C. placing   D. altering
8. A. enjoyment   B. happiness   C. torture   D. faint
9. A. all   B. none   C. each   D. both
10. A. reference   B. response   C. reaction   D. reduction

Unit Seven

IV. Read the following passage and choose the best answer for each question.

Many things make people think artists are weird. But the weirdest may be this: artists' only job is to explore emotions, and yet they choose to focus on the ones that feel bad. This wasn't always so. The earliest forms of art, like painting and music, are those best suited for expressing joy. But somewhere in the nineteenth century, more artists began seeing happiness as meaningless, phony or, worst of all, boring as we went from Wordsworth's daffodils to Baudelaire's flowers of evil.

You could argue that art became more skeptical of happiness because modern times have seen so much misery. But it's not as if earlier times didn't know perpetual war, disaster, and the massacre of innocents. The reason, in fact, may be just the opposite: there is too much damn happiness in the world today.

After all, what is the one modern form of expression almost completely dedicated to depicting happiness? Advertising. The rise of anti-happy art almost exactly tracks the emergence of mass media and with it, a commercial culture in which happiness is not just an ideal but an ideology.

People in earlier eras were surrounded by reminders of misery. They worked until exhausted, lived with few protections, and died young. In the West, before mass communication and literacy, the most powerful mass medium was the church, which reminded worshippers that their souls were in danger and that they would someday be meat for worms. Given all this, they did not exactly need their art to be a bummer too.

Today the messages your average Westerner is surrounded with are not religious but commercial, and forever happy. Fast-food eaters, news anchors, text messengers, all smiling, smiling, smiling. Our magazines feature beaming celebrities and happy families in perfect homes. And since these messages have an agenda—to lure us to open our wallets—they make the very idea of happiness seem unreliable. "Celebrate!" commanded the ads for the arthritis drug Celebrex before we found out it could increase the risk of heart attacks.

What we forget—what our economy depends on us forgetting—is that happiness is more than pleasure without pain. The things that bring the greatest joy carry the greatest potential for loss and disappointment. Today, surrounded by promises of easy happiness, we need someone to tell us, as religion once did, *Memento mori*: remember that you will die, that everything ends, and that happiness comes not in denying this but in living with it. It's a message even more bitter than a clove cigarette, yet, somehow, a breath of fresh air.

1. By citing the example of poets Wordsworth and Baudelaire, the author intends to show that _____.
   A. poetry is not as expressive of joy as painting or music
   B. art grows out of both positive and negative feeling
   C. poets today are less skeptical of happiness
   D. artists have changed their focus of interest

2. The word "bummer" (Paragraph 4) most probably means something _____.
   A. religious   B. disappointing   C. entertaining   D. commercial

3. In the author's opinion, advertising _____.
   A. emerges in the wake of the anti-happy art
   B. is a cause of disappointment for the general public
   C. replaces the church as a major source of information
   D. creates an illusion of happiness rather than happiness itself

4. We can learn from the last paragraph that the author believes _____.
   A. that happiness more often than not ends in sadness
   B. that anti-happy art is distasteful but refreshing
   C. that death and pain should be accepted rather than denied
   D. that anti-happy art flourishes when economy booms

5. Which of the following is true, according to the text?
   A. Religion once functioned as a reminder of misery.
   B. Art provides a balance between expectation and reality.
   C. People feel disappointed at the realities of morality.
   D. Mass media are inclined to cover disasters and deaths.

V. Read the following passage and decide whether each statement is TRUE or FALSE.

Along with the rapid progress of society, the advertising industry has undergone remarkable development. Every day we are surrounded by all kinds of ads and commercials, which have a profound influence on our daily lives. As a result, there arises a fierce debate concerning the proposal that we should ban all kinds of advertisements.

On one hand, some people are in favor of the idea that advertising should not be banned, that instead it should be further developed. They are of the opinion that advertising is a good channel which helps promote exchanges of information. In an era of information, everyone can benefit a lot from advertisements, not only the manufacturers but also the customers. Moreover, advertisements enable people to catch up with the amazing advances in all fields. From the mushrooming of advertising, people get to know the newest products and the trends of consumption. Also, advertising, to some extent, is not only an industry but an art. Many advertisements are elaborate works of art, full of ingenuity and originality, which render great aesthetic pleasure to the viewers and add to the vitality of modern life. To sum up, advertising is a blessing for modern people.

Despite the benefits advertising has brought us, many people strongly condemn it, saying that they are fed up with all kinds of frivolous ads. They call for a comprehensive ban on advertising based on the following reasons. First, many advertisements are misleading, causing confusion and even leading to the injury and death of some customers. Second, they are inconvenient. For example, who is pleased with a mailbox stuffed with unwanted ads or a wonderful film on TV being interrupted frequently? Furthermore, the non-standard use of language in advertising damages the integrity and purity of our language. Consequently, advertising exerts a disastrous impact on the literacy of our younger generations. In some people's eyes, advertising is a genie out of the bottle.

Frankly, it is quite impossible for people to reach an absolute consensus on most controversial issues. In my mind, a total ban on advertising is not an ideal and practical choice. Can we imagine all advertisements vanishing overnight? The disadvantages should by no means make us lose sight of the benefits advertising has brought us. A more workable and rational attitude should be adopted—that is, to eliminate the false and retain the true. Always bear in mind the old saying: "Never throw away the baby with the bath water."

1. According to some people, manufacturers benefit more from advertisements than do customers.
2. Many advertisements can evoke pleasant feelings in viewers' minds.
3. Some people hate advertisements which frequently interrupt a wonderful movie or TV program.
4. The non-standard use of language in advertisements will enrich our language instead of damaging its integrity and purity.
5. The author of this article strongly suggests banning all advertisements on TV.

Part Four: Oral Expression: Asking for and Expressing Opinions

I. Dialogues

Dialogue 1

Husband: Oh, look at that vase over there. It's beautiful. Don't you think so?
Wife: Yes, I do. I think it's lovely.
Husband: But it's a little too expensive, isn't it?
Wife: Do you think so? I am thinking it's very reasonable. What's your opinion, Kate?
Kate: I'm not very familiar with prices for such things, but it seems fairly reasonable to me.
Husband: Then we'll buy this vase. I think it can go in our living room.

Dialogue 2

Mary: Are you looking forward to your trip, Susan?
Susan: Yes. But I'm scared of the journey. My husband insists on flying, but I want to sail. Planes make me nervous.
Mary: There's nothing to be frightened of. How often do you hear of a crash? Once or twice a year?
Susan: But planes fly so high and fast that once is enough.
Mary: Look, there are more road casualties per day than air deaths per year. Air transport is really safe compared with road transport.
Susan: I'd still prefer to go by sea. Ships may not travel fast but at least you can relax.
Mary: It's fine if you are a good sailor, but have you ever traveled far in a rough sea?
Susan: No. I've only been in a boat once. I sailed down the River Thames on a sightseeing tour. But in any case I'd rather be seasick than dead.

Dialogue 3

A: You're going to get into a lot of trouble if you do that.

B: What makes you say that?
C: I don't see anything wrong with what we're doing.
A: That's just the problem. In these kinds of things the trouble doesn't always appear at first.
B: But everything has been so easy!
C: Everything has gone as smooth as clockwork (像钟表一样平稳)—just as we planned.
A: That may be true. But I warn you. There's trouble on the horizon (即将出现).
B: You always say that!
C: Yeah. You never look at the positive side of things.
A: Okay. Have it your way, but don't say I didn't warn you.

II. Useful Expressions

Asking for Advice	Giving Advice
• What do you think of...? • How do you like...? • How do you feel about...? • What's your opinion of...? • What about / How about...? • Thanks for the advice, but this is something I have to figure out myself. • That's just what I was looking for. • What about your opinion?	• Personally, I think... / As far as I am concerned... • From my point of view... / As I see it... / Why not...? • Don't you think...? / It would seem to me that... • You'd better... / It's best to... / If I were you, I would... • If you want my advice, I don't think you should go. • My feeling is that you ought to stay home tonight. • I suggest that you tear up the letter and start over again. • It's only a suggestion, and you can do what you please. • Please don't take offense. I only wanted to tell you what I think. • Good try, but not quite right.

III. Exercises

1. Dialogue Completion

(1) Man: Before an exam, do you think I should eat lots of sugar and drink lot of coffee to give myself energy?

Woman: _____

A. I should warn you that the exam is very difficult. So you should work extra hard to pass it.

B. If I were you, I would avoid all that. Eat high-protein foods such as milk, fish, and eggs. They help to stimulate the brain.

C. Yes. Go straight ahead, and then turn right. You will find the food section.

D. Really? You should read this research from Harvard University. It says that vegetarian mothers are more likely to give birth to girls.

(2) Man: I love surfing, but isn't it rather dangerous with all the sharks you get in the sea?

Woman: _____

A. The sea is pretty safe as far as sharks are concerned. You need to be much more careful of dangerous currents.

B. Well, there's McDonald's, and Pizza Hut. But Baylis Street Bistro has got a special children's menu.

C. I think the best thing to do is to get the ferry to Manly from Circular Quay. It takes you across the harbor east of the bridge.

D. If you travel by Qantas, you get discounts on domestic air routes.

2. Dialogue Comprehension

(1) Woman: I'd appreciate your professional opinion. Do you think that I should sue the company?

Man: Not really. I think that we can settle this out of court.

Question: What is the probable relationship between the two speakers?

A. Student and Teacher.

B. Patient and Doctor.

C. Customer and Waiter

D. Client and Lawyer.

Unit Seven

(2) Man:　　Jane, would you please read this letter of application I've just written? I'd like to have your opinion.

Woman:　I'd be glad to have a look.... It looks fine to me, but personally I believe a business letter should include much more information about your work experience.

Question: What does the woman mean?

A. The man's letter of application is perfect.
B. The man's letter of application includes too much information.
C. The man should add more information about his work experience in the letter.
D. The man should not focus too much on his work experience in the letter.

Key to Part Three and Part Four

Part Three:

I. Vocabulary:	1. A	2. B	3. D	4. A	5. C
	6. D	7. A	8. C	9. B	10. D
	11. B	12. C	13. A	14. D	15. C
II. Expression:	1. D	2. A	3. B	4. D	5. D
	6. C	7. B	8. C	9. A	10. A
	11. B	12. C	13. B	14. C	15. D
III. Cloze:	1. A	2. D	3. D	4. A	5. B
	6. B	7. B	8. C	9. A	10. D
IV. Reading:	1. B	2. B	3. D	4. C	5. A
V. Reading:	1. F	2. T	3. T	4. F	5. F

Part Four:
1. Dialogue Completion:　　　(1) B　　(2) A
2. Dialogue Comprehension:　　(1) D　　(2) C

Unit Eight

Text A

Nora Quealey

Part One: Language Points

I. Vocabulary

1. Their papers and their <u>junk</u> that they made from kindergarten on up—they were my total, whole life. (Para. 1)

    译文：他们的作业、试卷纸还有从幼儿园开始堆积起来的废物就是我的全部生活。

    junk: *n.* old or unwanted things, usually of low quality or little use or value   废旧杂物

    e.g.   *This is just a load of old junk.*
    这不过是一堆旧东西。

2. The only thing he told me was if I was gonna work with a lot of men, that I would have to listen to <u>swearwords</u> and some of the <u>obscene</u> things,   but still act like a lady, or I'd never fit in. (Para. 4)

    译文：他唯一告诉我的是，如果我要和很多男人一起干活，我就不得不听骂人的话还有一些脏话，但是我仍然要表现得像位淑女，要不然永远也不能与他们打成一片。

    swearword: *n.* a word considered offensive or shocking by most people   咒骂，骂人的话

e.g. *His talk was full of vile swearwords.*
他的讲话中充斥着骂人的脏话。

obscene: *adj.* highly offensive according to accepted standards of morality, 猥亵的,下流的

e.g. *Mike made an obscene gesture.*
麦克做了一个下流的手势。

3. You can still be treated like a lady and act like a lady and work like a man. So I just tried to fit in. It's worked, too. The guys come up and they'll tell me jokes and tease me and a lot of them told me that I'm just like one of the guys. Yet they like to have me around because I wear make-up and I do curl my hair, and I try to wear not really frilly blouses, see-through stuff, but nice blouses. (Para. 4)

   译文: 你可以被人家当成淑女对待,自己表现得像淑女,但要像个男人一样地干活。所以我尽量和大家打成一片。我也做到了。男工友们走过来给我讲笑话,开我的玩笑,他们很多人说我就像他们中间的一分子。然而他们喜欢聚在我身旁是因为我化妆而且烫了头发,我尽量不穿带花边的衬衫和特别薄的衣服,但是我穿的衬衫都很好看。

   tease: *v.* to make jokes about or laugh at unkindly or playfully 取笑,戏弄,拿……开玩笑

   e.g. *They teased me at school because I wore glasses.*
   由于我戴眼镜,所以他们在学校里取笑我。

   make-up: *n.* cosmetics worn on the face, by either actors or primarily by women for improving or changing one's appearance 化妆品

   e.g. *Too much make-up looks unnatural.*
   浓妆艳抹看上去不自然。

   see-through: *adj.* of a garment made of semi-transparent fabric 透明的

   e.g. *This nightgown is practically see-through.*
   这件睡衣几乎是透明的。

4. I was moved into the motor department after the big layoff. At that time we were doing ten motors a day. Now we're up to fourteen without any additional help. When we were down, the supervisor came to me and said we had to help fill in and give extra help to the other guys, which is fine. (Para. 6)

   译文: 在大裁员后,我被分到了发动机部。那时我们一天要装十台发动机。现在,在没有任何帮助的情况下,我们可以装十四台。我们干完了自己的活,工作总管就会来到我身边,让我们给其他的工人帮忙。这没什么。

layoff: *n.* the suspension of a worker's employment at a time when there is little work   临时解雇,失业期

e.g. *Textile companies announced 2000 fresh layoffs last week.*
   各纺织公司上周宣布再次裁员2000人。

down: *adj.* finished, already dealt with   完成了的;已处理的

e.g. *The students reported to his parents on his exams: five down and two to go.*
   那个学生向他父母汇报了考试情况:已考完五门,还剩两门。

5. They've got two guys that are supposed to fill in when you get behind, but I'm stubborn enough that I won't go over and ask for help. (Para. 6)

   译文: 他们找了两个男工人在有人落后的时候帮忙,但是我太固执,不愿意去找他们。

   stubborn: *adj.* determined, especially to an unreasonable degree, having a strong will   固执的,倔强的

   e.g. *She's so stubborn that she'll never listen to your advice.*
   她太倔强了,绝对不会听从你的忠告。

6. They wouldn't put me anywhere else, which is ridiculous, with all the small parts areas that people can sit down and work in while they are restricted. (Para. 7)

   译文: 他们不愿意把我派到别处去,这真荒谬。(厂里)有那么多零部件车间,当人们行动不便时,可以在那里坐着干活。

   ridiculous: *adj.* silly and deserving to be laughed at   荒谬的,可笑的

   e.g. *She looks ridiculous in those tight trousers.*
   她穿着那条紧身裤,样子很滑稽。

7. People could be rotated and moved rather than being cramped in the same position, like in the sleeper boxes, where you never stand up straight and stretch your neck out. (Para. 8)

   译文: 人们可以忍受旋转和移动,但却无法忍受整天被挤在一个位置,比如在卧箱里,在那里你无法站立,连脖子也无法伸直。

   cramp: *v.* to restrict, to limit, or prevent the movement, growth, or development of   限制,阻碍

   e.g. *A lack of good education cramped his chances of getting a good job.*
   缺乏教育使他得不到好的工作。

8. I'm gonna be put in some moldy, old, stinkin' nursing home. (Para. 8)

   译文: 我会被送到某家发霉的、陈旧的疗养院。

   moldy: *adj.* of or covered with mould   发霉的

e.g. *The house has been empty for years, and smells rather <u>moldy</u>.*
这座房子好些年没人住,发出一股子霉味。

9. It really hurt and I get very <u>confused</u> still. (Para. 10)

   译文：这真让我伤心,我到现在也想不明白。

   confused: *adj.* mixed up, not knowing what to think　迷惑的,糊涂的

   e.g. *I thought I knew what to do, but now I'm <u>confused</u>.*
   我原以为我知道该做什么,可是现在我被搞糊涂了。

10. I want my fingernails long and clean. I want to not go up to the bathroom and find a big <u>smudge</u> of grease across my forehead. I want to sit down and be <u>pampered</u> and pretty all day. (Para. 10)

    译文：我希望我的指甲留得长长的,保持得干干净净。我不想在到洗手间去的时候看到自己前额上有一大块油迹。我也想坐着,整天打扮得漂漂亮亮,有人宠爱。

    smudge: *n.* a dirty mark　污迹

    e.g. *You've got a <u>smudge</u> on your cheek.*
    你脸上有一块灰。

    pamper: *v.* to pay excessive attention to making (someone) comfortable and happy　宠,娇惯

    e.g. *Traditionally man will pamper his sweetheart with chocolates, red roses and champagne on Valentine's Day.*
    传统上,男人会在情人节用巧克力、红玫瑰和香槟酒来满足他的恋人。

II. Expressions

1. I put an application in and got hired <u>on the spot</u>. (Para. 3)

   译文：我提交了申请,当场就被录用了。

   on the spot: 1) at once　立即,即刻;2) at the place of the action　在现场

   a) *Anyone breaking the rules will be asked to leave <u>on the spot</u>.*
   任何违反规则的人都要被责令立即离场。

   b) *The thief was caught <u>on the spot</u> and received several strokes of the whip.*
   小偷被当场抓住,挨了几鞭。

   c) *When Mary again missed the deadline for a report, the boss hit the ceiling and fired her <u>on the spot</u>.*
   玛丽又一次没按时交报告,老板一怒之下当场炒了她的鱿鱼。

2. The only thing he told me was that I would have to listen to swearwords and some of the obscene things, but still act like a lady, or I'd never fit in. (Para. 4)

   译文：他唯一告诉我的是，如果我要和很多男人一起干活，我就不得不听骂人的话还有一些脏话，但是我仍然要表现得像位淑女，要不然永远也不能与他们打成一片。

   fit in: to (cause to) match or agree; to harmonize　适应

   a) *The application is a chance for the applicants to show the employer they understand what the job and company are all about and that they will fit in.*
   申请表对申请人来讲是向雇主展示他们对工作和公司的了解以及他们能够适应的一个机会。

   b) *After Forrest Gump joined the army, he really fit in like a fish in water.*
   阿甘成了一名士兵，他在军队里如鱼得水。

3. These last two weeks have been really tough. I've been way behind. (Para. 6)

   译文：过去的两周真不容易。我已经远远落后了。

   way behind: very far behind　远远落在后面

   a) *She is way behind the schedule.*
   她比预定的落后了。

   b) *Demand is way behind supply in most areas.*
   在很多领域供给远远大于需求。

   c) *When he turned around, he found the other runners were way behind him.*
   他回头一看，其他的赛跑选手都远远地落在后面。

4. I don't even remember putting parts on. I just go from one to the other, just block everything out. (Para. 6)

   译文：我甚至想不起来已经把部件装好了。我装了一件又一件，别的事都想不起了。

   block out: to stop yourself thinking about something or remembering it　把……摈弃在外

   a) *The memory of the ten-year turmoil is so terrible that she tries her best to block it out.*
   十年动乱的回忆是如此痛苦，令她不堪回首。

   b) *He shut his eyes as tight as he could and put his hands over his ears. He just wanted to block everything out.*
   他紧闭双眼，用手捂住自己的耳朵。他想把一切都置之度外。

Unit Eight

5. When we were down, the supervisor said we had to help <u>fill in</u> and give extra help to the other guys. (Para. 6)

   译文：我们干完了自己的活,工作总管就会来到我身边,让我们给其他的工人帮忙。

   fill in: to take someone's place　代替

   a) *I'm here to <u>fill in</u> for Mr. Smith as he's ill.*
   史密斯先生病了,我来代替他。

   b) *Could you <u>fill in</u> for Steve tonight to preside over the meeting?*
   今晚你能替史蒂夫主持会议吗?

   c) *John is an understudy. He got a chance to <u>fill in</u> for the regular performer yesterday.*
   约翰是个临时演员,他昨天得到了一个替代正式演员的上场机会。

6. If they can't see I'm <u>going under</u>, then I don't care. And I'll take five or ten minutes to just go to the bathroom, sit on the floor, and take a couple of deep breaths, just anything to <u>get away</u>. (Para. 6)

   译文：如果他们看不出我快晕倒了,那么我才不在乎。我会在洗手间呆上五到十分钟,坐在地板上,做上几个深呼吸,只要能得到休息。

   go under: to fail, be defeated, or get into difficulties, to become unconscious　失败,垮掉,破产

   a) *The filling station <u>went under</u> because there were too many others on the street.*
   这个加油站破产了,因为在这条街上有很多家其他的加油站。

   b) *The doctor injected something into my arm and I immediately felt myself going under.*
   医生在我的胳膊里注射了某种药物,我马上感觉到自己开始晕沉。

   get away: to succeed in leaving　走开,离开;脱身

   a) *I'm sorry I'm late; I was in a meeting and couldn't <u>get away</u>.*
   对不起我迟到了,我刚才在开会脱不开身。

   b) *The bank robbers used a stolen car to <u>get away</u>.*
   抢银行的盗贼用一辆偷来的车逃走了。

   c) *The thieves <u>got away</u> with jewellery worth over £50,000.*
   窃贼带着价值五万英镑的珠宝逃走了。

7. I <u>backed off</u> and said it wouldn't work. By this time I'd gotten the shop steward there, but he didn't do anything. (Para. 7)

   译文：我不愿意干了,说这样不行。这时候我已经请了厂方的工人代表到那

里,但他什么也没做。

back off: to stop supporting something, or decide not to do something you were planning to do   打退堂鼓,放弃原来的主张,放弃前言

a) *I saw that he was right, so I had to back off.*

我看到他是正确的,所以我只好放弃原来的主张。

b) *John backed off when he realized how much work was involved.*

当约翰得知工作量很大时,他退缩了。

c) *The manager backed off when it was pointed out by the government investigators that this was a violation of federal laws.*

当政府视察员指出这违反了联邦法律时,经理让步了。

8. He came but felt left out because there was always an inside joke or something that he couldn't understand. He resented that and the fact that I made more money than he did. And my not being home bothered him. But he never said, "I want you to quit," or "We'll make it on what I get." If he had said that I probably would have quit. Instead we just muddled on. (Para. 9)

译文:他来了,但觉得格格不入,因为总是有他听不懂的内部笑话,或者他没法明白的事情。对此他很不高兴,而且他也不满我挣钱比他多。我不在家让他心烦。但他从来没说过:"我想让你辞职,"或者"我挣的钱能养活一家人。"如果他这样说了,我可能早就辞职了。相反我们就这样凑合着过。

be/feel left out: to feel that you are not accepted or welcome in a situation   觉得不受重视,感到被冷落

a) *Come to the party with us, I don't want you to feel left out.*

和我们一起去参加派对吧——我不希望你觉得被冷落了。

b) *Mary felt left out when all her girl friends were invited by boys to the party.*

玛丽所有的女朋友都被男孩子约去参加舞会,她觉得自己受了冷落。

muddle on/along: to continue in a confused manner, without a clear plan   混日子,得过且过

a) *The project just muddled on till they appointed a new manager.*

直到他们任命了一位新经理,该项目一直进行得马马虎虎。

b) *Many of the students complained that they were left to muddle along on their own.*

很多学生都抱怨他们在混日子,没人管。

9. With me working, the whole family had to pitch in and help. When I come home

at night my daughter has dinner waiting, and I do a couple loads of wash and everybody folds their own clothes. (Para. 9)

译文： 由于我要上班，全家人都不得不来帮忙。我晚上回到家，女儿已经做好了饭等我，我负责洗几大堆衣服，大家各自叠自己的衣服。

pitch in: to join others and help with an activity 协力，作出贡献

a) *If we could ask more people to pitch in, we'll be able to finish the task on time.*
如果我们邀请更多的人加入出力的话，我们就可以按时完成任务。

b) *They all pitched in and enough money was collected within a few days.*
他们全都出钱，几天内就筹到了足够的钱。

10. He found another lady that didn't work, had four kids, and was on welfare. (Para. 9)

译文： 他另找了个女人，这个女人没有工作，带着四个孩子，靠救济生活。

on welfare: money that is paid by the government in the US to people who are very poor or unemployed 接受政府(或私人组织)福利救济的

a) *Most of the families in this neighborhood are on welfare.*
这一带的大多数家庭都领政府的福利救济。

b) *The fact that so many millions are on welfare, they believe, is a sure sign of a poor work ethic, laziness, immorality.*
他们认为成千上万的人接受福利救济的事实是工作道德败坏、懒惰和不道德的明确标志。

11. When the truck came to me, I'd have to hook up a little air-condition-pump-type. (Para. 5)

译文： 当卡车开到我身边时，我必须把一个空调泵之类的小部件接上。

hook up: to connect a piece of electronic equipment to another piece of equipment or to an electricity supply 把(收音机、电话机等的部件)装接起来

a) *The telephone will be hooked up in a few days.*
电话将在几天内装好接通。

b) *I hooked up my new DVD player to my TV using a video cable, but I got no picture.*
我用一根视频线把DVD播放机跟电视连接了起来，但收不到图像。

III. Grammar

1. But the minute production went up, I still had to do my own job plus putting on parts for three different guys. (Para. 6)

译文： 但是产量一上升，我除了干自己的工作外还要给另外三个人安装零件。

the minute: the minute (that) 一……就(= as soon as)。类似的用法还有 the moment (that)。

e.g. I'll tell him the minute he gets here.
他一来我就告诉他。
She wired her father the moment (that) she reached the hotel.
她一到旅馆就给她父亲发了电报。

2. When I joined the bowling team, I tried to get him to come and meet the guys I worked with. (Para. 5)

   译文: 我参加了保龄球队,并试图让他来见见跟我一块儿工作的搭档。

   get sb. to do sth.: 让某人做某事。动词与带 to 的不定式和名词(代词)构成复合结构,在英语中有很多。类似的动词还有:ask, leave, expect, encourage, advise, persuade 等。

   此外在 make, let, have, see, hear, watch, notice, feel 等动词后的复合宾语中,不定式都不带 to。

   e.g. I'll get someone to repair the radio for you.
   我去找个人来帮你们修收音机。
   She asked me to call again.
   她请我再去一次电话。
   I'll leave him to solve the problem for himself.
   我将让他自己去解决这个问题。
   What make you give up this opportunity?
   什么使你放弃了这个机会?

3. With me working, the whole family had to pitch in and help. (Para. 9)

   译文: 由于我要上班,全家人都不得不来帮忙。

   with: because of something   因为,由于

   e.g. With John away at university we've got more room in the house.
   由于约翰上了大学,我们房子里的地方宽敞一些了。

Unit Eight

Part Two: Key to Exercises

I. Suggested Answers to *Topics for Discussion*

1. What are Nora Quealey's attitudes toward domesticity? Toward work? Toward money and success? Is she a traditional woman or a feminist?

    Nora is a very traditional woman and she is not a feminist. She longs for a normal family life as do most ordinary women. She wants to have a happy family, living with her husband and children in a cozy and comfortable atmosphere. She has a serious attitude toward work. She works hard and is self-reliant to a fault. Nora does care about money. With a big family to support, she is strapped for money. She has to work hard to earn money to support herself and her girls. Struggling to make ends meet, she has no opportunity to realize her worth at a higher level. After working extremely hard at a truck factory and damaging her back and shoulder, her dream is to reestablish her family with a nice man and live a stable life.

2. Quealey's life is in some ways tragic. What are the greatest blows she has suffered? Could she have avoided any of them? How—and at what price?

    She is disappointed when she suffers from pain in her neck, back, and shoulder and receives no attention from her supervisor and the trade union. She could have avoided injury if she had not worked so hard. But if she had not worked so hard, she would have lagged far behind other workers and might have been fired. The biggest blow in her life is that her husband has left her for another woman who had four kids and lived on welfare. She might have avoided this if she had not gone out to work. But if she had not worked, she would not have had extra money to support her children.

3. What motivates Quealey to persevere in the face of the difficulties she encounters? List as many motivations as you can and review the text to find evidence for them.

    Her family, her self-esteem, and her desire to live a better life are motivations for Quealey to stick it out. For example, in Paragraph 2, we learn that the reason for her working out was to earn extra money for her family. And in Paragraph 8, she is very worried about her and her children's future if she becomes paralyzed from the neck down. This demonstrates that she is a responsible person. She cares about her children, and she wants to better off. In Paragraph 6, she is worn out by her work, but she refuses to ask for help. This shows she has a strong sense of self-worth and independence.

II. Key to Exercises
Text A
A.

1. These are the reasons Quealey goes to work: a) She feels worried and empty about her future. b) The life of a housewife is boring. c) She needs more money for her family. However, it is hard for a woman without a high school diploma to find a decent job. She can only find a position as a blue-collar worker on the truck line.
2. Although a woman has to work as hard as her male counterparts, she should never forget she is a woman. She must conduct herself as a woman and expect to be respected as a woman.
3. a) The workload is too heavy. Although she works extremely hard, she cannot keep up with her coworkers. b) She is too stubborn to ask for help from her colleagues. c) She suffers pain in her neck, back, and shoulder. The working conditions are very harmful to her health. d) Her supervisor and the work union show no sympathy for her. She is worried that they will not pay her anything if she becomes paralyzed.
4. In my opinion, it is not sensible for Quealey to work so hard. Maybe she is just too proud to be left behind. Her motivation to work so hard is to get her work done in time and do as well as her male co-workers. Finally she adjusts herself by learning to work as hard as she can but not caring whether she can get the job done or not.
5. Her health has been deteriorating while working on the truck line. She is worried that she will not get any compensation from her company or the work union if she becomes paralyzed. To make things worse, her husband has left her and lives with a woman on welfare. She is worried no one will take care of her and her three children in the future.

6. C   7. C   8. A   9. D
10. (1) T   (2) T   (3) F   (4) T   (5) F

B.
1. grown up ... left ... housewives ... neighborhood ... got together ... went bowling
2. high school diploma ... application ... until ... diploma ... G.E.D. ... on the spot

Unit Eight

3. fits in ... tease ... around ... make-up ... frilly ... see-through
4. way ... stubborn ... ask for help ... pushed ... in a trance ... every once in a while
5. muddled on ... pitch in ... waiting ... a couple ... on welfare

C.
1. B   2. B   3. D   4. A   5. B   6. C   7. D

D.
1. B   2. D   3. B   4. A   5. A   6. B   7. A   8. C   9. A   10. B

E.
1. muddled on   2. pitch in   3. went under   4. got away   5. fill in   6. fit in
7. on the spot   8. backed off   9. On welfare   10. being left out

F.
1. in a trance   2. a bunch of   3. end up   4. from the waist down   5. hooked up
6. cares about   7. once in a while   8. push himself hard   9. was jealous of
10. take breaks

G.
1. C   2. D   3. A   4. C   5. A   6. B   7. A   8. B   9. D   10. B   11. D   12. C
13. A   14. C   15. B   16. A   17. B   18. D   19. A   20. C

H.
1. When the fighting started, policemen and reporters were soon on the spot.
2. Some people's mode of thinking is outdated. They should try to move with the times so as to better fit into modern society.
3. The rabbit feels very proud because the tortoise is way behind him.
4. I'm filling in for Jack for a few days, since he's gone to Brazil.
5. The patient went under as soon as he breathed the anaesthetic.
6. Linda caught a butterfly, but it managed to get away from her.
7. He said he could swim, but he backed off when we got to the lake.
8. He felt he was left out because nobody would listen to him in the meeting.
9. There's no point in muddling on in the same old job forever.
10. Everyone ought to do his or her part and pitch in to keep this park clean.

I.
1. 突然有一天,我意识到当他们长大成人,离开家门,完成学业并结婚成家时,我将会一无所有。我想许多妇女也都和我一样。作为家庭主妇,她们从来不知道邻里以外的人事。我是说,街坊里的人会一周聚上一次,喝喝咖啡,或许还会打打保龄球,但仅此而已。

173

2. 如果我颈部以下瘫痪了,公司不会在乎,工会也不会在乎,谁来照顾我?谁来照顾我的女儿们?我会被送到某家发霉的、陈旧的、臭气烘烘的养老院。我才 37 岁,还能再活上三四十年。谁会真正关心我?
3. 噢,我不知道。我觉得自己现在着魔般地讨厌肮脏。我想把指甲留得长长的、干干净净的。我不想到洗手间的时候发现自己前额上有一大块油迹。我也想歇着,有人宠,整天打扮得漂漂亮亮。

Text B
B.
1. D   2. A   3. C   4. A   5. C

Part Three: Self-check

I. Choose the word closest in meaning to the underlined word in each sentence.

1. Their papers and their junk were my total, whole life.
   A. food   B. clothes   C. trash   D. pen
2. If I was gonna work with a lot of men, that I would have to listen to swearwords and some of the obscene things.
   A. curses   B. compliment   C. encouragement D. criticism
3. If I was gonna work with a lot of men, that I would have to listen to some of the obscene things.
   A. playful   B. offensive   C. funny   D. brave
4. The guys come up and they'll tell me jokes and tease me.
   A. lay into   B. make a fool of   C. make fun of   D. play with
5. Yet they like to have me around because I wear make-up and I do curl my hair.
   A. paint   B. cosmetics   C. mask   D. crayon
6. I try to wear not really frilly blouses, see-through stuff, but nice blouses.
   A. piercing   B. dressy   C. obvious   D. semi-transparent
7. I was moved into the motor department after the big layoff.
   A. dismissal   B. fire   C. pause   D. disarmament

Unit Eight

8. When we were down, the supervisor came to me and said we had to help fill in and give extra help to the other guys, which is fine.
   A. behind   B. not operating   C. worried   D. backward
9. I'm stubborn enough that I won't go over and ask for help.
   A. strong   B. obstinate   C. capable   D. control
10. They wouldn't put me anywhere else, which is ridiculous, with all the small parts areas that people can sit down and work in while they are restricted.
    A. interesting   B. reasonable   C. clever   D. unreasonable
11. People could be rotated and moved rather than being cramped in the same position.
    A. depressed   B. confined   C. impressed   D. laid
12. I'm gonna be put in some moldy, old, stinkin' nursing home.
    A. fresh   B. comfortable   C. stale   D. poisonous
13. It really hurt and I get very confused still.
    A. painful   B. embarrassed   C. mixed   D. baffled
14. I want to sit down and be pampered and pretty all day.
    A. spoiled   B. encouraged   C. cared   D. flattered
15. I want to not go up to the bathroom and find a big smudge of grease across my forehead.
    A. smear   B. dust   C. glimpse   D. trail

II. Choose the expression that best completes each sentence.

1. I put an application in and got hired _____.
   A. on the spot   B. in public   C. on the ground D. behind the doors
2. The only thing he told me was that I would have to listen to swearwords and some of the obscene things, but still act like a lady, or I'd never _____.
   A. put in   B. fit in   C. suit in   D. cut in
3. These last two weeks have been really tough. I've been _____.
   A. well in advance   B. ahead of schedule
   C. under way   D. way behind
4. I don't even remember putting parts on. I just go from one to the other, just everything _____.
   A. flock ... out B. break ... out   C. let ... out   D. block ... out
5. When we were down, the supervisor said we had to help _____ and give extra help to the other guys.

    A. hand in   B. fill in   C. turn in   D. fit in

6. If they can't see I'm _____, then I don't care.

    A. going under   B. laying into   C. sitting up   D. making up

7. I'll take five or ten minutes to just go to the bathroom, sit on the floor, and take a couple of deep breaths, just anything to _____.

    A. get up   B. get away   C. get around   D. go around

8. I _____ and said it wouldn't work.

    A. backed out   B. backed up   C. backed into   D. backed off

9. He came but felt _____ because there was always an inside joke or something that he couldn't understand.

    A. driven off   B. knocked out   C. left out   D. frozen out

10. If he had said that, I probably would have quit. Instead we just _____.

    A. went on   B. muddled on   C. sputtered on   D. marched on

11. With me working, the whole family had to _____ and help.

    A. pitch in   B. come in   C. step in   D. hand in

12. He found another lady that didn't work, had four kids, and was _____.

    A. in welfare   B. on welfare   C. by welfare   D. with welfare

13. When the truck came to me, I'd have to _____ a little air-condition-pump-type.

    A. hook up   B. connect with   C. contact with   D. join in

III. Read the following passage and fill in each blank with one of the words or expressions given.

    The most frequently expressed complaint women have about men is that men don't listen. Either a man completely __1__ her when she speaks, or he listens for a few beats (片刻), accesses what's bothering her, and then he proudly puts on his Mr. Fix-it hat, and offers her a solution to make her __2__ better. No matter how many times she tells him that he's not listening, he doesn't __3__ it, and he keeps doing the same thing. She wants sympathy, he thinks she wants solutions.

    The most frequently expressed complaint men have about women is that women are always trying to __4__ them. When a woman loves a man, she feels responsible to assist him in growing and tries to help him improve the way he does things. She forms the Home Improvement Committee, and he becomes her primary focus. No matter how much he resists her help, she persists, __5__ an opportunity to help him or to tell him what to do.

Unit Eight

Men value power, competency, efficiency, and achievement. Their sense of self is defined ___6___ their ability to achieve results. And for him to feel good about himself, he must achieve the goals ___7___, by himself. To offer a man unsolicited advice is to presume that he doesn't know what to do or that he can't do it ___8___. Women are very intuitive. They pride themselves ___9___ being considerate of the needs and feelings of others. A sign of great love is to offer help and assistance without even being asked. Without insight into the ___10___ of men, it's very easy for a woman to unknowingly and unintentionally hurt and offend the man she loves most.

Love is magical, and it can last if we remember our differences.

1. A. ignores   B. knows   C. understands   D. amuses
2. A. feeling   B. feel   C. felt   D. to feel
3. A. get   B. make   C. learn   D. touch
4. A. change   B. set   C. arrange   D. judge
5. A. waiting   B. wait   C. waiting for   D. wait for
6. A. on   B. through   C. with   D. to
7. A. lonely   B. alone   C. lone   D. along
8. A. by his own B. with his own   C. on his own   D. in his own
9. A. of   B. in   C. by   D. on
10. A. nature   B. person   C. character   D. characteristic

IV. Read the following passage and choose the best answer for each question.

Every year, *Fortune* magazine celebrates (歌颂,赞美) women in the top echelons (等级,阶层) of corporate (公司的) America by publishing a list of the Fifty Most Powerful Women in Business. Their titles are impressive—CEO, chairman, president—and photos portray them as polished (光彩照人的) and confident.

What an inspiration they could be to the young women following them.

But what if those young women don't aspire to a corner office? A week after the Fortune list appeared on newsstands (报摊儿,杂志摊儿), a major national study of teenagers revealed a surprising finding: While ninety-seven percent of girls polled expect to work to support themselves or their families, only nine percent want careers in business. Among boys, the figure is fifteen percent.

"Girls of this generation are quite ambitious, which is exciting," says Fiona Wilson, a professor at Simmons College School of Management and author of the study, which polled more than 3,000 girls and 1,200 boys in middle school and high school. She finds it encouraging that half the girls prefer professions such as doctors, lawyers, and architects. "We're not going back to the stereotype (陈规,刻板模式) of their mothers' generation, where women were thinking about being nurses and teachers."

But why do girls shy away from business? The number of women applying to business schools has dropped off. By contrast, women make up half the students in medical and law schools.

Unlike boys in the study, who say they want to earn a lot of money, girls place great importance on helping others and improving society. But they don't see connections between those goals and business, which they equate with finance and numbers. And they're less confident than boys about their business-related skills.

Teen girls also place a high value on having enough time to spend with family and friends. In describing business, Professor Wilson says, "they used many images involving stress—images about dads having to make conference calls on vacation and moms always being tired when they got home or complaining about their bad bosses."

As it happens, mothers are primary sources of career advice for daughters. But parents' goals are often less well defined for girls than for boys.

"Mothers express their hope and aspirations for daughters in terms of wanting them to be happy and have a lot of options (选择), but they don't translate that directly into business opportunities," says Connie Duckworth, head of the Committee of 200, a national women's business leadership group that commissioned the study.

Wilson calls the lack of women at the top "alarming," adding that the study doesn't offer a lot of hope that future generations will swell the ranks of women in leadership positions.

1. According to the passage, why do girls shy away from business?

   A. They don't see the connections between business and making contributions.

   B. They want to have more time to spend with family and friends.

   C. They are less confident about their abilities to do business.

   D. All of the above.

2. According to the passage, which of the following statements is NOT true?
   A. Teen girls have stereotypes about business people.
   B. Girls of this generation are more ambitious than the last generation in choosing careers.
   C. Nowadays many girls want to follow the example of the fifty most powerful businesswomen listed annually in Fortune magazine.
   D. Mothers usually play an important role in giving career advice for daughters.
3. What does "corner office" (Line 1, Paragraph 3) mean?
   A. shabby office
   B. office at the corner of a building
   C. unnoticeable office
   D. prime office location, reserved for the most powerful
4. What can we learn from Professor Wilson's study?
   A. Not many girls want careers in business.
   B. Boys are more practical than girls.
   C. Girls are underprivileged in society.
   D. Good girls follow their mothers' steps.
5. What projection can we make according to Professor Wilson's study?
   A. We will have more women leaders in business in the future.
   B. Women will play a more and more important role in the business world.
   C. Women leaders are worried about their future positions.
   D. The number of businesswomen leaders will not greatly increase in the near future.

V. Read the following passage and decide whether each statement is TRUE or FALSE.

Confirming what women have long known, an American study released (发布) on Wednesday shows men are dragging their feet on getting married.

Researchers say one of the biggest reasons that men are delaying marriage is that more and more couples are choosing to live together before marriage. As a result, sex—traditionally one of the main reasons for men to marry—is relatively easily available, they say.

"In a sense, with cohabitation (同居) he gets a quasi-wife (准妻子) without having to commit," said David Popenoe, co-director of the National Marriage Project at Rutgers University in New Jersey.

"Another big thing in addition to cohabitation is that these men are very,

very concerned about divorce. It's not getting your heart broken ... the worst thing that could happen is that somebody could take their money," Popenoe adds.

The preliminary findings report on the attitudes toward marriage of sixty unmarried, heterosexual (异性恋的) men between the ages of 25–33. The participants, from different religious, ethnic and family backgrounds, were from four major metropolitan areas in northern New Jersey, Chicago, Houston, and Washington, D. C.

Researchers say both men and women are putting off getting married. The average age for men's first marriage is now twenty-seven, the oldest in history, the study shows. That compares to the average age of twenty-three in 1960, Popenoe said.

For women, the average age of their first marriage has risen to twenty-five, a full five years older than the 1960 average.

And giving women even more reason to be impatient that their boyfriends are dragging their feet, researchers say the trend favors men.

"Guys can afford to wait to marry. The older they get, the better their chances in some ways of getting married, while for women it's the reverse," Popenoe said.

"Once a woman gets into her thirties, it's more likely that she will have to marry a man who was married earlier. It's more likely that she will marry a man who brings kids and more likely that she will have a child by herself," Popenoe says.

1. According to the study, both men and women are delaying marriage.
2. The biggest reason why men delay marriage is that they have to earn a lot of money before getting married.
3. Men do not worry about divorce because they still have chances to find a nice wife in their second marriage.
4. Both men and women prefer to get married later because they want to find more suitable spouses.
5. Men have an advantage over women in the marriage market.

Unit Eight

Part Four: Oral Expression: Going to the Movies

I. Dialogues

Dialogue 1

Man: Would you like to go to the movies tonight?
Woman: Yes, I would love to.
Man: Good. I'll pick you up at your house at seven.
Woman: That would be fine.

Dialogue 2

Man: Are you free tonight?
Woman: Yes. I don't have any plans for tonight. Why do you ask?
Man: I don't have anything to do tonight, so I was wondering if we could go out somewhere.
Woman: Would you like to go to the movies?
Man: That would be great.
Woman: All right. You wait here. I'll go upstairs and change.
Man: Take your time. We are not in a hurry.

Dialogue 3

Man: Two tickets, please.
Woman: Sorry, the tickets are all sold out.
Man: Oh, no. What time does the next picture begin?
Woman: The next show time is nine o'clock.
Man: Oh well, I guess I'll have to wait till then. Can I buy a ticket ahead of time?
Woman: Sorry, sir. We don't sell tickets ahead of time.

II. Useful Expressions

Going to the Movies	Booking Tickets
• How long did the movie last? • The feature (正片) started at 6 p.m. and ended at 8:30. • What is the movie called? • It's called *My Fair Lady*. (窈窕淑女) • They say *My Fair Lady* is a great movie. • The movie was good and everybody enjoyed it. • I prefer to download the movie from the Internet. • It's really worth seeing.	• Hello, is this the box office of the Minorities Cultural Palace Theatre? • What prices are the tickets? • Where are the 80 RMB seats? • Well, they'll be at the end of the row. • Two tickets, please. • Sorry, the tickets are all sold out. • Could you pick the tickets up by Thursday, please?

III. Exercises

1. Dialogue Completion

(1) Man: Hey, Amy, would you like to go to the cinema with me this Friday night?

Woman: _____

A. That would be great.

B. I have to take care of my baby at home.

C. I have no time. Please ask somebody else.

D. Who is responsible for the tickets?

(2) Man: I'll pick you up at your house at seven.

Woman: _____

A. Thanks. That's unnecessary. I can take a taxi by myself.

B. That would be fine. See you then.

C. That's very polite of you. OK, I'll take your car.

D. No, no. I'll take a bus by myself. It's very convenient.

(3) Woman: Back so soon?
Man: Bad news: the tickets are all sold out.
Woman: Oh.
Man: _____

A. It's not my fault.
B. Could you tell me what to do?
C. Let's watch TV at home.
D. Don't be disappointed. We can still go to another theater.

2. Dialogue Comprehension

(1) Woman: I feel obliged to attend the meeting, but I'd much rather go with you to the cinema.
Man: I'm sorry that you can't. Everyone says Crazy Stone is a wonderful movie and it is really worth seeing.
Question: Where is the woman going?
A. Cinema.
B. Meeting.
C. Concert.
D. Party.

(2) Woman: What are the ticket prices?
Man: Up till five p.m., it is $3.00 for adults and $1.50 for children under twelve. After five p.m., it is $4.50 for adults and $2.75 for children.
Question: What is the ticket policy?
A. All tickets are cheaper before five p.m.
B. Children's tickets are more expensive than adult tickets after five p.m.
C. Adult tickets are cheaper than children's tickets before five p.m.
D. Tickets are cheaper after five p.m.

Key to Part Three and Part Four
Part Three:
I. Vocabulary:　　　1. C　　2. A　　3. B　　4. C　　5. B
　　　　　　　　　　6. D　　7. A　　8. B　　9. B　　10. D
　　　　　　　　　　11. B　　12. C　　13. D　　14. A　　15. A

II. Expression: 1. A   2. B   3. D   4. D   5. B
                 6. A   7. B   8. D   9. C   10. B
                 11. A   12. B   13. A
III. Cloze: 1. A   2. B   3. A   4. A   5. C
                 6. B   7. B   8. C   9. D   10. A
IV. Reading: 1. D   2. C   3. D   4. A   5. D
V. Reading: 1. T   2. F   3. F   4. F   5. T
Part Four:
1. Dialogue completion: (1) A   (2) B   (3) D
2. Dialogue comprehension: (1) B   (2) A

Unit Nine

Text A

How to Deal with a Difficult Boss

Part One: Language Points

I. Vocabulary

1. Over the next few months, as the account manager watched coworkers <u>cower</u> under the boss's browbeating, he realized that the tyrant fed on fear. (Para. 3)

   译文：以后几个月里，财务经理看着他的同事们(一个个地)屈服于老板的淫威时，他意识到员工的害怕助长了这个暴君的气焰。

   cower: *v.* to bend low and move back out of fear, cringe 畏缩

   e.g. *The children were <u>cowering</u> in a corner.*
   孩子们吓得缩在角落里。

2. "He was like a schoolyard bully," the manager recalls, "and I've known since childhood that, when <u>confronted</u>, most bullies back down." (Para. 3)

   译文："他就像个学校的霸王，"这位经理回忆道，"从小我就知道，真要遇到挑战，大多数恃强凌弱的人实际上是不堪一击的。"

   confront: *v.* to meet face to face in an angy or defiant manner 勇敢地面对，对抗

   e.g. *We must <u>confront</u> the future with optimism.*
   我们必须乐观地面对未来。

185

3. Some bosses have had a problem with temper control all their lives and are not pleased with this aspect of their personality. (Para. 5)

   译文：有些老板一辈子都很难控制他们的脾气，他们对此也颇感不安。

   personality: *n.* character, especially as shown in interactions with others　个性，性格

   e.g.　My sister has a lovely personality.
   　　　　我妹妹的性格很可爱。

4. Whatever strategy you choose, deal with the bully as soon as possible, because "once a dominant/subservient relationship is established, it becomes difficult to loosen," warns industrial psychologist James Fisher. (Para. 7)

   译文：无论你采取什么策略，请尽早对付霸道的老板，因为工业心理学家詹姆斯·费希尔警告说："这种控制或附庸的关系一旦确立，就将很难解除。"

   dominant: *adj.* most powerful; controlling　统治的，支配的

   e.g.　His boss had a very dominant nature.
   　　　　他老板生性喜欢支配别人。

5. By realizing that even the most intimidating people are vulnerable, you can more easily relax. (Para. 7)

   译文：意识到甚至那些最令人恐惧的人也很脆弱，你会更容易放松下来。

   vulnerable: *adj.* easily harmed or hurt　脆弱的，易受伤的

   e.g.　She looked so young and vulnerable.
   　　　　她看上去十分年轻而又脆弱。

6. If he responds angrily, reassure him that you will tackle any project first thing in the morning. (Para. 9)

   译文：如果他很生气，请安慰他你会在早晨第一时间首先处理相关项目。

   tackle: *v.* to take on a difficult problem　处理，对付

   e.g.　The computer can be programmed to tackle a whole variety of tasks.
   　　　　计算机可以通过程序编制处理各种各样的任务。

7. Finally, never relax with an abusive boss, no matter how charming he or she can be. (Para. 7)

   译文：最后，不管这个滥用职权的老板有多么迷人，对他都不要掉以轻心。

   abusive: *adj.* rude and cruel, harmful to the physical or emotional wellbeing of another　谩骂的，滥用的

   e.g.　His language was very abusive when he spoke to her.
   　　　　他对她讲话时用了辱骂的语言。

Unit Nine

8. Get him to set the priorities, so you can decide which tasks can wait. (Para. 9)

   译文：让他来决定什么是最重要的，以便你能够决定哪些任务可以暂时放一放。

   priority: *n.* position of first importance   优先考虑的事

   e.g. Government should make education a priority.
   政府应优先发展教育。

9. Then he'd ask a barrage of questions, ending with the one Ahlrichs dreaded most: "Are you sure you'll make the deadline?" (Para. 15)

   译文：接着他会连珠炮般地问上一大堆问题，最后的那个问题是令阿尔里希斯最害怕的："你肯定能按时完成任务吗？"

   dread: *v.* to anticipate with anxiety and reluctance   担心，畏惧

   e.g. The child dreads going back home alone in the dark.
   这孩子不敢一个人在黑暗中回家。

10. By keeping the perfectionist posted, you might circumvent constant supervision. (Para. 18)

    译文：让这个完美主义者时刻了解你工作的进程，你就可以避开无休止的监督。

    circumvent: *v.* to avoid or bypass, especially cleverly or illegally   回避，规避

    e.g. The company has opened an office abroad in order to circumvent Spanish tax laws.
    公司在海外开设了一个办事处，以避开西班牙的税法。

11. Many workers feel frozen out by their boss in subtle ways. (Para. 21)

    译文：很多员工都很微妙地觉得他们的老板排斥他们。

    subtle: *adj.* hard to detect; behaving in a skillful and clever way, especially using indirect methods or language   微妙的，巧妙的

    e.g. His whole attitude has undergone a subtle change.
    他的整个态度发生了微妙的变化。

12. Perfectionists can often prod you into exceeding your own expectations. (Para. 28)

    译文：完美主义者能经常激励你超越自己的期望。

    exceed: *v.* to go beyond, to be greater than   超过，超出

    e.g. He was fined for exceeding the speed limit.
    他因超速而被罚款。

II. Expressions

1. Over the next few months, as the account manager watched coworkers cower under the boss's browbeating, he realized that the tyrant <u>fed on</u> fear. (Para. 3)

   译文：以后几个月里，财务经理看着他的同事们（一个个地）屈服于老板的淫威时，他意识到越害怕老板他越猖狂。

   feed on: to use something in order to continue to exist or become stronger　以……为食物；以……为能源；受到某事物的滋养；因某事物而助长

   a) Both sides in the conflict <u>feed on</u> old suspicions.
   原有的怀疑使双方的冲突更加激化。

   b) Prejudice <u>feeds on</u> ignorance.
   无知助长偏见。

2. I've known since childhood that, when confronted, most bullies <u>back down</u>. (Para. 3)

   译文：从小我就知道，真要遇到挑战，大多数恃强凌弱的人实际上是不堪一击的。

   back down: to admit that one is wrong or that one has lost an argument　放弃原来的主张，声明取消前言，打退堂鼓

   a) Both sides have refused to <u>back down</u>.
   双方都拒绝让步。

   b) We could see that he would <u>back down</u> if we stood firm.
   如果我们立场坚定，我们会看到他会作出让步的。

3. <u>True to type</u>, the boss started to treat him with grudging respect. (Para. 4)

   译文：果然，这个老板开始勉勉强强尊敬他了。

   true to type / form: behaving badly, as expected　典型的，合乎本性的

   a) <u>True to form</u>, Henry turned up late.
   亨利又迟到了，他就这么个人。

   b) When that sort of person cheats at cards, I am not all surprised—they're just acting <u>true to type</u>.
   那种人打牌作弊的话，我一点也不会感到意外，因为这种行为合乎他们的本性。

4. Eventually, the young man <u>moved up</u> the ranks and was rarely <u>subjected to</u> his boss's outbursts. (Para. 4)

   译文：最后，这个年轻人被提了职，也几乎不用忍受老板的大发雷霆了。

   move up: to get a better job in a company or advance to a higher rank　升级，

Unit Nine

晋升

a) *To move up, you'll need the right training.*
为了得到晋升,你需要接受正确的培训。

b) *Share prices moved up this month.*
这个月股票上涨了。

be subjected to: to be forced to experience something very unpleasant, especially over a long time 经受,遭受

a) *All our products are subjected to rigorous testing.*
我们的所有产品都接受过严格的检测。

b) *These prisoners were taken to places where they would be subjected to interrogation through torture.*
这些犯人被带到其他地方,对他们进行刑讯逼供。

5. Although standing up to the bully often works, it could make matters worse. (Para. 5)

译文:尽管对霸道的老板进行抵制经常能够奏效,但也可能使事情变得更糟。

stand up to: to refuse to accept unfair treatment from a person or organization 勇敢面对,抵抗

a) *He'll respect you more if you stand up to him.*
如果你拒绝接受他不公正的待遇,他会更尊重你。

b) *The official tells people to stand up to terrorism.*
这位官员告诉人们要勇敢抵制恐怖主义。

6. Mardy Grothe recommends a different strategy: reasoning with him after he's calmed down. (Para. 5)

译文:马迪·格罗思推荐了另一种策略:在老板冷静下来后跟他讲道理。

reason with: to try to persuade someone to be more sensible 理喻,劝告

a) *We tried to reason with the worried mother, but she went out alone in the storm to look for the child.*
我们试图说服那位焦虑的母亲,但是她还是一个人冲进了暴风雨中去寻找孩子。

b) *You can't reason with people blinded by hate.*
你没办法跟被仇恨蒙蔽了双眼的人讲道理。

7. Fisher also suggests confronting your boss behind closed doors whenever possible, to avoid being disrespectful. (Para. 7)

译文：费希尔还建议要尽可能地关起门来和老板论理，以避免无礼。

behind closed doors: in private, not open to public observation　私下，秘密地，背地里

a) *It seems that the deal was made behind closed doors.*
看起来这个交易是在私下里达成的。

b) *Football authorities ordered the club to play its next two games behind closed doors after the riots in February.*
在二月份骚乱结束后，足球管理部门命令该俱乐部秘密进行下两场比赛。

8. The bully will worm his or her way into your heart as a way of positioning your face under his foot. (Para. 7)

译文：这些仗势欺人的老板会想法先骗取你的心再把你踩在脚下。

worm one's way into somebody's heart /affections/confidence: to subtly earn someone's love or trust　逐渐赢得某人的心／喜爱／信任

a) *He tried to worm his way into her heart as a friend.*
他设法骗得她的友谊。

b) *She was confident she could worm her way into their affections.*
她自信能够逐渐赢得他们的喜爱。

9. As a result, a secretary sat on important correspondence for over a month, risking a client's tax write-offs. (Para. 12)

译文：结果一个秘书把重要的来信压了一个多月，差点影响了一位客户的税金减免。

sit on: (informal) to delay dealing with something　拖延，搁下，压下

a) *I sent my application about six weeks ago and they've just been sitting on it.*
6个月前，我就发出了申请，但他们一直压着不予理睬。

b) *Are these people still sitting on your letter? It's time you had a reply!*
这些人还压着你的信没回吗？这时候你应该收到回信了！

10. "Tell the jellyfish: 'This is what I think I ought to be doing. What do you think?' You are taking the first step, without stepping on your boss's toes." (Para. 13)

译文："请告诉软蛋：'这是我想我应该做的。您觉得呢？'你迈出了第一步，而且也不会得罪你的老板。"

step on one's toes: (American English) to offend someone, especially by intruding on that person's responsibilities　触犯某人，得罪人

a) *If you criticize someone's job performance, you may step on his or her toes.*
如果你批评某人的工作表现，你可能会得罪他／她。

Unit Nine

b) *Mind you don't go stepping on Father's toes again by mentioning his trouble at work.*
当心,别再提你父亲工作上的麻烦得罪他了。

11. Often, a boss will let the work you've completed stand—especially when she realizes another project may be put on hold. (Para. 18)
译文:经常,老板会接受你已经完成的工作——尤其是当她意识到会耽搁别的项目时。

put on hold: to put aside to deal with at a later time   延迟,使停顿,阻碍

a) *Since having the kids, my career has been put on hold.*
自从有了孩子,我的事业就停滞不前了。

b) *Plans to sell genetically modified wheat in the U.S. have been put on hold by Monsanto, the agrobiotech giant in St. Louis, Missouri.*
在美国出售转基因小麦的计划被密苏里州圣路易丝市的农业生物技术巨头蒙桑托搁置了起来。

12. By keeping the perfectionist posted, you might circumvent constant supervision. (Para. 18)
译文:让这个完美主义者时刻了解你工作的进程,你就可以避开无休止的监督。

keep posted: to regularly tell someone the most recent news about something   向……提供最新消息,使充分了解

a) *I'll keep you posted on his progress.*
我会随时让你知道他的进展的。

b) *Mr. Hopkins, I want you to keep me posted on whatever happens while I'm off the job.*
霍普金斯先生,在我休假期间无论发生什么希望您都告知我。

13. Many workers feel frozen out by their boss in subtle ways. (Para. 21)
译文:很多员工都很微妙地觉得他们的老板排斥他们。

freeze out: to deliberately prevent someone from being involved in something, to exclude   排挤,逼走,逐出

a) *Other traders did everything they could to freeze us out of the business.*
其他的经商者竭尽全力想把我们挤出生意场。

b) *Give consumers the option to freeze out credit crooks.*
请给顾客赶跑信用骗子的权力。

191

14. At the core of every good boss is the ability to communicate expectations clearly. (Para. 21)

   译文：所有好老板的最核心的能力是能清楚地传达(自己的)期望。

   at the core of: at the most important or central part of something 位于……的核心，是……中最重要者

   a) Debt is at the core of the problem.
   债务是个核心问题。

   b) Dick Cheney has been at the core of some of the darkest activities in this country over the last four years.
   过去四年来迪克·切尼一直是这个国家一些最见不得人的活动主角。

15. No matter which type of bad boss you have, think twice before going over his head. (Para. 26)

   译文：不管你碰上了哪个类型的老板，在改变他的想法前请最好三思而行。

   think twice before doing: to very carefully consider the dangers or problems before deciding to do something 重新考虑，仔细考虑

   a) I'd think twice before taking out such a large loan.
   在申请这么一大笔贷款前，我还是应该仔细考虑考虑。

   b) Parents should think twice before making their backyard an extreme sports zone.
   在把后院变成一个极限运动区之前，父母应该三思。

16. The difficult boss is usually unaware of the problem and often is eager to make amends. (Para. 26)

   译文：难相处的老板通常会意识不到问题所在，而且也会经常急于补过。

   make amends: to do something conciliatory to show regret for hurting or upsetting someone 赔罪，赔偿

   a) He seized the chance to make amends for his behavior.
   他抓住机会为自己的行为赔罪。

   b) He should find a way to both make amends to the surviving relatives both in word and deed.
   他应该找到一种办法，向幸存的亲属们在语言和行为上赔罪。

17. Before embarking on any course of action, engage in some self-analysis. (Para. 27)

   译文：在开始任何行动前，先自我剖析一下。

   embark on / upon: to start something, especially something new, difficult, or exciting 从事,着手,开始工作

a) He <u>embarked on</u> a new career as a teacher.
他开始了做教师的新的生涯。

b) I should think twice before I <u>embarked on</u> such a hazardous project at that.
在就这样开始那样一个危险的项目之前,我应该认真考虑。

18. And the skills you sharpen to ease a tense relationship will <u>stand you in good stead</u> throughout your career. (Para. 30)

译文：你练就的缓和紧张关系的高超技巧将会使你的事业终身受益。

stand / serve / hold sb. in good stead: to be very useful in the future 对某人有用,对某人有利

a) His years of training were <u>standing him in good stead</u>.
他多年所受的训练对他很有帮助。

b) He said that lessons learned from their World Cup final defeat to Australia would <u>stand them in good stead</u> for the future.
他说他们从世界杯决赛负于澳大利亚队的失败中所学到的教训对他们未来的比赛很有帮助。

19. And because a difficult boss can cause rapid turnover, those who <u>stick it out</u> often advance quickly. (Para. 30)

译文：因为一个难对付的老板能造成快速的人员流动,那些能坚持住的人经常能得到快速的提升。

stick it out: to continue doing something that is difficult, painful, or boring 容忍,忍受,挺住

a) It wasn't a happy period of his life, but he <u>stuck it out</u>.
那不是他生命中一个快乐的时期,但他挺住了。

b) "I only wish people would see that more because he's had a very hard time and yet he's <u>stuck it out</u> and he's still very positive." (Prince William on his father, Prince Charles)
"我只希望人们能够更多地看到那一点,因为他经历了一个非常困难的时期,然而他挺了过来,并且仍然很积极。(威廉王子评其父——查尔斯王子)

III. Grammar

1. Finally, never relax with an abusive boss, <u>no matter how</u> charming he or she can be. (Para. 7)

   译文：最后，不管这个滥用职权的老板有多么迷人，对他都不要掉以轻心。

   no matter how (what, when, where, whether, who) = however; whatever, whenwever, wherever, wherever, whoever, etc.: 不管怎样（怎么，何时，哪里，是否，谁）

   e.g.　*No matter how hard I try, I can never catch up with him.*
   不管我怎样努力，我永远不能赶上他。

   　　　No matter what I say, he always thinks I'm wrong.
   不论我说什么，他总认为我不对。

   　　　No matter when the invaders come, they will be wiped out clean.
   无论侵略者什么时候来，他们必将被彻底消灭。

2. "My boss hires people with the <u>assumption that</u> we all know our jobs," says a woman who works for a small firm in New England. (Para. 11)

   译文：一位在一家在新英格兰小公司工作的女士说："我的老板在雇人的时候总认为我们都了解自己的工作"。

   assumption that...: 在某些名词，如 assumption, idea, fact, news, hope, belief, thought 等后可以用 that 或连接代（副）词引起同位语从句。

   e.g.　*I had no idea that you were here.*
   我不知道你也在这儿。

   　　　We are going on the assumption that the work will be finished tomorrow.
   我们是在根据明天可以完工这一假定办事。

   　　　Then arose the question where we were to get the machines needed.
   这时就产生了一个问题：我们到哪里去找所需要的机器。

3. <u>Chances are</u>, no matter how difficult your boss is, you are also contributing to the conflict. (Para. 27)

   译文：情况很可能是，不论你的老板多难相处，你也同样对冲突负有责任。

   chances are...: (chance 常作 ~s) 很有可能发生的情况

   e.g.　*Chances are ten to one that we'll succeed.*
   我们十有八九会成功。

Unit Nine

Part Two: Key to Exercises

I. Suggested Answers to *Topics for Discussion*

1. What strategies does the author suggest for dealing with each of the five types of bosses?

    a) To deal with a bully, one needs to be brave enough to stand up to him and reason with him. b) To deal with a workaholic, one needs to set limits on one's availability, making it possible to separate his or her home life from the office. c) To deal with a jellyfish, one needs to help a boss establish a pecking order in the office and build the indecisive boss's confidence. d) To deal with a perfectionist, one needs to keep his or her boss informed and get the boss to focus on the big picture. e) To deal with an aloof boss, one should decide on the best course of action, speak up to the boss, and try to prove one's value to the company.

2. Hogarty claims that "the worst bosses often have the most to teach you" (Paragraph 28). What examples does she give to support that point? Have you ever had a bad boss from whom you learned something? If so, what did you learn and how did you learn it?

    The author uses Harry Levinson's example to support her point that the worst bosses often have the most to teach you. The answers to the following two questions are open.

3. In general, is Hogarty's tone in discussing how to deal with difficult bosses pessimistic or optimistic? What specific details support your answer?

    Hogarty's tone is optimistic in discussing how to deal with a difficult boss. We can learn this from the humorous language used in the text such as "the boss turned beet red" and "If she's got a double chin, watch her flesh shake while she's yammering." Also, the point of the essay is to give suggestions for improvement. Implying that improvement is possible shows optimism.

II. Key to Exercises
Text A
A.

1. Please see the answer to question 1 in *Topics for Discussion*.

2. mention shout confess recall explain say yell scream repeat yammer discuss convince ask tell speak

3. A   4. B   5. D   6. C

7. The bully will use subtle strategies to win your heart as a way of controlling you.

8. First, the worst bosses often have the most to teach you. Bullies, for example, are frequently masters at reaching difficult goals. Perfectionists can prod you into exceeding your own expectations. Second, dealing with a difficult boss forces you to set priorities, to overcome fears, to stay calm under the gun, and to negotiate for better working conditions. Because a difficult boss can cause rapid turnover, those who stick it out often advance quickly. Last but not least, your bad boss can also teach you how not to deal with subordinates as you move up and how to one day be a better boss yourself.

9. They have learned a lot about how to handle difficult situations from their former demanding bosses. They are also tough enough to survive. They earn the respect of higher-ups for being able to manage a difficult situation.

10. (1) F   (2) F   (3) T   (4) F   (5) T   (6) F   (7) T

B.

1. Armed with ... matched ... True to type ... grudging respect ... subjected to
2. Whatever ... once ... established ... warns ... confronting
3. setting limits on ... reached ... at ... set ... first ... morning ... set ... priorities
4. fresh ... landed ... deadline day ... over ... barrage ... make ... deadline
5. missed ... single ... lack of confidence in
6. frozen out ... subtle ... key ... available ... At ... core ... communicate expectations ... wonder ... on ... mind
7. embarking on ... engage in ... Chances are ... contributing to ... you're contributing to

C.

1. C   2. B   3. D   4. A   5. C   6. B   7. A   8. A   9. A   10. D

D.

1. vulnerable   2. dreading   3. personality   4. subtle   5. cowered   6. circumvented
7. dominant   8. abusive   9. confronted   10. priority   11. exceeding   12. tackling

E.

1. reason with   2. moved up   3. backed down   4. sitting on   5. stand up to
6. stick it out   7. frozen out   8. embarking upon   9. step on her toes   10. feeds on

F.

1. think twice before   2. be subjected to   3. landed   4. Chances are
5. rise to the challenge   6. loom large   7. has good rapport with   8. at the core of
9. first thing   10. compensates for   11. been put on hold   12. suggest
13. behind schedule   14 raise his voice   15. meet the deadline

G.

1. C   2. C   3. B   4. C   5. A   6. C   7. B   8. A   9. B   10. A

H.

1. The company has been sitting on his report.

2. Does she have a problem with her learning method?

3. You must make amends to them for the insult.

4. The English teacher just couldn't convince him of the importance of learning English.

5. We cannot report the discussion, as it took place behind closed doors.

6. Nowadays people are always busy meeting deadlines.

7. He always keeps me posted about what he's doing.

8. I should have thought twice before accepting that offer; it sounded rather suspicious then.

9. She is fresh out of graduate school.

10. We can use lists to set priorities, plan activities, and measure progress.

I.

　　与难以取悦的老板打交道迫使你确定事情的先后顺序，克服恐惧，临危不惧，去争取更好的工作条件。而且你磨练出来的用以缓和紧张关系的技能会在你的职业生涯中随时起作用。"能够应对挑剔的老板的雇员因其处理困难的能力而常常赢得上级的尊敬，"莱文森说，"因为难以取悦的老板使人员流动很快，那些坚持下来的人往往就很快得到提升。"

Text B
B.

1. D   2. C   3. A   4. B   5. C   6. D

Part Three: Self-check

I. **Choose the word closest in meaning to the underlined word in each sentence.**

1. Over the next few months, as the account manager watched coworkers cower under the boss's browbeating, he realized that the tyrant fed on fear.
   A. entreat　　B. exit　　C. cringe　　D. fight

2. I've known since childhood that, when confronted, most bullies back down.
   A. opposed　　B. conflicted　　C. afflicted　　D. combated

3. Some bosses have had a problem with temper control all their lives and are not pleased with this aspect of their personality.
   A. characteristic　　B. congeniality　　C. character　　D. eccentricity

4. Once a dominant relationship is established, it becomes difficult to loosen.
   A. controlling　　B. pleasant　　C. unequal　　D. obedient

5. By realizing that even the most intimidating people are vulnerable, you can more easily relax.
   A. broken　　B. painful　　C. damaged　　D. susceptible

6. If he responds angrily, reassure him that you will tackle any project first thing in the morning.
   A. construct　　B. deal with　　C. control　　D. dismiss

7. Finally, never relax with an abusive boss, no matter how charming he or she can be.
   A. overbearing　　B. rude　　C. easygoing　　D. supportive

8. Get him to set the priorities, so you can decide which tasks can wait.
   A. rights　　B. series
   C. rank of importance　　D. breaks

9. Then he'd ask a barrage of questions, ending with the one Ahlrichs dreaded most.
   A. feared　　B. welcomed　　C. anticipated　　D. expected

10. By keeping the perfectionist posted, you might circumvent constant supervision.
    A. confront　　B. hide　　C. reveal　　D. avoid

11. Many workers feel frozen out by their boss in subtle ways.
    A. imperceptible　　B. accurate　　C. slow　　D. horrible

12. Perfectionists can often prod you into exceeding your own expectations.
    A. passing　　　　B. fulfilling　　　　C. surpassing　　　　D. failing

II. Choose the expression that best completes each sentence.

1. Over the next few months, as the account manager watched coworkers cower under the boss's browbeating, he realized that the tyrant _____ fear.
   A. fed back　　　　B. fed into　　　　C. fed off　　　　D. fed on

2. I've known since childhood that, when confronted, most bullies _____.
   A. back down　　　　B. back out　　　　C. back away　　　　D. back up

3. _____, the boss started to treat him with grudging respect.
   A. True to type
   C. Out of true
   B. Too good to be true
   D. True to life

4. Eventually, the young man _____ the ranks.
   A. moved away　　B. moved around　　C. moved up　　D. moved along

5. Eventually, the young man was rarely _____ his boss's outbursts.
   A. addicted to　　B. attached to　　C. entitled to　　D. subjected to

6. Although _____ the bully often works, it could make matters worse.
   A. living up to　　B. standing up to　　C. standing up for　　D. rising to

7. Mardy Grothe recommends a different strategy: _____ him after he's calmed down.
   A. reasoning out　　B. working out　　C. reasoning with　　D. speaking of

8. Fisher also suggests confronting your boss _____ whenever possible, to avoid being disrespectful.
   A. behind closed doors
   C. from door to door
   B. out of doors
   D. inside the door

9. The bully will _____ into your heart as a way of positioning your face under his foot.
   A. come his or her way
   C. have a way
   B. worm his or her way
   D. go his or her way

10. As a result, a secretary _____ important correspondence for over a month, risking a client's tax write-offs.
    A. sat by　　　　B. sat in　　　　C. sat on　　　　D. sat back

11. You are taking the first step, without _____ your boss's toes.
    A. stepping on　　B. stepping in　　C. stepping out　　D. stepping down

12. Often, a boss will let the work you've completed stand-especially when she realizes another project may be _____.
    A. put on hold   B. lose its hold   C. take a hold   D. get a hold
13. By _____ the perfectionist _____, you might circumvent constant supervision.
    A. keeping ... in   B. keeping ... posted
    C. keeping ... off   D. keeping ... down
14. Many workers feel _____ by their boss in subtle ways.
    A. taken out   B. kicked out   C. thrown out   D. frozen out
15. _____ every good boss is the ability to communicate expectations clearly.
    A. To the core   B. At the core of   C. In the centre of   D. On the point of
16. No matter which type of bad boss you have, _____ before going over his head.
    A. think twice   B. think of   C. think big   D. think aloud
17. The difficult boss is usually unaware of the problem and often is eager to _____.
    A. make a living   B. make amends   C. make mistakes   D. make troubles
18. Before _____ any course of action, engage in some self-analysis.
    A. focusing on   B. stepping on   C. embarking on   D. getting on
19. And the skills you sharpen to ease a tense relationship will _____ throughout your career.
    A. do in your stead   B. stand in your light
    C. stand you in good stead   D. take a stand against you
20. And because a difficult boss can cause rapid turnover, those who _____ often advance quickly.
    A. stick to their guns   B. stick to the point
    C. stick to the rules   D. stick it out

III. Read the following passage and fill in each blank with one of the words or expressions given.

While humor and kindness are important characteristics for bosses to have, work is serious business and must be __1__ with a serious attitude. A boss must be able to keep his/her employees working hard and on schedule (准时). He/She must __2__ rules, enforce them, and also personally adhere __3__ them. If the boss comes in late to work, leaves early, or spends all day joking with the co-workers, then the employees will neither respect nor work hard for him/her. A boss must have a serious and professional attitude that __4__ an example for all of the employees in the workplace.

To confront （对抗）the countless problems that arise every day in the workplace, a boss must be extremely creative. If a client needs the company to meet a deadline earlier than ___5___ , a boss must find ways to motivate employees to work faster and harder. A creative boss might spend a small ___6___ of money, and treat everyone to dinner at the office to encourage employees to stay late. In this way the company might meet the deadline, ___7___ quality, and keep employee morale （士气，精神面貌）high.

Finally, the most important quality that a good boss must ___8___ is flexibility. While needing to set serious, strict rules, he/she must also recognize that at times the rules need to be ___9___ or broken. For instance, a boss should strictly enforce attendance policies in the workplace. But if an employee with an excellent attendance record needs to take a day ___10___ for personal reasons, the boss should let him/her do it. In this way employees' loyalty to the company will be strengthened, and they will be more happy and productive in the workplace.

1. A. reached   B. approached   C. attached   D. detached
2. A. set down   B. turn down   C. knock down   D. put down
3. A. with   B. by   C. in   D. to
4. A. makes   B. sets   C. establishes   D. leads
5. A. assumed   B. known   C. expected   D. posted
6. A. number   B. load   C. deal   D. amount
7. A. preserve   B. persevere   C. claim   D. demand
8. A. owe   B. take   C. possess   D. seek
9. A. bowed   B. bent   C. forgotten   D. ignored
10. A. out   B. away   C. in   D. off

IV. Read the following passage and choose the best answer for each question.

Talking about money is something that can make even the most confident people feel uneasy. This important process can be done with confidence if you know how to go about it and have a clear sense of what you really want.

Morley offers these following tips （有用的意见；告诫）to help you understand your worth and negotiate for it with confidence.

"There is a variety of salary surveys that you as an individual can access over

201

the Internet," Morley says. "Research professional associations and HR (人力资源) web sites." He also suggests browsing job postings and classified ads. While ads don't always list salaries, you can often get ideas of the pay range (薪金范围) companies are willing to offer.

"You need to be honest with yourself about what you can and cannot do," Morley says. For example, you may be tempted to apply for a job that is offering a $60,000 salary, even if you don't meet the job requirements. One major part of being realistic about what you can make is being realistic about what skills you can bring to the table.

Certain advertisements can give job seekers false hope about salary and job potential, Morley warns. For example, education programs that promise that their graduates will make a certain amount of money often give figures that are atypical (反常的) or totally inflated (夸张的, 言过其实的). The bottom line is that you cannot always take everything you hear or read as the truth. Educate yourself to find out what the standard really is.

Morley says that he wants his clients to look at the big picture, not just one element of a job offer. "In a professional field, we caution people not to focus solely on compensation," he says. "The real thing to focus on is whether or not the job is right for you."

There are so many things to consider when taking a new job. From whether the company culture is suitable to whether or not the job is challenging (富有挑战性的) enough, you need to weigh all factors (选择). "Compensation is important and it has to be reasonable and fair, but focusing on compensation alone is a poor way to do a job search," Morley says.

Use a simple list, Morley suggests. On a piece of paper, write down all the things that are important to you in order of their rank. While cash for most is king, having a short commute (上下班路程) and good medical benefits might matter more than a few extra dollars. Or perhaps you'd be willing to trade a couple thousand dollars for more vacation time. Having this knowledge about yourself and the market will give you the confidence to negotiate effectively. Write down your desired salary and the benefits you most desire. Be ready to play hardball (强硬方式, 强硬手段), but give yourself a little wiggle room (回旋空间). Then if you have to negotiate, you can still achieve your bottom-line total compensation goal.

1. According to Morley, being honest with yourself means _____.
   A. not lying to yourself
   B. not lying to a company
   C. knowing what contribution you can make to a company
   D. not pretending to know what you do not know about a company
2. According to Morley, some education programs _____.
   A. create false expectations through misleading advertisements
   B. provide excellent job opportunities for their graduates
   C. grant fabulous scholarships to their students
   D. encourage their graduates to find best-paying jobs
3. Morley advises his clients that _____.
   A. they should refuse a job if the salary is not satisfactory
   B. they should know something about painting and drawing
   C. they should focus their time and energy on one aspect of a new job
   D. they should take many factors into account when accepting a job
4. What does "compensation" (Line 3, Paragraph 7) refer to?
   A. Salary plus benefits.
   B. Refund.
   C. Endowment.
   D. Money paid for loss or damage.
5. How do you understand "cash for most is king" (Line 2, Paragraph 8)?
   A. Most bosses want control over the company's cash.
   B. For most job seekers, a good salary is the determining factor.
   C. Most people want to pay in cash when shopping.
   D. Employees want to be paid in cold hard cash rather than with checks or electronic deposit.

V. Read the following passage and decide whether each statement is TRUE or FALSE.

You may be all these things at the office and more. But when it comes to getting ahead, experts say, the ABCs (基础知识) of business should include a "P" for politics, as in office politics.

Dale Carnegie suggested as much more than fifty years ago: Hard work alone doesn't ensure career advancement. You have to be able to sell yourself and your ideas, both publicly and behind the scenes (秘密地, 幕后). Yet, despite the obvious rewards of engaging in office politics—a better job, a raise, praise—many people are still unable or unwilling to "play the game."

"People assume that office politics involves manipulative (工于心计的) behavior," says Deborah Comer, an assistant professor of management at Hofstra University. "But politics is related to the word" polite. "It can mean lobbying (游说) and forming associations. It can mean being kind and helpful, or even trying to please your superior and then expecting something in return."

In fact, today, experts define office politics as proper behavior used to pursue one's own self-interest in the workplace. In many cases, this involves some form of socializing within the office environment—not just in large companies, but in small workplaces as well.

"The first thing people are usually judged on is their ability to perform well on a consistent basis," says Neil P. Lewis, a management psychologist. "But if two or three candidates are up for a promotion, each of whom has reasonably similar ability, a manager is going to promote the person he or she likes best. It's simple human nature."

Yet, psychologists say, many employees and employers have trouble with the concept of politics in the office. Some people, they say, have an idealistic vision of work and what it takes to succeed. Still others associate politics with flattery (奉承), fearful that, if they speak up, they may appear to be flattering their boss for favors (恩惠).

Experts suggest altering this negative picture by recognizing the need for some self-promotion.

1. "Office politics" (Line 1, Paragraph 4) is used in the passage to refer to one's political views or beliefs about work and welfare.
2. People who are good at office politics are more likely to be rewarded.
3. To get promoted, it is important to have the ability to please one's boss.
4. Many people think it a must to master office politics in order to prove their worth.
5. The author holds a negative view about office politics.

Unit Nine

Part Four: Oral Expression: Internet

I. Dialogues

Dialogue 1

A: You look sleepy.
B: Yes. I didn't go to bed until two o'clock this morning.
A: Why?
B: I was sitting at the computer.
A: Were you chatting with your friend online?
B: Yes. How did you know that?
A: Everyone knows you are fond of online chatting.

Dialogue 2

A: I should say that chatting online is a waste of time.
B: Maybe you are right. But it's very interesting.
A: That's why you just can't give it up?
B: You are partly right. But the most important reason is that I practice my English as I chat online.
A. Really? But I suggest you spend less time chatting. There are lots of more important things to do, right?
B: I know. Thanks for your advice.

Dialogue 3

A: My computer is connected to the Internet. Let's search for information on Shakespeare.
B: Do you often surf the Internet for the information you need?
A: Yes, I do. The Internet is very interesting and useful. With it you can play games, read stories, do shopping, and send e-mails.
B: Yeah, I agree. It's a wonderful thing to have the Internet. Now we can easily get the information we want and do many interesting things.
A: Could you give me your email? I found a very interesting PowerPoint and I can send it to you if you like.
B: Great! My e-mail address is happyperson@yahoo.com.cn.

II. Useful Expressions

Surfing the Internet	Chatting On-line
• Do you often surf the Internet? • My computer is connected to the Internet. • Do you have your own homepage? • You can send me an e-mail. • My e-mail address is goodluck@yahoo.com.cn. • Use the search engine and you can find the information you want. • The information superhighway goes all around the world. • You notebook computer can connect you to the information highway while you travel.	• I think chatting online is a waste of time. • I have no desire to talk on a network with a bunch of strangers. • A private session lets you talk alone. • The online chat program lets you talk about anything with anyone, without prejudice because you can't see the other person. • I'm afraid surfing the Internet will take up too much of my time. • Being in front of the computer for a long time will harm my eyes. • I think it is fun to talk over the Internet.

III. Exercises

1. Dialogue Completion

(1) Man: I find playing computer games is a waste of time.
   Woman: Take it or leave it. It's up to you. But _____.
   A. I find it relaxing and it takes my mind off my work
   B. you don't have to listen to other people's opinions
   C. computer games are so boring that it makes me sleepy
   D. you can just follow your own course and let people talk

(2) Man: I have no desire to talk on a network with a bunch of strangers.
   Woman: That's the whole point. _____
   A. Don't shy away from strangers.
   B. It's boring to talk with people you know.
   C. All your discomfort disappears because you can't see the other person.
   D. You can use the network to practice English with strangers.

Unit Nine

(3) Man: Have you tried any computer games? They are very fascinating.
Woman: _____

A. I don't know. I have no time to play games on the computer.
B. Oh, really? I'll try it. But I'm afraid it will take up too much time.
C. I don't believe it. You must be kidding.
D. Interesting. I'll give it a try.

2. Dialogue Comprehension

(1) Woman: Will you come to my home tonight? I'll show you how to chat online.
Man: Thanks, anyway. Sleep is more important for me. I must get up early tomorrow morning.
Woman: Poor you!
Question: What is the man going to do?
A. Chat online.
B. Visit the woman.
C. Go to the office.
D. Stay at home.

(2) Woman: What's all this?
Man: The company has decided to computerize.
Woman: But I don't know anything about computers.
Man: You don't have to know how to program one, just how to use one.
Woman: Oh, I guess that's not so bad.
Question: Where did this conversation most likely take place?
A. In a bank.
B. In an office.
C. In a hotel.
D. In a classroom.

Key to Part Three and Part Four
Part Three:
I. Vocabulary: 1. C 2. A 3. C 4. A 5. D
              6. B 7. B 8. C 9. A 10. D
              11. A 12. C

II. Expression: 1. D   2. A   3. A   4. C   5. D
                  6. B   7. C   8. A   9. B   10. C
                  11. A   12. A   13. B   14. D   15. B
                  16. A   17. B   18. C   19. C   20. D
III. Cloze: 1. B   2. A   3. D   4. B   5. C
                  6. D   7. A   8. C   9. B   10. D
IV. Reading: 1. C   2. A   3. D   4. A   5. B
V. Reading: 1. F   2. T   3. T   4. F   5. F
Part Four:
1. Dialogue Completion: (1) A   (2) C   (3) B
2. Dialogue Comprehension: (1) D   (2) B

Unit Ten

Text A

Was America a Mistake?

Part One: Language Points

I. Vocabulary

1. Later, in accounting for the intense contemporary <u>backlash</u> against Columbus, he concludes: ... (Introduction)

   译文：稍后，在解释当代针对哥伦布的强烈反应的原因时，他总结道：……

   backlash: *n.* (against) a strong but usually delayed feeling of opposition among many people towards a belief or practice, especially towards a political or social development （对重大事件的）强烈反应，对抗性反应

   e.g. *The continual rise in violent crime eventually provoked a <u>backlash</u> against the liberal gun-control laws.*

   暴力犯罪不断增加，终于引起了（人们）对不严的枪支管制法的强烈不满。

2. The anthropologist Jorge Klor De Alva once <u>speculated</u> that it might be something like contemporary India—a mixture of religions, languages, and castes, somehow extracting coherence out of incoherence. (Para. 1)

   译文：人类学家乔治·克劳·德·阿尔瓦曾经推测它有可能像当代的印度——一种宗教、语言和种姓制度的综合体，努力从一种无序状态中取得秩序。

   speculate: *v.* to think about or talk about a matter without having the necessary facts; to make guesses 猜测，推测

e.g. *The doctor speculated that a virus caused the disease.*
医生推测是某种病毒引起了这种疾病。

3. One must hope that by the twentieth century the Aztecs and the Incas would have learned to read and write and would have abandoned their commitment to torture, obsidian knives, and blood-stained pyramids. (Para. 2)

译文：人们一定相信，到20世纪，阿兹特克和印加人已经学会读写，并且已经放弃了对折磨、黑曜石刀和血迹斑斑方尖塔的信奉。

commitment: *n.* the state of being committed; deeply-felt loyalty to a particular aim, belief etc. 忠诚；信奉；支持；献身

e.g. *This is a novel of plot and structure and commitment.*
这是一部情节动人、结构严谨、主旨明确的小说。

4. But they would most likely have preserved their collectivist cultures and their conviction that the individual had no legitimacy outside the theocratic state, and the result would have been a repressive fundamentalism comparable perhaps to that of the Ayatollah Khomeini in Iran. (Para. 2)

译文：但是，他们很可能保留了他们的集体主义文化，以及个人在神权国家之外没有合理性的信仰。其结果很可能是像伊朗霍梅尼那样的压制性原教旨主义。

repressive: *adj.* (of a law, system of government etc) hard and cruel （法律、政治等）镇压的；压制的

e.g. *Under the general's repressive regime, thousands of people were imprisoned without trial.*
在这位将军的残酷政权下，成千上万的人民不经审判被投入了监狱。

5. The idea that the Americas could have survived in invincible isolation is fantasy. (Para. 3)

译文：美洲可能一直孤立存在下去的想法只能是幻想。

invincible: *adj. appreciative* too strong to be defeated [褒]不可战胜的；不能征服的

e.g. *There was an invincible reasonableness in his arguments.*
他的论据中有不能驳倒的合理成分。

6. It would not, could not, halt there. (Para. 3)

译文：它不会，也不可能停在那儿。

halt: *v.* to stop; to come or bring to a halt 暂停；使停止，制止

e.g. *The project halted for lack of funds.*
那项工程因缺乏资金下马了。

Unit Ten

7. In general, the European record in dealing with the indigenous peoples of the Americas was miserable—and indefensible. (Para. 4)

   译文：总的说来，欧洲人使美洲土著人非常悲惨———他们的行为也是无法辩解的。

   record: *n.* the facts known about a person's past   履历，经历

   e.g.   He has a very distinguished record.
   他一生显赫。

8. But it is not clear that Europeans in those war-wracked and religiously fanatical centuries were any more humane in dealing with their enemies at home. (Para. 4)

   译文：但是不清楚欧洲人在那些饱经战患和宗教狂热的世纪里对待本土的敌人是不是更多一点点的人道。

   wrack: *v.* to rack to cause great pain or anxiety to; to torment   使痛苦，使焦虑；折磨

   e.g.   Acute dysentery wracked and sapped life from bodies already weakened by hunger.
   急性痢疾把本已饿瘦的身体折腾得衰弱无力。

   fanatical: *adj.* motivated or characterized by an extreme, uncritical enthusiasm or zeal, as in religion or politics; rabid   (宗教或政治信仰等方面)狂热的，盲信的

   e.g.   He is a fanatical rebel.
   他是个狂热的造反者。

9. In their ignorance and arrogance the intruders did indeed bring about extreme ecological disruption. (Para. 5)

   译文：由于无知和傲慢，侵入者们确实给生态造成了极大的破坏。

   disruption: *n.* disorder   混乱

   e.g.   The state was in disruption.
   那个州当时一片混乱。

10. Is every culture equally sacred, no matter how sadistic and horrible? (Para. 6)

    译文：是不是每一种文化同样的神圣，不管它有多残酷和可怕？

    sadistic: *adj.* gaining pleasure from being cruel   虐待狂的

    e.g.   "I'm afraid you will never see your children again," he said with a sadistic smile.
    "恐怕你以后再也见不到你的孩子了，"他露出施虐狂般的笑容说。

11. What <u>animated</u> Columbus more than anything else, more than God or glory or gold, must surely have been those <u>primal</u> passions of curiosity and wonder, the response to the challenge of the unknown, the need to go where none had gone before. (Para. 7)

   译文: 使哥伦布(对探索新世界)充满激情的不仅仅是上帝、荣耀或黄金。在他体内涌动的(对新世界的)好奇与探险欲望,对未知世界的无畏挑战,促使他来到从未有人涉足过的地方。

   animate: *v.* (rather formal) to give life or excitement to; to enliven   赋予……以生命;使有生气;激励

   e.g. Laughter <u>animated</u> his face for a moment.
   笑使他脸上一时增添了生气。

   primal: *adj.* (as if) belonging to the earliest time in the world; original   (似乎)原始的,最初的

   e.g. Village life continued in its <u>primal</u> innocence.
   乡村生活以原始的简朴的方式继续着。

12. That everlasting quest for new frontiers continues today as <u>earthlings</u> burst terrestrial bonds and begin the endless voyage beyond planet and galaxy into the illimitable dark. (Para. 7)

   译文: 那种对新领域永恒的探索今天仍在继续,地球人突破地球的束缚,越过行星和星系,开始进入无边的黑暗进行永不停歇的旅行。

   earthling: *n.* (in science fiction stories) a human being, when addressed or talked about by a creature from another world   (科幻小说中外星人谈话时使用的)地球人

   e.g. "Take me to your leader, <u>earthling</u>," said the green creature from the spacecraft.
   乘宇宙飞船来的绿色生物说:"地球人,带我去见你们的领袖。"

13. But there are benefits, too, and these require to be factored into the historical <u>equation</u>. (Para. 9)

   译文: 但是(哥伦布发现美洲)也有有利之处,而且这些有利之处也应被放进历史的方程式中进行综合考虑。

   equation: *n.* a statement that two quantities are equal   等式,方程式

   e.g. Most people believe the factory would provide more jobs but the other side of the <u>equation</u> is the pollution it would cause.
   大多数人认为工厂可提供更多的工作职位,但问题的另一方面是工厂所造成的污染。(fig. 喻)

Unit Ten

II. Expressions

1. Revisionism <u>redresses the imbalance</u> <u>up to a point</u>; but, driven by Western guilt, it may <u>verge on</u> masochism. (Introduction)

   译文：修正主义(对此)作了某种程度上的修正。但是在西方负罪感的驱使下，它又可能接近受虐狂。

   redress the imbalance/redress the balance: to make things equal or fair (again) 恢复平衡；矫正不公平(或不合理)的状态

   a) *Affirmative action was meant to <u>redress the balance</u> (=make the situation fair) for minorities.*
   鼓励雇佣少数民族成员等的积极措施是为了能够给予少数民族成员一些较公正的机会。

   b) *The enemy has more missiles than we have, so we must find a way of <u>redressing the balance</u>.*
   敌人的导弹比我们多，所以我们必须找到一种改变力量不均衡局面的办法。

   up to a point: partly, but not completely　在一定程度上；部分地

   a) *I agree with you <u>up to a point</u>.*
   在某种程度上我同意你的看法。

   b) *That is true, but only <u>up to a point</u>.*
   这只能说在某种程度上是对的。

   verge on: to be near to (the stated quality or condition)　处在边沿(或边缘)；接近

   a) *Her strange behavior sometimes <u>verges on</u> madness.*
   她奇怪的行为有时几近疯狂。

   b) *Many of Lewis's activities <u>verged on</u> the illegal.*
   刘易斯的许多活动接近非法。

2. Let us for a moment suppose that the Americas could <u>have been</u> indefinitely <u>sealed off</u> from Europe. (Para. 1)

   译文：让我们假设一下美洲永远与欧洲隔绝(的情形)。

   seal off: to prevent people from entering an area or building　封闭；封锁

   a) *Following a bomb warning, police <u>have sealed off</u> the whole area.*
   爆炸警告之后，警察封锁了整个地区。

   b) *They <u>sealed off</u> their ancient country from the rest of the world.*
   他们把自己古老的国家与世界隔绝开来。

213

3. Aztec and Inca traditions offer little hope for the status of women, for equality before the law, for religious tolerance, for civil liberties, for human rights, and for other purposes <u>deriving</u> uniquely <u>from</u> European culture. (Para. 2)

   译文：在阿兹特克和印加传统中，很难谈得上妇女地位、法律面前人人平等、宗教自由、公民自由、人权以及其他来自欧洲文化的独特理念。

   derive from: to develop or come from something else　源于；来自

   a) *The word "deride" <u>derives from</u> Latin.*
      "deride(取笑；嘲笑)"这个词源自拉丁文。

   b) *My information <u>derives from</u> a very reputable source.*
      我的消息来源非常可靠。

4. As a practical matter, America by the fifteenth century was fated to be found by a Europe <u>bursting at the seams</u> with its own dynamism, greed, and evangelical zeal. (Para. 3)

   译文：事实上，15世纪的美洲注定会被一个充满活力、贪婪和基督教新教会福音派狂热的欧洲发现。

   burst at the seams: to be extremely and usually uncomfortably full　溢出

   a) *I've had so much to eat that I'm <u>bursting at the seams</u>.*
      我吃得肚子都快爆炸了。

   b) *The little hall was practically <u>bursting at the seams</u>. (=It was completely full of people.)*
      小小的教室挤满了人。

5. If the "discoverer" was not to be Christopher Columbus, then it would have been Amerigo Vespucci or John Cabot or some mute, inglorious mariner now <u>lost to</u> history. (Para. 3)

   译文：如果发现者不是克里斯托弗·哥伦布，那么他也许会是阿梅里戈·韦斯普奇，或者约翰·卡伯特，或者某个已经被历史遗忘了的默默无闻的航海家。

   lose sth. to sb./sth.: to stop having sth., because others have taken it from you
   在……面前失去……

   a) *We were losing customers <u>to</u> cheaper rivals.*
      由于对手开价低，我们失去了一些顾客。

   b) *She was about to <u>lose</u> her husband <u>to</u> a younger woman.*
      由于一位更年轻的女人(的存在)，她将要失去她的丈夫。

Unit Ten

6. Las Casas, alas, had <u>all too</u> few equivalents in the British and French colonies. (Para. 4)

   译文：可是,在英法殖民地,像拉斯·卡萨斯这样的人太少了。

   all too: very; much more than is desirable 太

   a) These scenes of violence are <u>all too</u> familiar.
   这些暴力场面太熟悉了。

   b) <u>All too</u> often it's the mother who gets blamed for her children's behavior.
   太多的时候,母亲替孩子的行为受过。

7. <u>In general</u>, the European record in dealing with the indigenous peoples of the Americas was miserable—and indefensible. (Para. 4)

   译文：整体上看,欧洲人使美洲土著人非常悲惨——他们的行为也是无法辩解的。

   in general: used when talking about the whole of a situation, group, or thing, rather than specific parts of it 大体上;总的来说

   a) These policies are unpopular with politicians and people <u>in general</u>.
   这些政策遭到政治家和老百姓的一致反对。

   b) We're trying to raise awareness about the environment <u>in general</u> and air pollution in particular.
   我们希望提高大家对环境(保护)的意识,尤其希望大家关注空气污染的问题。

8. And, assuming the answer is yes, is it possible to freeze history <u>in place</u> and immunize the world against what has heretofore seemed history's one constant—change? (Para. 6)

   译文：并且,假设答案是肯定的,有没有可能把历史冻结起来,使世界免于至今似乎是历史唯一的不变——变化?

   in place: in the proper or usual position 在所属的位置

   a) The chairs for the concert were nearly all <u>in place</u>.
   为音乐会准备的椅子几乎都在它们该在的位置上。

   b) The glass was held <u>in place</u> by a few pieces of sellotape.
   玻璃用透明胶带粘好了。

9. If we are compelled to give this anniversary a balance sheet, those costs <u>weigh heavily against</u> Columbus and even more against those who followed him. (Para. 8)

   译文：如果我们不得不给这个周年纪念日列一个资产负债表,这些代价对哥伦布非常不利。对他们的追随者来说,情况可能更糟。

weigh against: to influence people's opinion and the decision that they make 对……不利

a) *This unfortunate experience will weigh heavily against further investment in the area.*
这次不幸的经历将会对这个地区进一步的投资非常不利。

b) *The landlady's evidence weighed heavily against him.*
女房东的证据对他非常不利。

10. The opening of the Americas ushered in a new era of human history. (Para. 9)
    译文：美洲的开放开创了人类历史的新时代。

    usher in: to bring, especially by showing the way 开创；开始；开启

    a) *The bombing of Hiroshima ushered in the nuclear age.*
    对广岛的轰炸开启了核时代。

    b) *The song of birds ushers in the dawn.*
    小鸟的鸣叫迎来了黎明。

11. But out of anguish (out, too, of self-criticism and bad conscience) have evolved the great liberating ideas of individual dignity, political democracy, equality before the law, religious tolerance, cultural pluralism, artistic freedom—ideas that emerged uniquely from Europe but that empower people of every continent, color, and creed; ideas to which most of the world today aspires; ideas that offer a new and generous vision of our common life on this interdependent planet. (Para. 9)
    译文：但是从痛苦(也从自我批评和我们的负罪感)中，逐步形成了个人尊严、政治民主、法律面前人人平等、宗教信仰自由、文化多元化、艺术自由等诸多奇妙的自由思想。这些独特的思想产生于欧洲，但却能使各洲、各色、各种信仰的人受益。这是一些今天全世界大多数人都渴求的思想。它们为我们在这个相互依赖的行星上的共同生活提供了一种全新的、慷慨的视角。

    aspire to: to desire and work towards achieving something important 渴望(成就)

    a) *College graduates aspire to careers in finance.*
    大学毕业生渴望在金融界就业。

    b) *At that time, all serious artists aspired to go to Rome.*
    那时，所有严肃的艺术家都渴望去罗马。

12. The clash of cultures may yield in the end—not, certainly, to a single global culture (heaven forbid) but to a world in which many differentiated national cultures love side by side in reciprocal enrichment. (Para. 10)

Unit Ten

译文：文化的冲突最终当然不会让位于一个单一的全球文化(但愿不要这样)，而是可能让位于一个许多不同的民族文化共存互利的世界。

yield to = give way to: to be replaced by 让位给

a) *Their wine yields to ours.* 他们的酒比我们的差。

b) *Laughter quickly yielded to amazement as the show went on.*
演出继续进行，笑声很快被惊奇代替了。

heaven forbid (或 forfend): used to say that you very much hope something will not happen 老天不许，但愿不要这样

a) *What would you do financially if, heaven forbid, your husband died?*
如果(上帝保佑别这样)你丈夫死了，你经济上怎么办？

b) *A: I hope we don't have any problem with the car. B: Heaven forbid!*
甲：但愿我们的汽车不出毛病。乙：老天保佑千万别出！

side by side: closely together with each other and helping each other 肩并肩地；一起

a) *We've worked side by side for years.* 我们一起工作许多年了。

b) *I was running side by side with our captain.* 我和队长一起跑步。

III. Grammar

1. Aztec and Inca traditions offer little hope for the status of women, for equality before the law, for religious tolerance, for civil liberties, for human rights, and for other purposes <u>deriving</u> uniquely <u>from</u> European culture. (Para. 2)

   译文：在阿兹特克和印加传统中，很难谈得上妇女地位、法律面前人人平等、宗教自由、公民自由、人权以及其他来自欧洲文化的独特理念。

   v. + ing 分词形式作定语，限定前面的名词。

2. Columbus happened to make the decisive voyage, but he was not indispensable to that voyage's eventually <u>being made</u>. (Para. 3)

   译文：哥伦布恰巧作了这次决定性的航行，但并不是没有他就不能作出这次航行。

   v. + ing 动名词形式相当于名词，作介词 to 的宾语。

3. <u>Had</u> Columbus, like his brother Giovanni Pellegrino, <u>died</u> young, the quincentennial might have been delayed a few years, but would still be on its way. (Para. 3)

   译文：如果哥伦布像他的兄弟乔瓦尼·佩莱格里诺一样早逝，这次五百周年纪念也许会推迟几年，但它仍将到来。

217

倒装句,相当于 if 引导的条件状语从句。这句可以写成:If Columbus, like his brother Giovanni Pellegrino had died young, the quincentennial might have been delayed a few years, but would still be on its way.

4. In their ignorance and arrogance the intruders did indeed bring about extreme ecological disruption. (Para. 5)

   译文:由于无知和傲慢,闯入者们确实带来了极度的生态混乱。

   did 强调后面的动词。

5. And, assuming the answer is yes, is it possible to freeze history in place and immunize the world against what has heretofore seemed history's one constant—change? (Para. 6)

   译文:并且,假设答案是肯定的,有没有可能把历史冻结起来,使世界免于至今似乎是历史唯一的不变——变化?

   what: 关系代词,"……那样的事物(或人)",作前面句子的宾语,后面句子的主语。

Part Two: Key to Exercises

I. Suggested Answers to *Topics for Discussion*

1. Why does the author say that America by the fifteenth century was fated to be found by Europe?

   At that time Europe was full of dynamism, greed, and evangelical zeal. Many people were exploring new frontiers. That someone would find America was inevitable.

2. Respond to the suggestion that had it remained sealed off from Europe, America today "might be something like contemporary India—a mixture of religions, languages and castes..." Do you agree? If so, would such a land be preferable to the United States today? If not, what might an "un-Europeanized" America be like instead?

   The United States today is like contemporary India in that it too is a mixture of religions, ethnic groups, and languages. However, even though many languages are spoken in the United States, there is one official language—English. Also, there is mobility from one social class to another, a social system unlike the rigid caste system of India.

An America without any European infusion might be better than the contemporary America—it might be worse. The Aztecs and Incas might have abandoned some of their barbaric cruelties, but the Americas would not have benefited from the civilizing influences of European culture.

3. Why does Schlesinger believe it makes no sense to blame Columbus for the often bloody heritage of the Europeans in the Americas?

The opening of the Americas ushered in a new era of human history and the great liberalizing ideas that have benefited the entire human race—"individual dignity, political democracy, equality before the law, religious tolerance, cultural pluralism, artistic freedom" (Paragraph 2).

4. To what extent does Schlesinger condemn the Europeans for their actions in the New World?

Schlesinger condemns their cruel behaviors in the New World, calling them "unnecessary costs" of change.

II. Key to Exercises

Text A

A.

1. (1) The higher status of women (2) Equality before the law
   (3) Religious tolerance (4) Civil liberties
   (5) Human rights (6) individual dignity
   (7) political democracy (8) cultural pluralism
   (9) artistic freedom

2. It shows the rebellion of the Third World against economic exploitation, against political control, against cultural despoliation, against personal and national humiliation, even at times, against modernity itself. It shows the bad conscience of the West and the consequent re-examination of the Western impact on the rest of humanity.

3. We can reduce the costs of change, especially unnecessary costs in human suffering and destruction.

4. North America is a modern, highly developed area, whereas contemporary India is a mixture of religions and castes, somehow extracting coherence out of incoherence.

5. The individual has no legitimacy outside the theocratic state.

6. C   7. A   8. B   9. D

10. (1) T   (2) F   (3) T   (4) T   (5) F

B.

1. read and write ... commitment ... obsidian
2. record ... indigenous ... Americas ... miserable ... indefensible
3. assuming ... in place ... constant
4. quest ... earthlings ... planet and galaxy
5. preserving ... as ... as ... do
6. heaven ... but ... cultures ... enrichment

C.

1. B 2. D 3. A 4. C 5. A 6. B

D.

1. record 2. are speculating 3. repressive 4. earthling 5. backlash
6. commitment 7. primal 8. was wracked 9. sadistic 10. disruption (disorder)
11. invincible 12. equation 13. fanatical 14. halted 15. animated

E.

1. derive from 2. redress the balance 3. verged on 4. was ... ushered in
5. is (was) ... bursting at the seams 6. yield to 7. Up to a point 8. sealed off
9. aspired (aspires) to 10. in place 11. weighs ... against 12. Heaven forbid
13. lost ... to 14. of course 15. in the end

F.

1. something like 2. all too 3. go on 4. on its way 5. deal with 6. No matter how
7. is seen as, as 8. for a ... moment 9. in general 10. better off
11. are ... immunized against 12. obligation to 13. in ignorance 14. compelled to
15. response to

G.

1. B 2. A 3. C 4. D 5. A 6. B 7. D 8. C 9. A 10. D 11. A 12. B
13. C 14. A 15. B 16. C 17. A 18. B 19. D 20. C

H.

1. Such a remark verges on impertinence (impoliteness).
2. These factors weigh heavily against the effectiveness of scientific research in industry.
3. The consumer's viewpoint should be factored into decision making.
4. Broadcasters tried to abandon their native regional accents and aspired to BBC pronunciation.
5. Most of the films in this series were directed by men, so in order to redress the balance they are now showing some films by women directors.

6. There were so many people that the hall was bursting at the seams.

7. As soon as all the chairs are in place, we can let the people in.

8. His power derives mainly from his popularity with the army.

9. The French Revolution ushered in a new age.

10. Hard conditions of life yielded to more propitious (pleasant) circumstances.

11. I agree with you up to a point.

12. Police sealed off the area and questioned everybody closely.

13. Some people don't know when they're well off.

14. Accidents like this happen all too often.

15. This is a crucial year for your relationships in general and your love life in particular.

I.

但是,让我们现实一些吧。美洲一直会隔绝下去的想法只是个幻想。事实上,十五世纪的美洲注定会被一个充满活力、贪婪和基督教新教会福音派狂热的欧洲发现。哥伦布恰巧作了这次决定性的航行,但对这次航行本身,他并不是不可或缺的。欧洲西行的冲动已经让人们发现了马德拉群岛、加那利群岛以及亚速尔群岛。它不会、也不可能就此罢休。如果发现者不是克里斯托弗·哥伦布,那么他也许会是阿梅里戈·韦斯普奇,或者约翰·卡伯特,或者某个已经被历史遗忘了的默默无闻的航海家。如果哥伦布像他的兄弟乔瓦尼·佩莱格里诺一样英年早逝,这次五百周年纪念也许会推迟几年,但它仍将到来。

Text B

1. A 2. B 3. D 4. C 5. A

Part Three: Self-check

I. Choose the word closest in meaning to the underlined word in each sentence.

1. Later, in accounting for the intense contemporary backlash against Columbus, he concludes: ...

   A. recognition   B. opposition   C. eyelash   D. praise

2. The anthropologist Jorge Klor De Alva once speculated that it might be something like contemporary India—a mixture of religions, languages, and castes, somehow extracting coherence out of incoherence.
   A. supposed   B. wrote   C. revealed   D. told
3. One must hope that by the twentieth century the Aztecs and the Incas would have learned to read and write and would have abandoned their commitment to torture, obsidian knives, and blood-stained pyramids.
   A. fashion   B. debt   C. attachment   D. committee
4. But they would most likely have preserved their collectivist cultures and their conviction that the individual had no legitimacy outside the theocratic state, and the result would have been a repressive fundamentalism comparable perhaps to that of the Ayatollah Khomeini in Iran.
   A. encouraging   B. kind   C. reassuring   D. inhibiting
5. The idea that the Americas could have survived in invincible isolation is fantasy.
   A. inconquerable B. invisible   C. cold   D. far
6. It would not, could not, halt there.
   A. have   B. stop   C. justify   D. hesitate
7. In general, the European record in dealing with the indigenous peoples of the Americas was miserable—and indefensible.
   A. event   B. attitude   C. history   D. ruthlessness
8. But it is not clear that Europeans in those war-wracked and religiously fanatical centuries were any more humane in dealing with their enemies at home.
   A. stricken   B. indisposed   C. enthusiastic D. wrapped
9. But it is not clear that Europeans in those war-wracked and religiously fanatical centuries were any more humane in dealing with their enemies at home.
   A. friendly   B. political   C. correct   D. extremist
10. In their ignorance and arrogance the intruders did indeed bring about extreme ecological disruption.
    A. eruption   B. disorder   C. fiasco   D. war
11. Is every culture equally sacred, no matter how sadistic and horrible?
    A. primitive   B. blind   C. sad   D. cruel
12. What animated Columbus more than anything else, more than God or glory or gold, must surely have been those primal passions of curiosity and wonder, the response to the challenge of the unknown, the need to go where none had gone before.
    A. criticized   B. dwarfed   C. motivated   D. challenged

13. What animated Columbus more than anything else, more than God or glory or gold, must surely have been those primal passions of curiosity and wonder, the response to the challenge of the unknown, the need to go where none had gone before.
    A. extreme   B. outstanding   C. fundamental   D. proud
14. That everlasting quest for new frontiers continues today as earthlings burst terrestrial bonds and begin the endless voyage beyond planet and galaxy into the illimitable dark.
    A. human beings   B. animals   C. Europeans   D. explorers
15. But there are benefits, too, and these require to be factored into the historical equation.
    A. event   B. balance   C. moment   D. significance

II. Choose the expression that best completes each sentence.

1. Revisionism _____ up to a point; but, driven by Western guilt, it may verge on masochism.
   A. breaks the balance   B. redresses the balance
   C. strikes a balance   D. keeps the balance
2. Revisionism redresses the balance _____; but, driven by Western guilt, it may verge on masochism.
   A. up to a point   B. on edge
   C. out of proportion   D. on the flat
3. Revisionism redresses the balance up to a point; but, driven by Western guilt, it may _____ masochism.
   A. make game of   B. make a grab at
   C. drop in   D. verge on
4. Aztec and Inca traditions offer little hope for the status of women, for equality before the law, for religious tolerance, for civil liberties, for human rights, and for other purposes _____ uniquely _____ European culture.
   A. deriving...from   B. different...from
   C. consisting...of   D. leading...to
5. As a practical matter, America by the fifteenth century was fated to be found by a Europe _____ with its own dynamism, greed, and evangelical zeal.
   A. bursting at the seams   B. keeping up
   C. coming up   D. breaking up

6. If the "discoverer" was not to be Christopher Columbus, then it would have been Amerigo Vespucci or John Cabot or some mute, inglorious mariner now _____ history.
   A. lost to   B. remembered by
   C. recorded in   D. compared to
7. Las Casas, alas, had _____ few equivalents in the British and French colonies.
   A. much   B. a little   C. quite   D. all too
8. _____, the European record in dealing with the indigenous peoples of the Americas was miserable—and indefensible.
   A. In fact   B. In general   C. In the past   D. Up to a point
9. And, assuming the answer is yes, is it possible to freeze history _____ and immunize the world against what has heretofore seemed history's one constant—change?
   A. in the mill   B. out of nowhere
   C. in place   D. at a loss
10. If we are compelled to give this anniversary a balance sheet, those costs _____ heavily _____ Columbus and even more against those who followed him.
    A. weigh...against   B. set...against
    C. work...on   D. lean...against
11. The opening of the Americas _____ a new era of human history.
    A. set in   B. turned in   C. ushered in   D. cut in
12. But out of anguish (out, too, of self-criticism and bad conscience) have evolved the great liberating ideas of individual dignity, political democracy, equality before the law, religious tolerance, cultural pluralism, artistic freedom—ideas that emerged uniquely from Europe but that empower people of every continent, color, and creed; ideas _____ which most of the world today _____; ideas that offer a new and generous vision of our common life on this interdependent planet.
    A. for...replies   B. to...aspires
    C. like...looks   D. to...denies itself
13. The clash of cultures may _____ in the end—not, certainly, _____ a single global culture (heaven forbid) but to a world in which many differentiated national cultures live ride by side in reciprocal enrichment.
    A. stem...from   B. come...up
    C. ring...off   D. yield...to

14. The clash of cultures may yield in the end—not, certainly, to a single global culture (_____!) but to a world in which many differentiated national cultures live side by side in reciprocal enrichment.
    A. heaven forbid			B. never mind
    C. God bless you			D. wait and see
15. The clash of cultures may yield in the end—not, certainly, to a single global culture (heaven forbid!) but to a world in which many differentiated national cultures live _____ in reciprocal enrichment.
    A. one after another		B. side by side
    C. from time to time		D. con and pro

III. Read the following passage and fill in each blank with one of the words or expressions given.

In all the concern over what will happen to Hong Kong when it is taken over by China in 1997, business comment has tended to miss one of the key aspects of the pending transformation in one of the major business centers of the Asian region.

This is the quite simple question of what happens when China is ___1___ over by Hong Kong.

While businesses with trading relationships in Hong Kong have been asking anxiously ___2___ the Chinese Government will really be able to maintain the promised special status of the Hong Kong area, less attention has been paid to the likely ___3___ of the Hong Kong Chinese, with their financial, trade and manufacturing skills and established business connections, on the rest of China.

Yet according to some observers, Hong Kong is ideally ___4___ to become the New York of the Chinese region, offering concentrated facilities and entrepreneurial skills for other parts of China.

"Hong Kong could ___5___ as the financial capital of China," said a Hong Kong-based partner of accountants Price Waterhouse, Mr. David Human.

"I believe that Hong Kong will be the ___6___ economic and communications center for China because of its present and future skills base." It's an ___7___ port. It works, despite the politics.

"It's a great opportunity. Despite the ___8___ they got when Mrs. Thatcher announced they were going back to China, they've regained considerable ___9___, the property markets are strong, the top income tax rate is only 18.5 per cent, there's

225

no exchange control, trade figures are good, and there's a very __10__ financial industry, with over one hundred banks registered."

1. A. presided   B. taken   C. cheated   D. deleted
2. A. what   B. how   C. whether   D. that
3. A. impact   B. success   C. honesty   D. shortcoming
4. A. ruled   B. dominated   C. met   D. placed
5. A. come over   B. keep up   C. end up   D. set in
6. A. major   B. small   C. insignificant D. conventional
7. A. bad   B. excellent   C. wasted   D. forsaken
8. A. enthusiasm   B. happiness   C. joy   D. fright
9. A. territory   B. confidence   C. point   D. market
10. A. kind   B. simple   C. strong   D. hard

IV. Read the following passage and choose the best answer for each question.

Martin Both and Willard Seyb, two passengers on the tourist train called the Rocky Mountaineer, have the look of men who have found nirvana. They are sitting at the front of the dome car, the observation deck on the train, and they are watching everything that goes by.

Most of their fellow passengers are smartly dressed in expensive designer clothing. This is an excursion tour, an expensive way to travel—too expensive for back-packers. Martin and Willard, however, look relaxed in jeans and comfortable flannel shirts. They are wearing matching baseball caps, sporting the logo "20th Century RR (Rail Rovers) Club"—a train enthusiasts' society. Martin and Willard are train buffs.

Willard Seyb is seventy-one, a retired electrician from the suburbs of Chicago. He has some heavy binoculars and a 35mm camera round his neck. Martin Both is also from Chicago, where he is software quality controller for computer firm IBM. He has several things hanging from his neck, including a small personal radio. He is listening to it by using an earpiece.

"It's so we can listen to the engineers," he explains. "There's a lot of radio communication between the train and guys checking the track. Sounds like everything's okay." He looks wistful, almost disappointed that he hasn't heard of any runaway freight trains hurtling towards us.

Unit Ten

Like many train buffs, Martin and Willard spend their holidays pursuing dreams along the iron road.

They have been to New Zealand to ride on the TransAlpine Express, which takes travelers from one side of the spectacular Southern Alps to the other. They have been to Australia to travel on the famous Ghan railway which crosses the central desert on its way to the famous outback town of Alice Springs.

1. "Buffs" (Line 6, Paragraph 2) probably means _____.
   A. engineers   B. guests
   C. mountaineers   D. aficionados
2. From the passage we learn that Martin and Willard are _____.
   A. pessimistic   B. well traveled   C. forgetful   D. ungrateful
3. Where do they come from?
   A. Chicago.   B. Boston.   C. New York.   D. Washington, D.C.
4. Why is Martin almost disappointed?
   A. The train is not as luxurious as he expected.
   B. The scenery is not beautiful.
   C. The train is very crowded.
   D. He wants to see how the engineers and linemen would handle a crisis.
5. Why do they take such tourist trains?
   A. They have nothing else to do.
   B. They want to pursue dreams along the iron road.
   C. Their business requires them to do so.
   D. They cannot buy plane tickets.

V. Read the following passage and decide whether each statement is TRUE or FALSE.

Martin and Willard breathe train talk; they appear to be more interested in the train than in the scenery. Their obsession is rooted in nostalgia: Martin recalls a childhood spent so close to a railway line that he could hear the spooky whistle of passing trains at night.

The company which runs the Rocky Mountaineer caters to people's nostalgia for the golden age of the steam train. The Rocky Mountaineer has a diesel engine, but its heating is steam-generated. The train is wreathed in steam as we climb aboard it in the early morning at Banff, a railway and tourist town on the eastern side of the

Rocky Mountains. It will take us two days to complete the 832-km journey westwards to the coastal city of Vancouver.

We wind our way through mountain passes beneath peaks whose caps are dusted with snow. The peaks themselves are outlined in jagged relief against a dazzlingly clear sky. The terrain is so rugged that it must have been a grim task indeed for the men who laid this track more than a century ago.

The Canadian Pacific Railway Company spearheaded the construction of Canada's first 4600-km-long transcontinental railway. The track laying was pronounced complete on November 7, 1885, when the last spike was driven into the ground at the small settlement of Craigellachie in British Columbia. Some ten thousand laborers, mainly from China, built the railway. They were hired in California, where they had been doing similar work, and were paid a dollar a day for their muscle, sweat, and knowledge of explosives. The railway took four and a half years to construct—six years less than had been estimated.

Canadian Pacific President William Van Horne drove his workers to lay 800 km of track in a season last century. Today's tracklayers work in better conditions: it took ten years to lay 480 km of new track in the 1980s and 90s.

1. Martin spent his childhood so close to a railway line that he could hear the spooky whistle of passing trains at night.
2. People like Martin and Willard care little about the golden age of the steam train.
3. It will take three days to complete the 832-km journey.
4. Labourers mainly from China built the railway.
5. The railway took ten years to build.

Part Four: Oral Expression: Talking About Sports

I. Dialogues

Dialogue 1

A: What's your favorite sport?

B: Hmmm...it's hard to say. I like golf a lot—but I guess I like tennis better.

Unit Ten

A: Do you play much tennis?

B: Yes, quite a bit. How about a game sometime?

A: Sorry. I'm strictly a spectator (观众)—football, baseball, basketball, golf—I watch them all.

Dialogue 2

A: What do you do to keep fit?

B: Well, lately I've taken up yoga. It's very slow and tranquil and I am forced to just breathe and move slowly. I tend to move really fast in my daily life, and yoga seems to be a good balance for me. What about you?

A: I like to run and work out (锻炼) with weights, but mostly I like to play basketball. It's a lot of fun when you get to play with a lot of other people. I never get tired of it.

C: You know, they say that swimming is the best, most total, exercise because it works out your whole body, and it really engages your breathing fully. So when you're done, you feel tired, but in a very satisfying way. It's one of the safest ways that you can exercise.

D: I used to swim a lot. Then I decided to take up golf because friends of mine played. At first it was just for fun, and I wasn't interested in winning at all. Gradually though, as I improved, I became more and more competitive. Now I can't stand losing!

Dialogue 3

A: Would you please tell me something about the Beijing Olympic Games? Since you are a Beijinger, you must know a lot about this.

B: Oh, Sure! At the beginning, Beijing, Toronto, Osaka (大阪), Istanbul, and Paris were competing for the right to host the 2008 Summer Olympic Games, and finally Beijing won the bid (投标).

A: Great! You must have been very excited at the news then.

B: Yes. In the minds of millions of young Beijingers, the year 2008 represents dreams, pride, and wealth. Besides, Beijing's successful bid for the Olympics has also given our country the international prestige it has been seeking in recent years.

A: What can the Olympic Games bring to Beijing?

B: Our goal is to make the 2008 Olympic Games the "Green Olympics, High-tech Olympics, and People's Olympics." (绿色奥运、科技奥运、人文奥运) I believe the environmental protection, technical innovation, and cultural exchange will contribute to both the success of the Games and the prosperity of the city.

II. Useful Expressions

Recreation and Sports	About the Olympics
• Baseball is my favorite sport. What's your favorite? • My nephew is a baseball player. He is a catcher (接球手). • When you played football, what position did you play? • We played a game last night. The score was tied (打成平手) six-to-six. • I went to a boxing match last night. It was a good fight. • When I was on the track team (田径队), I used to run the quarter mile (跑接力赛). • My favorite winter sport is skiing. I belong to a ski club. • Would you be interested in going to the horse races this afternoon? • The hardest thing to learn is to be a good loser. • Be a good sport (输得起). Play according to the rules of the game. • Our family went camping last summer. We had to buy a new tent. • This afternoon we went to the gym for a workout. We lifted weights (举重). • What do you do for recreation	• Athens is the birthplace of the ancient Olympics. • The modern Olympic Games were initiated by Baron Pierre De Coubertin. • Barcelona was chosen to be host of the 1992 Olympic Games. • "Swifter, Higher, Stronger" is the Olympic motto (格言). • The slogan of the Beijing 2008 Olympic and Paralympic Games (残奥会) "One World One Dream" fully reflects the essence and the universal values of the Olympic spirit—Unity, Friendship, Progress, Harmony, Participation, and Dream. • Fuwa (福娃) will serve as the official mascots (吉祥物) of Beijing 2008 Olympic Games, carrying a message of friendship and peace—and good wishes from China—to children all over the world. • Carl Lewis established himself as one of the greatest track and field (田径) athletes as he won four gold medals in the Los Angeles Olympics. • He was caught cheating during the Seoul Olympics and humiliatingly stripped of his title.

| (休闲娱乐)? Do you have a hobby?
• My muscles are sore (痛的) from playing baseball. | • Her only aim is to represent China at the Olympics. |

III. Exercises

1. **Dialogue Completion**

    (1) Man: Would you like to go running?
       Woman: I'd enjoy that. Where would you like to go?
       Man: _____

       A. Good. Just let me change.
       B. We could go to the park. There shouldn't be many people there now.
       C. Did the doctor suggest that you lose weight?
       D. Oh, if I kept doing that, I would increase my chances of having a heart attack.

    (2) Man: How about going hiking with us? Let's go up to the mountains. It should be beautiful there.
       Woman: Sounds good to me. _____

       A. Where do you want to go?
       B. I love fresh air if you don't mind.
       C. Why don't we go down to the lake? It's not too far from here.
       D. Just give me a few minutes to get ready.

2. **Dialogue Comprehension**

    (1) Woman: Have you seen Jim around? We're supposed to play tennis.
       Man: Well, his racket is here on the table.
       Question: What does the man imply about Jim?

       A. He is probably nearby.
       B. He should pick up his things.
       C. He broke his racket.
       D. He might be playing tennis right now.

    (2) Woman: Joe, do you want to go swimming with me today?
       Man: Sure, but I can't leave yet. I have lost my room key and have to wait for the security guard to let me back in.

Question: Why must Joe wait?
A. He won't go swimming without a lifeguard.
B. He has lost his money.
C. He has to wait for his roommate.
D. He is locked out of his room.

Key to Part Three and Part Four

Part Three:

I. Vocabulary:	1. B	2. A	3. C	4. D	5. A
	6. B	7. C	8. A	9. D	10. B
	11. D	12. C	13. C	14. A	15. B
II. Expression:	1. B	2. A	3. D	4. A	5. A
	6. A	7. D	8. B	9. C	10. A
	11. C	12. B	13. D	14. A	15. B
III. Cloze:	1. B	2. C	3. A	4. D	5. C
	6. A	7. B	8. D	9. B	10. C
IV. Reading:	1. D	2. B	3. A	4. D	5. B
V. Reading:	1. T	2. F	3. F	4. T	5. F

Part Four:
1. Dialogue Completion: (1) B (2) D
2. Dialogue Comprehension: (1) A (2) D

Unit Eleven

Text A

Any More Like You at Home?

Part One: Language Points

I. Vocabulary

1. Though my father <u>yearned</u> to travel, he never managed in all of his 83 years to escape very far from Pecan Island. (Para. 1)

   译文：尽管我的父亲渴望旅行，但他在 83 年的生命中从未远离过山核桃岛。

   yearn: *v.* to have a strong desire for somebody or something, especially when the desire is tinged with sadness 渴望，期望

   e.g. He <u>yearned</u> for her daughter to return.
   他盼望他的女儿回来。

2. He was constantly almost <u>overwhelmed</u> by the problems of trying to support a family of 20 on the often less than $ 350 a year he made from farming and trapping. (Para. 1)

   译文：用靠他种植和狩猎挣来的不到 350 美元来养活 20 人的家庭给他带来的问题，常常几乎要把他压垮。

   overwhelm: *v.* to overpower somebody emotionally or physically, provide somebody with huge amount; to surge over somebody or something 使陷入某种情绪；压倒，制服

   e.g. An <u>overwhelming</u> majority voted against the proposal.
   占压倒多数的人投票反对这项议案。

233

3. They were too big to fight, and I ran home furious, on the verge of tears. (Para. 2)

   译文: 他们太强,我斗不过就气愤地跑回家,几乎就要哭出来。

   furious: *adj.* extremely or violently angry 满腔愤怒的,大发雷霆的

   e.g. She was furious to find that they had gone without her.
   她发现他们没有带自己去,顿时愤怒极了。

4. "Stop that sniveling and come with me." Papa said sternly. (Para. 3)

   译文: 爸爸严厉地说:"别哭哭啼啼了,跟我来。"

   stern: *adj.* rigid, strict, and uncompromising; grim, austere, or forbidding in appearance 严厉的,苛刻的,不苟言笑的 **sternly:** *adv.*

   e.g. The policeman sternly warned the thief not to make a mistake again.
   警察严厉地警告小偷不要再犯错误。

5. If my father ever resented his hard lot or felt the least twinge of self-pity, he never showed it. (Para. 7)

   译文: 即使我的父亲曾经怨恨过命运的不如人意或者感到过哪怕是一点点的自怜自艾,他也从没表露过。

   resent: *v.* to feel aggrieved about something or toward somebody, often because of a perceived wrong or injustice 感到愤恨、怨恨或气愤

   e.g. I strongly resent her attempts to interfere in my work.
   我非常讨厌她企图干涉我的工作。

6. When, at the end of the last day, I flopped into the pirogue exhausted, Papa put his hand on my shoulder. (Para. 10)

   译文: 最后一天干完活后,我筋疲力尽,一下瘫倒在小船里,这时爸爸把他的手搭在了我的肩膀上。

   exhaust: *v.* to tire out, to use up completely (使)筋疲力尽,(使)完全耗尽

   e.g. My patience is exhausted. 我忍无可忍了。

7. Papa tried to get the donation from old Chapie Marceau, a well-to-do rancher and friend of the family. (Para. 16)

   译文: 爸爸试图得到老 Chapie Marceau 的捐赠——他是一个富有的牧场主也是我们家的朋友。

   donation: *n.* the act of donating or something donated 捐赠,捐赠物

   e.g. The rich people would give large donations when natural disasters take place.
   当发生自然灾害的时候,富人们愿意慷慨捐献。

8. He's calling us to worship and do something good today. (Para. 18)

   译文：他正在召唤我们去做礼拜,并且今天要行善。

   worship: *v.* to treat somebody or something as divine and show respect by engaging in acts of prayer and devotion; to take part in a religious service; to love, admire, or respect somebody or something greatly and perhaps excessively or unquestioningly 崇拜,做礼拜,爱慕

   e.g. We worship regularly at that church.
   我们经常在那个教堂做礼拜。

9. There didn't seem to be a chance for us six younger Veazeys to get high school diplomas. (Para. 20)

   译文：对于我们六个小维萨们来说,似乎没有得到高中毕业证书的机会了。

   diploma: *n.* a certificate given by a high school, college, university, or professional organization, indicating that somebody has completed a course of education or training and reached the required level of competence （毕业)证书,文凭

   e.g. She has a diploma in Education. 她拥有教育学文凭。

10. His approach was anything but subtle. (Para. 22)

    译文：他的方法一点也不含蓄。

    approach: *n.* the act of approaching, a way of getting, a method of doing something, an act of speaking to someone 靠近,通道,方法,接触

    e.g. We have made approaches to them with a view to forming a business partnership.
    为了要和他们建立商业伙伴关系,我们开始同他们打交道。

11. He even borrowed a highwheeled marsh buggy and personally surveyed a line to Little Prairie. (Para. 24)

    译文：他甚至借了一辆高轮子的沼泽独轮车,亲自勘测了一条通往小草原的路线。

    survey: *v.* to look at, examine, consider as a whole 审视,鉴定,勘测,调查

    e.g. We surveyed the view from the top of the hill.
    我们从山顶放眼眺望景色。

12. Papa became almost fanatical in his pleas for the road. (Para. 25)

    译文：爸爸为了那条道路苦苦哀求,几乎着了魔。

    fanatical: *adj.* excessively enthusiastic about a particular belief, cause, or activity 狂热的,异想天开的,古怪的

    e.g. Your proposals are utterly fanatical; we couldn't possibly afford them.
    你的那些建议太不切实际了,我们实在无法接受。

13. My father agreed to lease his land to the company, and he urged our suspicious neighbors to lease theirs. (Para. 26)

   译文：我的父亲同意把土地租给那家公司，并且催促我们的那些怀有疑虑的邻居也把他们的土地出租了。

   suspicious: *adj.* suspecting guilt or wrongdoing, not trusting, causing one to suspect guilt　猜疑的，疑心的，多疑的，可疑的

   e.g.　If you see anything suspicious, inform the police at once.
   　　　你要是看到什么可疑的东西马上通知警方。

14. That started the fulfillment of Papa's biggest dream—work and prosperity for the people on Pecan Island. (Para. 29)

   译文：它开始实现了爸爸最大的梦想——为居住在山核桃岛上的人民带来工作和繁荣。

   fulfillment: *n.* the act of fulfilling or state of being fulfilled　实现，完成，履行，满足感

   e.g.　After many years, our plans have come to fulfillment.
   　　　我们的计划在许多年后终于实现了。

15. Rousing again, he said, with something like his old authority... (Para. 34)

   译文：再次直起身来的时候，带着惯有的权威，他说……

   authority: *n.* the power, power to influence, right to control or command　权利，权威，威信

   e.g.　He enjoys exercising his authority over his staff.
   　　　他喜欢对自己的职员指手画脚。

II. Expressions

1. He was further shut off from the outside world by the fact that he couldn't read even the simplest newspaper headline, and could write only two words—his name, Ulysse Veazey. (Para. 1)

   译文：他的生活愈加与世隔绝，因为他甚至读不懂最简单的报纸标题，他也仅仅会写两个单词——他的名字，Ulysse Veazey。

   shut off: to isolate; separate　孤立，隔离

   a) The village was shut off by mountains from the rest of the world, yet many young villagers still dreamed of going beyond the mountains to the outside world one day.
   　　那个村子被群山与外面的世界隔离，然而许多年轻人仍旧梦想有一天能够走出大山。

Unit Eleven

b) *Living in the countryside has shut him off from the city life.*
乡下的生活把他和城市生活隔离了。

2. *This family included 11 children of his own and the seven in-laws he took upon himself to raise.* (Para. 1)
译文：那个家庭有他自己的11个孩子和他承担起抚养责任的7个亲戚的孩子。

take sth. upon oneself: to assume as a responsibility or obligation　以……为己任，主动承担(责任等)，把(过错)归咎自己

a) *As a teacher, she takes it upon herself to help each student with their homework after class.*
作为一个老师，她以辅导每一位同学的课后作业为己任。

b) *One mustn't take upon oneself the right to make every decision on the committee.*
任何人决不能认为自己有权利做委员会的每一项决定。

3. *Yet Papa refused to be hemmed in by circumstances, or to let us be.* (Para. 1)
译文：然而爸爸不愿意让自己或者是我们受到环境的限制。

hem in: to enclose or confine　限制住，围住

a) *The enemies were hemming our troops in.*
敌人正把我们的队伍团团包围。

b) *I always felt hemmed in by conventions.*
我总是感觉被成规所限制。

4. *We hadn't gone far before the high marsh grass closed around us, curtaining off familiar landmarks.* (Para. 3)
译文：我们没有走多远，就被高高的沼泽草团团包围，那些熟悉的地标完全被挡住了。

curtain off: to separate or divide by means of a curtain or curtains　用帘子把……隔开

a) *One corner of the room was curtained off as a wardrobe.*
房间的一角被帘子隔成一个衣柜。

b) *A tall building was erected in front of our house, curtaining off the mountain view from us.*
在我们的房前立起一栋高楼，挡住了群山的景色。

5. *The house he had grown up in as a boy, he liked to remind us, had had a dirt floor, no panes in the windows, and no lighting but candles.* (Para. 7)

237

译文：他喜欢提醒我们，小时候他住的房子，地板是泥土铺的，窗户上没有玻璃，没有照明设备只有蜡烛。

grow up: to be or become fully grown; attain maturity 成长，长大

a) *He grew up listening to country music.*
   他是听着乡村音乐长大的。

b) *What are you going to do when you grow up?*
   你长大后打算做什么？

6. Take, *for instance*, what happened during my Christmas holidays when I was 11. (Para. 8)

译文：举个例子，那是发生在我11岁过圣诞节时的事情。

for instance: as an example; for example 举例

a) *His spelling is terrible! For instance, look at this word!*
   他的拼写很糟糕，例如，看这个单词。

b) *There was something strange about James; for instance, he could not speak.*
   詹姆斯有些奇怪，比如，他不会说话。

7. If you don't do good in school, you can look forward to another 50 years of this kind of work. (Para. 14)

译文：如果你在学校里不好好学习，那么你就等着再干50年同样的事情吧。

look forward to: to expect, to look into future with expectation 期待，渴望

a) *Christmas is coming, children are looking forward to a pleasant holiday with lots of gifts from parents.*
   圣诞节即将来临，孩子们正期待着从父母那收到许多礼物，度过一个快乐的节日。

b) *If you don't finish the work today, you could look forward to another difficult day.*
   如果你今天不能完成工作，那么你明天还会有许多事要做。

8. After that, my schoolwork picked up considerably. (Para. 14)

译文：从那以后，我的功课有了很大的起色。

pick up: to make progress; to improve 取得进步，改善

a) *Sooner or later our production will pick up as we continue working hard.*
   只要我们继续努力工作，我们的生产迟早会提高。

b) *We've been through some difficult time, but things will be picking up quickly.*
   我们是度过了一段困难的时期，但事情会很快得到改善。

Unit Eleven

9. Papa tried to get the donation from old Chapie Marceau, a <u>well-to-do</u> rancher and friend of the family. (Para. 16)

    译文： 爸爸试图得到老 Chapie Marceau 的捐赠——他是一个富有的牧场主也是我家的朋友。

    well-to-do: having more than adequate financial resources　富有的

    a) *They looked like a group of <u>well-to-do</u> tourists, purchasing all sorts of souvenirs wherever they went.*

    他们看起来像一群富有的游客，走到哪里都购买各种各样的纪念品。

    b) *Students from <u>well-to-do</u> families are shocked by what they saw in the poverty-stricken areas.*

    来自富裕家庭的学生们被他们在极度贫困地区看见的境况所震惊。

10. Even when he went to spend a weekend with Chapie, he <u>made a point of</u> not mentioning it. (Para. 17)

    译文： 甚至当他和 Chapie 一起共度周末时，他都特意不再提起这件事。

    make a point of: to do something because one feels necessary or important　特别注意做某事

    a) *I always <u>make a point of</u> checking spelling and grammar before I hand in my English paper.*

    我在交英语试卷前总是要特别注意检查拼写和语法。

    b) *We <u>make a point of</u> being punctual whenever attending an activity.*

    参加活动时，我们特别注意做到准时。

11. His approach was <u>anything but</u> subtle. (Para. 22)

    译文： 他的方法一点也不含蓄。

    anything but: definitely not　根本不，绝不，一点也不

    a) *The hotel was <u>anything but</u> satisfactory.*

    那个旅馆一点也不令人满意。

    b) *The joke he told was <u>anything but</u> funny.*

    他讲的那个笑话一点也不逗。

12. He <u>talked up</u> the idea to governors and senators who came to hunt with him. (Para. 24)

    译文： 他向那些和他一起打猎的州长们、参议员们热情地建议(修路)这件事。

    talk up: to promote sth. with enthusiasm, to make sth. appear more important　积极促成，深入谈论

    a) *Tom <u>talked up</u> the idea of giving more rights to the students at the meeting.*

    在会上，汤姆积极提议要给学生更多的权利。

b) *He will use the chance of hosting a television program to talk up his latest book.*
   他将利用主持一档电视节目的机会大谈他的新书。

13. My cousin and I, the first islanders given the opportunity to try out as roustabouts, were plenty nervous as we set forth from home that first morning. (Para. 28)

    译文：我和我的堂兄，作为第一批有机会成为普通工人的岛民，在离家的那天早上异常紧张。

    try out: to compete for a position or a role by taking part in a trial or test 争取

    a) *Nancy tried out for the leading role in the play.*
       南茜争取在这部戏剧中扮演主要角色。

    b) *You won't join the team if you don't try out.*
       如果你不争取，你将不能加入团队。

    set forth: to start a journey; to make sth. known 启程，出发，触发；衬托，使……更明显

    a) *When will you set forth on your trip to the mountains?*
       你们什么时候动身去山里？

    b) *The President set forth the aims of government in a television broadcast.*
       总统在电视讲话中明确了政府的目标。

14. Papa gave us a pep talk. (Para. 28)

    译文：爸爸给我们做了战前动员。

    pep talk: a talk intended to fill the listeners with an urge to complete something well 激励性讲话，鼓舞士气的简短讲话

    a) *Before I stepped onto the stage, my parents gave me a pep talk.*
       当我迈上舞台之前，我的父母为我鼓气。

    b) *It is typical of the manager to excite his staff with a pep talk first thing in the morning.*
       通常经理早晨做的第一件事就是讲一番话，鼓舞他的员工。

15. You'll be competing against veterans who know their stuff. (Para. 28)

    译文：你将要和精通业务的老手们展开竞争。

    know one's stuff: to be competent or well-informed especially in a particular field; to be knowledgeable 精通本行业务

    a) *His colleagues see him as a gifted teacher, who knows his stuff.*
       他的同事把他看作一位精通教学的天才老师。

    b) *What I expected of her was nothing more than knowing her stuff.*
       我只是希望她精通业务。

16. The manager called in my cousin and me, and asked, "You got any more Webfeet like you at home?" (Para. 29)

    译文：经理把我和我的堂兄请去，然后问我们："你们家里还有像你们一样的蹼足吗？"

    call in: to ask for help with difficult situation 请……帮忙

    a) *The government then called in troops to stop the disturbances.*
       政府召来军队平息暴乱。

    b) *It is too late to call in a technician to fix your computer at this time.*
       那时请技术人员来修理你们的计算机已经晚了。

17. "Strange," he said, eyes clouding with troubled wonder, as if what he was about to say had just occurred to him. (Para. 33)

    译文："奇怪"，他说，眼睛里浮起一层迷雾，好像他打算说的事情是刚刚才想到的。

    occur to sb.: come into sb.'s mind 浮现于脑海，被想起

    a) *It just occurred to me that he might know how to find her.*
       我刚好想起他或许知道如何找到她。

    b) *It never occurred to her to ask anyone.*
       她从没想过要问别人。

18. His voice trailed off, and this time didn't come back. (Para. 34)

    译文：他的声音渐渐微弱下去，这次他没有再醒来。

    trail off: to become gradually weaker and fade away 渐渐微弱，消逝

    a) *His interest in work has never trailed off, which is really admirable.*
       他对工作的兴趣从未减少过，这真的令人敬佩。

    b) *The baby cried bitterly in Mom's arms, his voice trailing off before he fell asleep.*
       那个婴儿在妈妈的怀抱里号啕大哭，声音渐渐微弱直到睡去。

III. Grammar

1. I must have been about seven when I first heard that nickname. (Para. 2)

   译文：我头一次听到这个绰号的时候肯定是七岁左右。

   must 是情态动词，表达的是非常肯定的推断，当被推断的事实发生在过去的时候，要求其后的动词用完成时态。

2. Because if I weren't, neither one of us would ever find our way out of this swamp! (Para. 6)

   译文：因为假如我要不是个蹩足的话，我们两个就谁也别想找到走出这沼泽的路了。

   此句是个虚拟语气复合句，表达了与当下事实相反的假设和其后果。从中可以推断出：父亲恰恰是个所谓的蹩足，而且正因为是个蹩足，才能找到走出沼泽回家的路。

3. If my father ever resented his hard lot or felt the least twinge of self-pity, he never showed it. (Para. 7)

   译文：即使我的父亲曾经怨恨过命运的不如人意或者感到过哪怕是一点点的自怨自艾，他也从没向任何人表露过。

   ever 表示"曾经"除了经常出现在上面的条件(让步)句中，还经常用于疑问句和否定句，如：Have you ever been to China? He's never ever tasted a drop of wine before. 但是在一个陈述事实的肯定句中表达"曾经"的意义，常用 once，如：I once lived in Beijing. They once learned English by memorizing words in a dictionary.

4. When, at the end of the last day, I flopped into the pirogue exhausted, Papa put his hand on my shoulder. (Para. 10)

   译文：最后一天干完活儿后，我筋疲力尽地一下瘫倒在小船里，这时爸爸把他的手搭在我的肩膀上。

   exhaust：使筋疲力尽，它的现在分词形式 exhausting 表示令人筋疲力尽，如 What an exhausting day! (多么令人筋疲力尽的一天啊！) 而它的过去分词 exhausted 表示筋疲力尽，忍无可忍，如 My patience was exhausted. (我忍无可忍。)

5. What could have been more fitting than for you, who adore children, to have given the bell? (Para. 18)

   译文：有什么能比由您这样一个喜爱孩子的人捐出钟这件事更合适的呢？

   句中两处使用完成时态，主句中 what could have been more fitting 是对已发生事件的推测，than 的不定式宾语 for you to have given the bell 表达的是已完成的事情。父亲如此使用时态，是在引导牧场主想象他捐了钟之后的情景。如果换成现在时 what could be more fitting than for you to give the bell? 给人以强加的感觉，使人心里不舒服。

Unit Eleven

Part Two: Key to Exercises

I. Suggested Answers to *Topics for Discussion*

1. What distinguishing characteristics do you find in the father in the story?

    We find in him strength and ability, self-respect and self-reliance, wisdom and courage, ambition and industry, selflessness and devotion—a treasured heritage which fills his son with confidence and inspiration.

2. The father is a good teacher and psychologist, although he is illiterate and has few experiences in the outside world. What makes him a good psychologist?

    He teaches by his own experience and practice that hard work can produce progress. "A warm understanding of human nature not to be learned from books" (Paragraph 16) makes the father a good psychologist.

3. How do you understand the title of the text?

    The title "Any More Like You at Home?" is taken from the oil field manager's asking the Veasey brothers for more "Webfeet" like them. This question shows the change in outsiders' attitudes toward the islanders: once disdained for being "Webfeet," now the islanders are becoming desirable workers. Papa's biggest dream—work and prosperity for the islanders—is taking off.

II. Key to Exercises

Text A

A.

1. (1) Teaching him a lesson in a harsh way on the importance of education

    (2) Persuading an old man in a friendly way to donate for the church

    (3) Papa's contribution to setting up a local high school for the kids of the islanders

    (4) The realization of Papa's dream: work and prosperity for the islanders

    (5) The blessed life of Papa and his hope for his children

2. He would work hard and keep his eyes open for any chance to change his situation.

3. He takes two steps. First, he does not bring up the donation throughout an entire weekend with Chapie, when Chapie expects to be beseiged. Second, when Chapie Marceau cannot hold out any longer, Father appeals to Chapie's pride in being remembered as the benefactor of the community.

4. He approaches the mainlanders directly and appeals to their sense of fairness.
5. Father thinks that he and Mama have been blessed—nine of their children still living and most of their forty-eight grandchildren and great-grand-children going to college. Even without money and education, he has worked for progress on the island and betterment for his family. His life has meant something.
6. A   7. D   8. A   9. C
10. (1) T   (2) F   (3) F   (4) F   (5) F

B.
1. yearned ... life ... shut off ... overwhelmed ... on ... farming and trapping
2. had never sat in the classroom ... quite ... a warm understanding...psychologist
3. as far as
4. If you don't do good in school ... you can look forward to another fifty years of this kind of work.

C.
1. C   2. D   3. B   4. A   5. C   6. B

D.
1. overwhelmed   2. resented   3. fanatical   4. prosperity   5. drudgery
6. solace   7. yearned   8. blurted   9. subtle   10. quite

E.
1. to talk up   2. pick up   3. to be shut off   4. to make a point of
5. to take upon himself   6. made it   7. to be hemmed in   8. look forward to
9. call in   10. simmer

F.
1. on the verge of   2. hard lot   3. in the depths of   4. anything but
5. on a strong note   6. A pep talk   7. well-to-do   8. get around   9. jeered at
10. in thanks

G.
1. A   2. C   3. C   4. B   5. A   6. A   7. D   8. A   9. B   10. A   11. B   12. C
13. A   14. C

H.
1. Being shut off from pressure during working hours makes one feel comfortable.
2. These volunteers take it upon themselves to make it possible for those rural kids to receive education.
3. Books are scattered everywhere in the room, and I am almost hemmed in by them.

4. My son said he would like to be a basketball coach when he grew up.
5. If we don't finish the work in time this year, we will look forward to another hard year.
6. After training, the English level of the kids picked up quickly.
7. In order to improve his academic achievements, he made a point of spending enough time on study.
8. It makes one happy to be successful. It makes one admired to make it without much effort.
9. What is crucial is to talk up this new idea to the leaders at the meeting.
10. Only after you try out will you know whether you can join the team.

I.

但是，我本该知道爸爸在讲一番语重心长的话时，最后总是有一个强调的表示。果然，他再次坐直了身子，又开始说话，带着他惯有的一家之长的威严。"听着，儿子，我在银行里给你们每人留了一点钱，还有几英亩地，我不想看到你们为了这一点点东西争吵不休。我想看到你们个个都成为我们希望的那样的人。记住，每次你们家庭聚会的时候，你妈妈和我都会和你们在一起，你知道吗？"他说道，脸上光彩照人，"我们并不会离开你们半步。不会的。我们一直都会在这儿，就在这里，看着你们，听你们说话，为你们骄傲……"他的声音小下去了，越来越弱，这一次没有再回来。

爸爸永远都不能不是我们的一家之主，永远也不会改变，尽管他现在是从一把空椅子上瞧着我们。

Text B

B.
1. B 2. D 3. D 4. C 5. B 6. C 7. A 8. C

Part Three: Self-check

I. Choose the word that is closest in meaning to the underlined word in each sentence.

1. Though my father yearned to travel, he never managed in all of his eighty-three years to escape very far from Pecan Island.

    A. longed   B. liked   C. decided   D. went

2. He was constantly almost overwhelmed by the problems of trying to support a family of twenty on the often less than $350 a year he made from farming and trapping.
   A. fought   B. overcome   C. annoyed   D. disturbed
3. They were too big to fight, and I ran home furious, on the verge of tears.
   A. angered   B. shameful   C. humiliated   D. sorrowful
4. "Stop that sniveling and come with me," Papa said sternly.
   A. impatiently   B. grimly   C. happily   D. leniently
5. If my father ever resented his hard lot or felt the least twinge of self-pity, he never showed it.
   A. hated   B. was bitter at   C. appreciated   D. loved
6. When, at the end of the last day, I flopped into the pirogue exhausted, Papa put his hand on my shoulder.
   A. weak   B. mad   C. quick   D. tired
7. Papa tried to get the donation from old Chapie Marceau, a well-to-do rancher and friend of the family.
   A. commission   B. present   C. contribution   D. reward
8. He's calling us to worship and do something good today.
   A. adore   B. admire   C. go to church   D. go to school
9. There didn't seem to be a chance for us six younger Veazeys to get high school diplomas.
   A. graduation certificates   B. examination papers
   C. vocational education   D. entrance examinations
10. His approach was anything but subtle.
    A. road   B. strategy   C. aim   D. proposal
11. He even borrowed a high-wheeled marsh buggy and personally surveyed a line to Little Prairie.
    A. researched   B. investigated   C. sought   D. plotted out
12. Papa became almost fanatical in his pleas for the road.
    A. obsessive   B. indifferent   C. strange   D. loyal
13. My father agreed to lease his land to the company, and he urged our suspicious neighbors to lease theirs.
    A. lend   B. borrow   C. rent   D. entrust

Unit Eleven

14. That started the <u>fulfillment</u> of Papa's biggest dream—work and prosperity for the people on Pecan Island.

    A. achievement　　B. promise　　　C. production　　D. engagement

15. Rousing again, he said, with something like his old <u>authority</u>.

    A. organization　　B. right　　　　C. command　　　D. citation

II. Choose the expression that best completes each sentence.

1. He was further _____ from the outside world by the fact that he couldn't read even the simplest newspaper headline and could write only two words—his name, Ulysse Veazey.

    A. shut off　　　B. left off　　　C. taken off　　　D. broken off

2. This family included eleven children of his own and the seven in-laws he _____ to raise.

    A. put on himself　　　　　　B. took over
    C. took upon himself　　　　D. lent a hand

3. Yet Papa refused to be _____ by circumstances, or to let us be.

    A. cut in　　　　B. set in　　　　C. turned in　　　D. hemmed in

4. We hadn't gone far before the high marsh grass closed around us, _____ familiar landmarks.

    A. curtaining off　　B. cutting off　　C. going off　　　D. turning off

5. Papa tried to get the donation from old Chapie Marceau, a _____ rancher and friend of the family.

    A. well-done　　　B. well-known　　C. well-to-do　　　D. well-informed

6. You'll be competing against veterans who _____.

    A. know their stuff　　　　　B. mind their own business
    C. tell left from right　　　D. make a difference

7. Papa gave us a _____.

    A. short talk　　B. pep talk　　　C. particular talk　　D. baby talk

8. His voice _____ and this time didn't come back.

    A. set off　　　B. took off　　　C. saw off　　　　　D. trailed off

9. The house he had _____ in as a boy, he liked to remind us, had had a dirt floor, no panes in the windows, and no lighting but candles.

    A. grown up　　B. stood up　　　C. gotten up　　　　D. brought up

10. Take, _____, what happened during my Christmas holidays when I was eleven.
   A. for all   B. for instance   C. for good   D. for ever
11. If you don't do good in school, you can _____ another fifty years of this kind of work.
   A. look after   B. look down upon
   C. look up   D. look forward to
12. After that, my schoolwork _____ considerably.
   A. stepped up   B. made up   C. picked up   D. went up
13. Even when he went to spend a weekend with Chapie, he _____ not mentioning it.
   A. was in a point of   B. made a point of
   C. was on the point of   D. was to the point of
14. He _____ the idea to governors and senators who came to hunt with him.
   A. talked up   B. gave up   C. came up   D. stood up
15. My cousin and I, the first islanders given the opportunity to _____ as roustabouts, were plenty nervous as we set forth from home that first morning.
   A. look out   B. find out   C. work out   D. try out
16. The manager _____ my cousin and me, and asked, "You got any more Webfeet like you at home?"
   A. called on   B. called off   C. called in   D. called up
17. My cousin and I, the first islanders given the opportunity to try out as roustabouts, were plenty nervous as we _____ from home that first morning.
   A. set forth   B. called forth   C. brought forth   D. came forth
18. His approach was _____ subtle.
   A. something like   B. anything but   C. anything like   D. nothing but
19. "Strange," he said, eyes clouding with troubled wonder, as if what he was about to say had just _____ him.
   A. occurred to   B. gotten to   C. turned to   D. moved to

III. Read the following passage and fill in each blank with one of the words or expressions from the table below.

Today's way of conducting business is informal, so that's what we should aim for in our email business writing too—a friendly, conversational style. We should

Unit Eleven

use short words and simple expressions, short sentences and paragraphs which are clear and concise __1__ still courteous. The only place for standard overused clichés __2__ "Please find attached herewith" and "Please be advised" is the recycle bin.

Messages which are sent without much thought or planning, with important details __3__, or with spelling and punctuation errors, create a very bad impression. Similarly, the common courtesies of a greeting and sign-off should not be __4__ for the sake of speed. Finally, a moment taken to fill in the "Subject" line will be appreciated by a busy __5__, who will be able to see what your email is about before they decide to open it.

High on the list of annoyances when I did some research recently was the overuse of abbreviations and __6__ punctuation. Using abbreviations is fine with a friend who you know will understand them, but should __7__ be limited to those that are already common to the English language, such as FYI (for your information) and BTW (by the way). As far as punctuation is __8__, a row of exclamation or question marks after an important point may be acceptable for __9__ with friends, but could look out of place in other contexts. The main point is: Don't overdo it.

Last but not __10__, remember that it's not a computer you're talking to, it's a real __11__ human being. Some people seem ignorant of the fact that writing in capitals is the equivalent of SHOUTING and should be avoided __12__ you intend to convey excitement: "WE WON!"

1. A. if   B. not   C. but   D. even
2. A. like   B. alike   C. unlike   D. likely
3. A. blank   B. vacant   C. gapped   D. missing
4. A. neglected   B. observed   C. criticized   D. highlighted
5. A. caller   B. receiver   C. sender   D. writer
6. A. excessive   B. obsessive   C. possessive   D. successive
7. A. likewise   B. otherwise   C. however   D. furthermore
8. A. used   B. known   C. concerned   D. observed
9. A. chatting   B. consulting C. identifying   D. quarreling
10. A. best   B. worst   C. most   D. least
11. A. live   B. alive   C. lively   D. living
12. A. lest   B. unless   C. so that   D. even though

IV. Read the following passage and choose the best answer to each question.

Whale watching allows humans a glimpse of magnificent creatures in their natural habitat. But as the pastime becomes more popular, a new study suggests, noise from boat traffic may be drowning out the animals' ability to hear one another's calls.

Rus Hoelzel of the University of Durham in England and his colleagues examined the vocalizations made by killer whales in the coastal waters of Washington State, analyzing calls uttered in the presence and absence of boat engine noise from recordings made during three time periods over the past twenty-five years. They observed no difference in whale calls recorded about twenty-five years ago and fifteen years ago. But the most recent set of recordings, made between 2001 and 2003, reveals that whales change the characteristics of their calls when boats are around, making them fifteen percent longer compared to the calls they make without such background noise. Boat traffic in the region increased fivefold during the 1990s, the team notes, with groups of killer whales now followed by as many as twenty-two tourist vessels a day. The results of the study, published today in the journal Nature, suggest that there exists a critical level of noise beyond which the animals' performance becomes weakened, forcing them to adapt their behavior in order to be heard above the noise.

Killer whales are highly social animals and are thought to call to one another while jointly searching for food. Although there is no direct evidence that the increased level of engine noise interferes with communication, the researchers note that the killer whale population in the area they study has been declining since 1996. "Whale watching is a really constructive thing," Hoelzel says. "It educates the public and it's a good conservation tool. But we need to do the research to see the kind of impact we're having and to regulate it effectively."

1. What is the main idea of the first paragraph?
   A. Whales are magnificent sea animals.
   B. Whale watching has become more and more popular.
   C. People now prefer to watch whales in their natural habitat.
   D. Noises from whale watching boats may affect whales' behavior.
2. What did Hoelzel and his colleagues do according to the passage?
   A. They observed killer whales three times a day.

B. They recorded boat engine noises.
C. They studied whale calls produced in different contexts.
D. They tried to interpret the vocalizations of killer whales.
3. Which of the following is the important finding of the scientists?
   A. Boat traffic in the region increased fivefold in the 1990s.
   B. As many as twenty-two tourist vessels follow killer whales every day.
   C. Whales produce fifteen percent longer calls than usual when boats are around.
   D. Whale calls of twenty-five years ago and those of fifteen years ago are nearly the same.
4. The results of the study suggest that _____.
   A. whales are forced to adapt to boat noises
   B. ordinary tourists can hardly hear whale calls now
   C. tourist whale watching does not impair whales' performance
   D. scientists encourage whale watching
5. What does Hoelzel think of whale watching?
   A. Harmful.   B. Healthy.
   C. Effective.   D. Educational.

V. Read the following passage and decide whether each statement is TRUE or FALSE.

Where do you go when you want to know the latest business news, follow commodity prices, keep up with political gossip, find out what others think of a new book, or stay abreast of the latest scientific and technological developments? Today, the answer is obvious: you log on to the Internet. Three centuries ago, the answer was just as easy: you went to a coffeehouse. There, for the price of a cup of coffee, you could read the latest pamphlets, catch up on news and gossip, attend scientific lectures, strike business deals, or chat with like-minded people about literature or politics.

The coffeehouses that sprang up across Europe, starting around 1650, functioned as information exchanges for writers, politicians, businessmen, and scientists. Like today's websites, blogs, and discussion boards, coffeehouses were lively and often unreliable sources of information that typically specialized in a particular topic or political viewpoint. They were outlets for a stream of newsletters, pamphlets, and advertising freesheets. Depending on the interests of their customers, some coffeehouses displayed commodity prices and shared prices and shipping lists, whereas others provided foreign newsletters filled with coffeehouse gossip from abroad.

Rumors, news, and gossip were also carried between coffeehouses by their patrons, and sometimes runners would run from one coffeehouse to another within a particular city to report major events such as the outbreak of a war or the death of a head of state. Coffeehouses were centers of scientific education, literary and philosophical speculation, commercial innovation, and, sometimes, political reformation. Collectively, Europe's interconnected web of coffeehouses formed <u>the Internet of the Enlightenment era</u>.

The kinship between coffeehouses and the Internet has recently been underlined by the establishment of wireless "hotspots" which provide Internet access, using a technology called WiFi, in modern-day coffee shops. T-Mobile, a wireless network operator, has installed hotspots in thousands of Starbucks coffee shops across America and Europe. Coffee shop WiFi is particularly popular in Seattle—home to both Starbucks and such leading Internet firms as Amazon and Microsoft.

Such hotspots allow laptop-using customers to check their email and read the news as they sip their coffees. But history provides a cautionary tale for those hotspot operators that charge for access. Coffeehouses used to charge for coffee, but gave away access to reading materials. Many coffee shops are now following the same model, which could undermine the plan for fee-based hotspots. Information, both in the seventeenth century and today, wants to be free—and coffee-drinking customers, it seems, expect it to be.

1. Old-time coffee-houses functioned as information exchanges in science, literature, business, and politics.
2. By "the Internet of the Enlightenment era" (Paragraph 3), the author refers to the inspirations that one customer drew from another.
3. The wireless "hotspots" were installed in thousands of coffee shops by Amazon and Microsoft.
4. Coffee houses are reluctant to charge customers for hotspots.
5. The text is mainly about the web of coffee houses in America.

Unit Eleven

Part Four: Oral Expression: Compliments/ Thanks and Responses

I. Dialogues

Dialogue 1

A: What a wonderful performance! You finished such a huge task in such a short time.
B: I'm lucky. Please accept my deep gratitude for your support.
A: Oh! It's my pleasure.

Dialogue 2

A: Congratulations, Mr. Alright! I have received the good news that you have been named outstanding manager.
B: Thank you, Mr. Black.
A: I really feel happy for you. I know you deserve the honor.
B: It's very kind of you to say so.

II. Useful Expressions

Compliments/Thanks	Responses
• What a wonderful (nice)...	• I'm lucky.
• Please accept my gratitude for...	• It is my pleasure.
• Congratulations!	• Thank you!
• You deserve the honor (grade)...	• It's very kind of you to say so.
	• I really studied hard for it...

III. Exercises

1. Dialogue Completion

(1) Man: _____. You certainly did quite well and I must say you deserve that grade.

Woman: Well, I really studied hard for that exam. I've been preparing for it more than a month. Now I can relax for a while.

A. Congratulations!   B. Excuse me!

C. I'm sorry!   D. Thanks a lot!

(2) Man: What a nice pen! _____

Woman: It came in the mail yesterday from my dad.

A. Could I borrow it?   B. Where did you get it?

C. Don't you think so?   D. Am I right?

2. **Dialogue Comprehension**

(1) Woman: Thanks for returning the books.

Man: I thought you needed them to study over the weekend. Thanks for letting me use them.

Question: What has the man done?

A. He has bought some books.

B. He has loaned the woman some books.

C. He has read some books over the weekend.

D. He has borrowed some books from the woman.

(2) Woman: These bookshelves look much more beautiful. It must have taken you a long time to paint them.

Man: Yes. If Bob hadn't helped me, I wouldn't have finished painting them so soon.

Question: What does the man say about the bookshelves?

A. Bob asked someone to paint them.

B. He painted them by himself.

C. Both he and Bob painted them.

D. They look more beautiful than before.

(3) Man: Maggie, your article in the *Campus News* was excellent.

Woman: I only wished they had published the entire thing.

Question: What do we learn from Maggie's response?

A. The newspaper printed another article of hers.

B. She could have written a better article.

C. Her publishing career has just begun.

D. The article was actually longer.

Unit Eleven

Key to Part Three and Part Four

Part Three:

I. Vocabulary:	1. A	2. B	3. A	4. B	5. A
	6. D	7. C	8. C	9. A	10. B
	11. D	12. A	13. C	14. A	15. C
II. Expression:	1. A	2. C	3. D	4. A	5. C
	6. A	7. B	8. D	9. A	10. B
	11. D	12. C	13. B	14. A	15. D
	16. C	17. A	18. B	19. A	
III. Cloze:	1. C	2. A	3. D	4. A	5. B
	6. A	7. B	8. C	9. A	10. D
	11. A	12. B			
IV. Reading:	1. D	2. C	3. C	4. A	5. D
V. Reading:	1. T	2. F	3. F	4. T	5. F

Part Four:

1. Dialogue Completion: (1) A (2) B
2. Dialogue Comprehension: (1) D (2) C (3) D

Unit Twelve

Text A

The Real Generation Gap

Part One: Language Points

I. Vocabulary

1. What all these statistics tell us is that the gap between generations is wider than ever before. (Para. 4)

   译文：所有这些数据告诉我们的是，现在的代沟比以前任何时候都要大。

   ever: *adv.* (used mostly in questions, negatives, comparisons, and sentences with if) at any time （主要用于疑问句、否定句及表示比较的句子或 if 引导的条件句中）在任何时候；在某时；有时；从来

   e.g. Nothing ever makes him angry.
   从来没有任何事会使他生气。

2. It is also a matter of public record that national ACT and SAT college entrance test scores are steadily declining despite "adjustments" designed to boost them artificially. (Para. 5)

   译文：大家也都知道，尽管（我们）做了一些"调整"来人为地提高分数，全国 ACT 和 SAT 大学入学考试分数在持续下降。

   boost: *v.* to increase; to raise 推动；提高

   e.g. These changes will help to boost demand.
   这些变化将有助于提高需求量。

256

Unit Twelve

3. Because grade inflation, which occurs at every level of education, is rampant.

   译文：因为充斥着教育界各个层次的分数膨胀非常盛行。(Para. 6)

   rampant: *adj.* prevailing or unchecked; widespread, rife 无约束的；猖狂的

   e.g. Sickness was rampant in the area.
   这个地区疾病流行。

4. Without missing a beat, Sarah replied, "Oh, they're much dumber." (Para. 8)

   译文：没有片刻的犹豫，萨拉回答道："唉，他们比我笨多了。"

   beat: *n.* the click of a timepiece （时计的摆或摆轮的）摆动；摆动声，滴答声

   e.g. At midnight, I can hear the beat very clearly.
   夜深人静的时候，我能非常清楚地听到钟摆的声音。

5. On the most recent International Math and Science Survey, which tests students from forty-two countries, one-third of all American high school seniors could not compute the price of a $1,250 stereo that was discounted by 20 percent. (Para. 8)

   译文：最近一项对来自四十二个国家的学生的国际数学和科学测试显示，三分之一的美国中学毕业班学生不知道打了八折的1,250美元立体声音响器材的价格是多少。

   discount: *v.* to offer for sale or sell at a reduced price 削价出售

   e.g. That store discounts all its unsold merchandise.
   那家商店降价出售所有卖不掉的商品。

6. One of the most popular history textbooks, produced as a result of the campaign for national education standards in the late 1980s, disparages the "Father of Our Country." (Para. 10)

   译文：在其中最流行的一本历史教科书里（此书是在20世纪80年代末（提高）全国教育水平的运动时出版的），"我们的国父"遭到了诋毁。

   campaign: *n.* a systematic course of aggressive activities for some specific purpose 运动

   e.g. She fought a successful election campaign.
   她的竞选活动很成功。

   disparage: *v.* to speak of or treat slightly, belittle 贬低

   e.g. He tends to disparage the efforts of conservationists.
   他总是贬低自然资源保护者的种种努力。

7. I made a great many charts, and I did a lot of little projects with painting. (Para. 14)

   译文：我制作了许多图表，还做了许多带图画的小作业。

project: *n.* （大型）作业

e.g. *In their geography class, the children are doing a special project on Native Americans.*
在地理课上，孩子们正在做一个有关北美印第安人的特别作业。

8. The literary shorthand of our culture is being lost. (Para. 16)

   译文： 在我们的文化中，文学的隐晦的表达方法正在消失。

   shorthand: *n.* (for) a shorter and often purposely less clear way of expressing something （对某事的）简短且常为故意搞得隐晦的表达方法

   e.g. *He's been "relocated," which is government shorthand for "given a worse job a long way away."*
   他已经被"调离"，这个官方词的意思就是"发落到边远地区做苦差"。

9. It shows a little girl declaring to her mother that her day in school was a bust. (Para. 17)

   译文： 漫画画的是一个小女孩跟她妈妈说她在学校的日子毫无用处。

   bust: *n.* a failure, bankruptcy 失败；倒闭；无价值之物

   e.g. *His new play is a complete bust.*
   他的新剧本写得糟透了。

10. Credit card debt, which has skyrocketed in recent years, is mainly held by those whose annual income exceeds $50,000. (Para. 22)

    译文： 近些年猛增的信用卡债务，主要是由那些年收入超过五万美元的人欠下的。

    skyrocket: *v.* (informal) (especially of a price, amount etc.) to go up suddenly and steeply （非正式）（尤指物价、数量等）突升，猛涨，剧增

    e.g. *He skyrocketed to national prominence.*
    他一举成为全国知名人物。

11. But now there is preemptive whining. (Para. 23)

    译文： 但是现在他们先发制人地抱怨。

    preemptive: *adj.* done before other people have a chance to act, and in order to prevent them from doing so 先发制人的，抢先的

    e.g. *The army launched a preemptive strike (=attack) against the enemy.*
    军队对敌人发起了先发制人的攻击。

12. Even before the semester begins, even before papers and tests are handed back, students come into my office at Arizona State University with a laundry list of complaints. (Para. 23)

Unit Twelve

译文：学生们甚至在一学期还没开始，论文和考卷还没交上来前，就拿着抱怨清单闯进我位于亚利桑那州立大学的办公室。

laundry list: *n.* a list of things one needs （美，非正式）所需物品的清单细目

e.g. *The Pentagon presented Congress with a laundry list of new weapons.*
五角大楼向国会提交了一份他们所需的新式武器的细目清单。

13. They are infected with an entitlement mentality. (Para. 24)

译文：他们深受一种权力心态的影响。

infect: *v.* to imbue with some pernicious belief, opinion, etc. 使受影响；以感染的方式来影响

e.g. *She infected the whole class with her enthusiasm.*
她以她的热诚感染了全班。

mentality: *n.* a person's habitual way of thinking; character 心态

e.g. *I can't understand the mentality of anyone who says such callous things.*
我无法理解说出这种无情的话的人是什么样的心态。

II. Expressions

1. Unfortunately, they do know about broken homes and "single-parent families." (Para. 1)

译文：不幸的是，他们确实知道离婚家庭和"单亲家庭"是什么样的。

know about: to have information about 知道……的情况；了解，知道

a) *The council has known about the leak for six months.*
委员会知道这个泄漏已六个月了。

b) *I know about the restaurant business.*
我略微知道一点饭店是如何经营的。

2. When she enrolled in an algebra class in the eighth grade, I offered to help her with her homework. She took me up on this offer one evening when we were sitting together at the kitchen table. (Para. 7)

译文：她八年级上了一个代数课时，我提出我可以帮她做作业。一天晚上我们坐在饭桌旁时，她（决定）接受我的帮助。

take up on: to accept an invitation or suggestion 接受（挑战、建议等）

a) *I must be going. I'll take you up on your invitation to lunch later.*
我得走了。下回（换个时间）我再接受你的午餐邀请。

b) *She paused for a moment, in case he might care to take her up on her offer.*
她停了一会儿，说不定他愿意接受她的提议。

3. She not only didn't know the answer, but she didn't know that this percentage could be expressed as "one-quarter" or "one-fourth." (Para. 7)

   译文：她不仅不知道答案,而且不知道这个百分比可以用"四分之一"来表示。

   not only...but.../ not only...(but) also...: used to emphasize that something else is also true 不但……而且……

   a) *She not only wrote the text but also selected the illustrations.*
      她不但写了文本,而且选了插图。

   b) *Shakespeare was not only a writer but an actor.*
      莎士比亚不仅是个作家,还是个演员。

4. Much is made of Thomas Jefferson's subjective observation that Washington was possessed of "a heart that was not warm in its affections." (Para. 10)

   译文：课本过于强调托马斯·杰佛逊关于华盛顿没有一颗温暖的心的主观评述。

   make much of: to treat a person or thing as very important or special 很重视;很尊重;强调

   a) *The press made much of the discovery.*
      新闻界非常重视这一发现。)

   b) *They've always made much of their nephews and nieces.*
      他们一直很重视他们的姪子和姪女。

   be possessed of: to have a particular quality or ability 拥有……的,具有……的

   a) *He was possessed of great self-confidence.* 他极有自信。

   b) *Anne is possessed of an acid tongue.* 安妮说话尖酸刻薄。

5. How is Generation X ever going to find out that Washington the general did more than any individual to win the war that established our nation? (Para. 11)

   译文：X代人究竟如何才能知道华盛顿将军在赢得建立我们民族的那场战争中做得比任何人都多?

   find out: to learn information 找出;发现;查明(真相等)

   a) *A number of tests have been carried out to find out if these drugs have any effect.*
      已经进行了一系列测试来验证这些药物是否有效。

   b) *I found out that he was having an affair with another woman.*
      我发现他与另一女人有染。

6. It certainly isn't going to learn such important lessons from a textbook that claims Washington was not much of a man because he did not, in modern lingo, "feel our pain." (Para. 11)

Unit Twelve

译文：这一代人当然不会从这样一本教材中学到如此重要的内容。这本教材宣称华盛顿并不是什么了不起的人，因为，用现代的行话来说，他"感觉不到我们的痛苦"。

not be much of: to not be a good example of something or not be very good at something <口> 不是什么了不起的,不是十分好的

a) I'm <u>not much of</u> a dancer, I'm afraid.
恐怕我不是什么了不起的舞蹈演员。

b) It <u>wasn't</u> really <u>much of</u> a storm.
这实际上并不是多大的暴风雨。

7. Special sections in each chapter feature biographies of people who have <u>made a difference</u> in history. (Para. 12)

译文：每一章节都留有专栏特载一些历史上有影响的人物的传记。

make a / the difference: to have an important effect or influence on something or someone 有关系;有影响;起(重要)作用

a) <i>No matter what she did, it <u>made no difference</u>.</i>
无论她做了什么,都没有关系。

b) <i>One more person wouldn't <u>make any difference</u> to the arrangements.</i>
再加一个人对整个安排不会有任何影响。

8. Famous religious leaders are also ignored, although the authors do <u>bow to</u> the ancient gods of primitive peoples. (Para. 13)

译文：著名的宗教领袖也忽略不提,但是作者们确实尊崇古代原始部落的神。

bow to: to bend the knee or body or incline the head toward, as in reverence, submission, or salutation 鞠躬

a) She avoided his eyes and <u>bowed to</u> him.
她避开他的目光,向他鞠了一躬。

b) The actors <u>bowed to</u> the audience at the end of the play.
演出结束时演员们向观众鞠躬。

9. Pre-Columbian cultures like the Toltecs are praised for their lavishly decorated temples, their calendars, their games—<u>so what</u> if they practiced human sacrifice? (Para. 13)

译文：在哥伦布(到达美洲)之前的像托尔特克这样的文化因为他们装潢考究的寺庙,他们的日历,以及他们的运动而倍受推崇——即便他们用人做祭品,那又如何？

so what: used to say that something does not matter 那又怎么样呢？那又有什么关系呢？

261

      a) *So what if we're a little late?*

         即使我们迟了一点又怎么样呢?

      b) *"She might tell someone." "So what? No one will believe her."*

         "她可能会告诉某个人。""那又怎么样呢?没有人会相信她。"

10. While I was still in a state of shock we arrived at the Old North Church and listened to a tour guide tell the story of Paul Revere. (Para. 13)

    译文:在我仍然吃惊不已之时,我们来到了老北教堂,听一个导游讲解保罗·里维尔的故事。

    arrive at: to get to a destination   抵达,到达

      a) *Elaine should be arriving at the station now.*

         伊莱恩现在应该到车站了。

      b) *He soon arrived back at his mother's house.*

         他很快返回了他母亲的家。

11. I do not mean to pick on Sarah. (Para. 15)

    译文:我不想指责萨拉。

    pick on: to behave in an unfair way to someone, e.g., by blaming or criticizing them unfairly   <口>找……的岔子;对……唠叨指责(= pick at)

      a) *Why don't you pick on someone else for a change?*

         你为什么不换个人唠叨?

      b) *He always picks on the newest member of his staff to criticize.*

         他对新来的职员总是横加指责。

12. At some colleges and universities, professors deliver lectures on the "The Apostle Paul as a Homosexual" and "Jesus Acted Up: A Gay and Lesbian Manifesto." (Para. 15)

    译文:在某些院校,教授讲授这样的课目:"同性恋使徒保罗"和"耶稣劣迹:同性恋好色宣言"。

    act up: to behave badly, to not work properly   耍脾气;捣蛋

      a) *He's a tough kid and he acts up a lot.*

         他是个无法无天的孩子,经常捣蛋。

      b) *This computer frequently acts up.*

         那台电脑经常出问题。

13. I cannot say, "Methinks thou dost protest too much," or at least one will inevitably respond, "Excuse me, Professor Jennings, shouldn't that be, 'I thinks?'" (Para. 16)

    译文:我不能说:"本人认为汝确实抗议太多了。"否则至少有一个学生会不可避免地反驳:"对不起,詹宁斯教授,是不是应该说'我认为'?"

Unit Twelve

at least: not less than a particular number or amount 至少

a) It will take you <u>at least</u> twenty minutes to get there.
你至少要二十分钟才能到那儿。

b) He had been dead for <u>at least</u> a fortnight.
他死了至少两星期了。

14. Look, the problem is that you have a lack of depth when it <u>comes to</u> your studies. (Para. 25)

    译文：瞧，你学习上的问题就是缺乏深度。

    come to: to concern 涉及

    a) *When it <u>comes to</u> politics I know nothing.*
    关于政治我一窍不通。

    b) *Now we <u>come to</u> the section on health.*
    现在我们来讲关于健康问题的那一节。

15. <u>Live up to</u> your obligations. (Para. 32)

    译文：履行你的义务。

    live up to: to keep to the high standards of 保持……的高水平；遵守；实践（原则等）；符合，不辜负（期望等）

    a) *Did the film <u>live up to</u> your expectations?*
    这部影片符合你的期望(合你的意)吗？

    b) *The new house didn't <u>live up to</u> expectations.*
    这幢新房子不合意。

III. Grammar

1. Because grade inflation, <u>which</u> occurs at every level of education, is rampant. (Para. 6)

    译文：因为充斥着教育界各个层次的积分膨胀非常盛行。

    which 引出非限定性定语从句，它并非限定前面的名词，而起补充说明作用。

2. George Washington was not, <u>the authors of *The United States: In the Course of Human Events* contend</u>, really successful as a soldier, as a politician, or as a human being. (Para. 10)

    译文：《人类事件中的美国》的作者声称，乔治·华盛顿其实并不是一个成功的士兵、政治家或人。

    划线部分为插入语，补充信息。

3. This is no small loss either, <u>for</u> words are symbols of important ideas. (Para. 16)

    译文：这也不是个小损失，因为单词是重要思想的符号。

for: 因为，由于……的缘故。比 because 更正式，较少用于口语中，但语气比 because 弱；不用以回答 why 问题，可在句首用以提供对上文的因果解释。

Part Two: Key to Exercises

I. Suggested Answers to *Topics for Discussion*

1. In what areas is the generation gap most pronounced?

   The generation gap is most obvious in the areas of skills, knowledge, critical thinking, work, and morality.

2. What is the price of a $1,250 stereo that is discounted by twenty percent?

   $1000.

3. What is the underlying reason for the increasing generation gap?

   With differences of age, culture, and wealth, generations are naturally different.

4. What can account for the skyrocketing credit card debt in recent years?

   The willingness to save and to delay gratification, the drive for success, and the concern for reputation are fast disappearing in a culture that condones irresponsible spending.

II. Key to Exercises

Text A

A.

1. (1) She thinks they are very poor in their skills.

   (2) She thinks they are terribly lacking in knowledge.

   (3) She thinks that indoctrination has seriously hindered their critical thinking.

   (4) She thinks that this generation is lazy and arrogant.

   (5) She thinks that Generation X lacks a solid foundation for its views on school, work, marriage, family, and community.

2. He did more than any individual to win the war that established America. He risked his reputation and career to ensure that Americans would have limited government, a sound economy, and a virtuous citizenry. He also performed acts of kindness and charity for others.

3. In her classroom, when she draws from what used to be common knowledge, students often do not understand her.

4. More and more mothers work outside their homes.

5. She made a great many charts, and she did a lot of little projects with painting.

6. B   7. A   8. C   9. D

10. (1) T   (2) F   (3) T   (4) F   (5) T

B.

1. flunk ... test ... pass ... remedial
2. flesh and blood ... help ... dumb ... replied
3. text ... was not much of ... lingo
4. bring on ... apocalypse

C.

1. B   2. C   3. A   4. D   5. A   6. B

D.

1. shorthand   2. beat   3. infected   4. project   5. disparage   6. ever   7. bust
8. laundry list   9. preemptive   10. mentality   11. boost   12. rampant   13. senior
14. campaign   15. grievous

E.

1. As a result of   2. So what   3. In the course of   4. make much of
5. not only ... but ...   6. not much of   7. bow to   8. was possessed of   9. acted up
10. take ... up on   11. at least   12. In terms of   13. find out   14. no longer
15. along with

F.

1. know what it is like to   2. attend church   3. start his own business   4. know about
5. a glimpse of   6. brought about   7. enrolled in   8. at all   9. part of
10. without exception   11. passed the test   12. It appears that   13. a lot
14. hovered between ... and ...   15. on a fast track

G.

1. A   2. B   3. D   4. A   5. C   6. A   7. B   8. D   9. A   10. C   11. B
12. B   13. B   14. D   15. B   16. A   17. C   18. B   19. D   20. A

H.

1. He will live up to what his parents expect of him.
2. His illness was brought on by poor diet.
3. The police are determined to find out who was the killer.

4. This bicycle is incapable of repair.

5. To sum up, within our society there still exist rampant inequalities.

6. Why are you making so much of such a trifling matter?

7. The speaker referred to him as an up-and-coming politician.

8. They contributed tactlessly to a general discontent.

9. Finally we had to bow to his greater experience.

10. He went on the journey along with his two friends.

11. You should take the insurance company up on their guarantee.

12. Such work is not only devalued in that country, but its nature is widely misunderstood.

13. He was possessed of great self-confidence whenever he spoke of music.

14. I hated the house but the new furniture made all the difference.

15. A: "He doesn't like you."
    B: "So what?"

I.

老师对学生思想的灌输是造成代沟的部分原因。这在教育中并不是什么新趋势。当我还在上学的时候，老师就教我们"全球变冷"，老师预测地球会在一个新的冰川世纪被冻起来。今天，我的孩子们被告知全球变暖将会导致生态灾难。而且，思想灌输的程度在大幅度提高。环保问题已经成为 X 代学生的老师日思夜想的事情。他们不断地用一些关于污染、资源短缺和天气灾害的不详警告对学生进行狂轰滥炸。最近的一幅漫画最能表示学生目前的态度。漫画中一个小女孩对她妈妈说她在学校只是混日子："我们不做任何拯救人类或环境的事情。我们把每天都浪费在阅读和数学上。"

Text B

1. D 2. C 3. B 4. A 5. C

Unit Twelve

Part Three: Self-check

I. Choose the word closest in meaning to the underlined word in each sentence.

1. What all these statistics tell us is that the gap between generations is wider than <u>ever</u> before.
   A. from time to time   B. at one time
   C. at any time   D. all the time

2. It is also a matter of public record that national ACT and SAT college entrance test scores are steadily declining despite "adjustments" designed to <u>boost</u> them artificially.
   A. raise   B. multiple   C. reduce   D. drop

3. Because grade inflation, which occurs at every level of education, is <u>rampant</u>.
   A. famous   B. unchecked   C. notorious   D. terrible

4. Without <u>missing a beat</u>, Sarah replied, "Oh, they're much dumber."
   A. breathing   B. hesitation   C. continuing   D. regret

5. On the most recent International Math and Science Survey, which tests students from forty-two countries, one-third of all American high school seniors could not compute the price of a $1,250 stereo that was <u>discounted</u> by twenty percent.
   A. sold at a reduced price   B. sold at half price
   C. sold at wholesale   D. sold at a retail price

6. One of the most popular history textbooks, produced as a result of the <u>campaign</u> for national education standards in the late 1980s, disparages the "Father of Our Country."
   A. company   B. drive   C. organization D. events

7. One of the most popular history textbooks, produced as a result of the campaign for national education standards in the late 1980s, <u>disparages</u> the "Father of Our Country."
   A. foretells   B. honors   C. belittles   D. gratifies

8. I made a great many charts, and I did a lot of little <u>projects</u> with painting.
   A. a series of events   B. a chain of thoughts
   C. items of clothes   D. assignments, often done in collaboration

267

9. The literary shorthand of our culture is being lost.
   A. a shorter way of expression   B. a short cut
   C. verbal symbolism   D. the upper hand
10. It shows a little girl declaring to her mother that her day in school was a bust.
    A. not worthwhile   B. worthwhile
    C. beneficial   D. necessary
11. Credit card debt, which has skyrocketed in recent years, is mainly held by those whose annual income exceeds $50,000.
    A. dropped   B. exploded   C. soared   D. stopped
12. But now there is preemptive whining.
    A. perfect   B. preventive   C. empty   D. rounded
13. Even before the semester begins, even before papers and tests are handed back, students come into my office at Arizona State University with a laundry list of complaints.
    A. length   B. item   C. piece   D. list
14. They are infected with an entitlement mentality.
    A. ingrained   B. bribed   C. marketed   D. printed
15. They are infected with an entitlement mentality.
    A. reality   B. mindset   C. reverence   D. rust

II. Choose the expression that best completes each sentence.

1. Unfortunately, they do _____ broken homes and "single-parent families."
   A. know about   B. bring about
   C. distinguish between   D. knock about
2. She _____ me _____ this offer one evening when we were sitting together at the kitchen table.
   A. put...up on...   B. took...up on...
   C. look...up on...   D. gave...up on...
3. She _____ didn't know the answer, _____ she didn't know that this percentage could be expressed as "one-quarter" or "one-fourth."
   A. not only...but...   B. in spite of...but...
   C. as...as...   D. so...that...

Unit Twelve

4. _____ Thomas Jefferson's subjective observation that Washington was possessed of "a heart that was not warm in its affections."
   A. Thanks to   B. Coming to ourselves
   C. Much is made of   D. Owing to

5. Much is made of Thomas Jefferson's subjective observation that Washington _____ "a heart that was not warm in its affections."
   A. played with   B. was proud of   C. was put on   D. was possessed of

6. How is Generation X ever going to _____ that Washington the general did more than any other individual to win the war that established our nation?
   A. freeze out   B. find out   C. plant out   D. pop up

7. It certainly isn't going to learn such important lessons from a textbook that claims Washington _____ a man because he did not, in modern lingo, "feel our pain."
   A. was not much of   B. did not make up
   C. did not let out   D. was a bit of

8. Special sections in each chapter feature biographies of people who have _____ in history. Almost all are politically correct minorities and/or females.
   A. trailed off   B. passed away
   C. made a difference   D. made tracks

9. Famous religious leaders are also ignored, although the authors do _____ the ancient gods of primitive peoples.
   A. make fun of   B. fill up   C. forget about   D. bow to

10. Pre-Columbian cultures like the Toltecs are praised for their lavishly decorated temples, their calendars, their games— _____ if they practiced human sacrifice?
    A. so what   B. as it were
    C. go it alone   D. thank God

11. While I was still in a state of shock, we _____ the Old North Church and listened to a tour guide tell the story of Paul Revere.
    A. came up   B. arrived at   C. arrived in   D. went up

12. I do not mean to _____ Sarah. She and her peers are victims of a pernicious system that has turned traditional liberal arts education on its head.
    A. stamp on   B. spark off   C. pick on   D. slow down

13. He's a tough kid and he _____ a lot.
    A. acted up   B. ran up   C. acted out   D. watched out

14. I cannot say, "Methinks thou dost protest too much," or _____ one will inevitably respond, "Excuse me, Professor Jennings, shouldn't that be, 'I thinks?'"
   A. in addition   B. by chance   C. at best   D. at least
15. Look, the problem is that you have a lack of depth when it _____ your studies.
   A. goes for   B. comes to   C. calls on   D. gets across

III. Read the following passage and fill in each blank with one of the words or expressions given.

Living in a foreign country can be extremely enriching. To be sure, __1__ time abroad gives a person a chance to experience another culture firsthand. Perhaps as important, though, time overseas provides a person with a valuable perspective in thinking about his own country. __2__, during my four fascinating years in this ancient land, I believe I have learned as much about the United States as I have about China. During this period, I have come to recognize not only differences between the two countries I hadn't expected, __3__ important commonalities which I had previously overlooked. At the same time, I've identified a __4__ of aspects of Chinese culture and society which I admire—and which I think Americans would do well to note.

Most Americans would agree that one of the United States' most pressing social problems is the __5__ of the two-parent family. Today, millions of American children grow up without fathers, often in poverty. Too often, these children lack the love and guidance they desperately need—and which they would ordinarily receive from two __6__ parents. Traditionally, American parents have placed the needs of their children above their own, often delaying their own gratification or sacrificing material comforts __7__ their children's future. At present, however, nearly one half of all new marriages end in divorce, with often troubling __8__ for the children involved. Worse, every year, thousands of teenage, unmarried Americans become mothers outside the context of wedlock altogether, with generally disastrous results for the mothers and children __9__ for American society more generally. In refreshing contrast, Chinese continue to value intact marriages. This is not to say that Chinese marriages are all perfect—they certainly are not, judging from increasing rates of divorce and __10__ affairs—but the willingness of Chinese to set aside their own needs and stay together for the sake of the children is admirable and worthy of study.

Unit Twelve

1. A. spending	B. keeping	C. using	D. having
2. A. Unfortunately	B. Still	C. Indeed	D. However
3. A. and	B. so	C. therefore	D. but also
4. A. part	B. number	C. amount	D. side
5. A. emergence	B. construction	C. lack	D. breakdown
6. A. irresponsible	B. responsible	C. absent-minded	D. kind
7. A. in exchange	B. in the interests of	C. in opposition	D. with respect to
8. A. consequences	B. benefits	C. disadvantages	D. shortcomings
9. A. so	B. still	C. as well as	D. alike
10. A. illegal	B. premarital	C. extramarital	D. romantic

IV. Read the following passage and choose the best answer for each question.

Families, in whatever form they take, are important to Americans. If one were to ask a group of Americans what is dearest to them, the overwhelming majority would say "family." And yet, so many Americans spend much more time at work—that is, beyond the formal forty-hour workweek—than they do with their own families. Obviously, the American economy is one of the most vibrant and powerful in the world, owing in large measure to a strong American work ethic and high efficiency. But frequently, a strong work ethic and high efficiency become "workaholism." It seems to me that Chinese generally find a better balance between work and family needs than many Americans do. I don't see the number of workaholics in China that I do in the United States (or in American organizations in China). Instead, average Chinese tend to head home right after work (in the office or field), have meals together, and spend time with their spouses and children. In addition, the Chinese tend to make more time for grandparents, uncles, aunts, and cousins (at least when they live in relative proximity) than many Americans; in many cases, multi-generational families live together. Of course, like many facets of Chinese society, this is all changing; increasing numbers of "New Chinese" are working longer hours and spending less time with their families than ever before. Still, while Americans do genuinely value their loved ones, I think we have something to learn from the Chinese about finding the proper balance between work and family.

Both the strengths and weaknesses of the American educational system are well known to many, and they are the source of vigorous debate in the United States. A product of American public education myself, I wouldn't trade the American system for any other I have encountered. Even so, I have been very impressed with the industry and discipline of the Chinese students I have met. Most invest a great deal of time and effort in their studies and many even speak English fairly well by the time they graduate from high school. Many American students devote much less attention to their schoolwork, with predictable and troubling results. I am certain that the emphasis in the United States on the well roundedness of the student is a major strength of the American system, but it must be coupled with the student's commitment to—and parental support for—academic excellence. I think Americans can learn from the Chinese in terms of seriousness of purpose in the classroom.

1. According to the author, who is better at finding the balance between work and family?
   A. Americans.   B. Chinese.   C. French.   D. Spanish.
2. Why is the American economy one of the most vibrant and powerful in the world?
   A. Americans are lazy.
   B. Americans are good at learning from other countries.
   C. Americans have a strong work ethic and high efficiency.
   D. Americans pay much attention to families.
3. According to the author, what is a major strength of the American educational system?
   A. The creativity of the students.
   B. The cooperation of the students.
   C. The high marks of the students.
   D. The well-roundedness of the students.
4. What is dearest to the overwhelming majority of Americans?
   A. Families.   B. Money.   C. Friends.   D. Love.
5. How many hours do many Americans work every week?
   A. 24 hours.   B. 50 hours.   C. 40 hours.   D. More than 40 hours.

V. Read the following passage and decide whether each statement is TRUE or FALSE.

More broadly, I have always enjoyed the relative safety of Chinese cities. Since the 1960s, violent crime has been a tragic fact of American life. The majority of violent crimes in the United States involve handguns. In the 1980s, in particular, gun-related violence soared to all-time highs in major cities across the United States: from Washington D. C. in the east to Detroit in the north, from Houston in the south to Los Angeles in the west, gunfire became a familiar sound to millions who were living in America's most crime-ridden neighborhoods. Like most foreign residents of China, I have never worried about violent crime in this country; it's very rare, relative to the United States. One of the reasons this is so is the absence of handguns. Though the U. S. Constitution guarantees Americans the right to own guns—I own a rifle, myself—I think Americans should study China's policy of "zero-tolerance" for violent crime and of strict gun control.

With regard to personal health, I believe Americans have much to learn from the Chinese. Americans, myself included, generally have poor eating habits. Many skip breakfast on a daily basis; frequently miss other meals or eat at very odd hours in order to accommodate busy work or social schedules; eat a lot of unhealthy fast-food and, even worse, junk food, such as potato chips, candy bars, and soft drinks; and fail to exercise regularly, preferring instead to sit in front of a television. As a result, Americans simply aren't in the health they should be. The Chinese, however, tend to have breakfast daily; eat other meals regularly, regardless of how busy they may be on a particular day; avoid excessive amounts of fast-food—though, with the rise of McDonald's and other chains, this is changing dramatically—and junk-food; and maintain a naturally active lifestyle (to date, at least, the majority of Chinese ride their bicycles every day, for example). Chinese medicine, especially preventive medicine, also plays an important role in keeping the Chinese healthy. I have always admired the Chinese people for their fitness and health. That's why I think Americans have a lot to learn from the Chinese people regarding their approach to diet, exercise, and medicine. In the meantime, one can only hope that the Chinese won't pick up all of the bad habits of Americans in these areas. With China developing the way it is, though, it appears to be a losing cause.

1. Compared with American cities, Chinese cities are relatively safe.
2. People can easily get guns in China.
3. The author thinks that Americans are healthier than Chinese.
4. According to the author, potato chips, candy bars and soft drinks are junk food.
5. The author doesn't think much of Chinese medicine.

Part Four: Oral Expression: Discussing Different Points of View

I. Dialogues

Dialogue 1

A: Would you agree that British English and American English are the same?

B: It's true that they are almost the same, but it is clear that they are different in some pronunciations. What's more, it is very difficult to understand the different accents.

A: Well, you have a point there, but in my opinion, not all speak with a strong accent.

B: Really?

A: Yes, you see, generally speaking, American people are more easily understood than English people.

Dialogue 2

A: I love football. I think we should have more football on TV.

B: I don't agree. There should be more sports programs on TV, but I think one football match a week is enough. Tennis is also exciting to watch.

A: But tennis is sometimes slow and dull on TV.

B: I'm afraid I can't go along with you on that. Tennis matches are quite wonderful if you get into them.

A: Well, let's agree to disagree.

Dialogue 3

A: What are your views on crime and punishment?

B: In my opinion, criminals must pay for their crimes. For a small crime, a man might have to go to jail. But for murder, he ought to pay with his life.

A: I disagree. The aim shouldn't be to make criminals "pay" for crimes, but to educate them so that they don't commit more crimes. Society has to first change its attitude. Criminals should be made to do something constructive and useful—like community service.

B: That's fine, but you will never solve the problem of crime until you deal with the root causes, such as poverty, crowded accommodation, poor schools, and broken homes.

II. Useful Expressions

Agreement	Disagreement
• I quite agree with you.	• I cannot agree with you on this point.
• I share your view on that.	• I'm afraid I have a different opinion.
• I'm with you there.	• That's not how I see it.
• Oh, yes, I couldn't agree more.	• I'm afraid we don't see eye to eye on this. (恐怕我们在这一点上达不成共识。)
• You can say that again.	
• I think I'll go along with your proposal. (我想我支持你的提议。)	• I don't see any point in discussing the question any further.
• That's just what I was thinking.	• You must be joking.
• Yes, you have a point there. (对, 你说的这一点有道理。)	• You can't be serious.
	• Well, it depends. (这得视情况而定。)
• That's one way of looking at it, I admit. (我承认可以从这个角度看问题。)	• All right, let's agree to differ on this topic. (好吧, 我们在这个问题上保留各自的观点。)

III. Exercises

1. **Dialogue Completion**

   (1) Man: There's nothing I like better to get myself started in the morning than a big breakfast—eggs, bacon, potatoes....

   Woman: _____ All that fatty food would give me a stomachache. I prefer something light, like fruit or yogurt.

   A. Exactly!
   B. You bet!
   C. Not me!
   D. Absolutely!

(2) Man: Tomorrow we are having our first test in my history class. I'm really worried about it. You've taken one of Dr. Parker's tests, haven't you? I hear they're impossible to pass.

Woman: I don't know whom you've been talking to.

A. We have to think of our priorities.

B. I didn't enjoy taking history with Dr. Parker.

C. Dr. Parker is no longer teaching history.

D. My experience was just the opposite.

2. **Dialogue Comprehension**

(1) Woman: Isn't this a terrific painting? It looks great on the wall in my office.

Man: To be honest, I don't know what you see in it.

Question: What does the man mean?

A. He doesn't like the painting.

B. He hasn't seen the woman's office.

C. He'll hang the painting on the wall.

D. He doesn't know where to put the painting.

(2) Woman: So, what did you think about the discussion at lunch? I didn't realize people have such strong feelings about politics.

Man: Are you kidding? That subject always touches a nerve.

Question: What does the man mean?

A. No one was interested in the discussion.

B. Politics is a sensitive topic.

C. The woman is not being serious.

D. People avoided discussing politics.

(3) Woman: Let's see. Another thing we need to do is to show the new students around town, you know, show them all the highlights of the area.

Man: I don't see why we need to do that ourselves. I understand the Visitors' Center offers a wonderful bus tour.

Question: What does the man suggest they do?

A. Meet the new students at the Visitors' Center.

B. Send the new students on a bus tour of the city.

C. Visit the new students to make them feel welcome.

D. Walk downtown with the new students.

Unit Twelve

Key to Part Three and Part Four

Part Three:

I. Vocabulary: 1. C   2. A   3. B   4. B   5. A
              6. B   7. C   8. D   9. C   10. A
              11. C 12. B 13. D 14. A 15. B

II. Expression: 1. A   2. B   3. A   4. C   5. D
               6. B   7. A   8. C   9. D   10. A
               11. B 12. C 13. A 14. D 15. B

III. Cloze: 1. A   2. C   3. D   4. B   5. D
            6. B   7. B   8. A   9. C   10. C

IV. Reading: 1. B   2. C   3. D   4. A   5. D

V. Reading: 1. T   2. F   3. F   4. T   5. F

Part Four:

1. Dialogue Completion: (1) C   (2) D
2. Dialogue Comprehension: (1) A   (2) B   (3) B